Improvisation

Improvisation

The Drama of Christian Ethics

Samuel Wells

BrazosPress

Grand Rapids, Michigan

Published by Brazos Press
a division of Baker Publishing Group
P.O. Box 6287, Grand Rapids, MI 49516-6287
www.brazospress.com

Printed in the United States of America

Library of Congress Cataloging-in-Publication Data
Wells, Samuel, 1965-
    Improvisation : the drama of Christian ethics / Samuel Wells.
        p.   cm.
    Includes bibliographical references. (p.   ) and index.
    ISBN 10: 1-58743-071-1 (pbk.)
    ISBN 978-1-58743-071-8 (pbk.)
    1. Christian ethics. I. Title.
BJ1251.W45 2004
241—dc22

2004004004

To Jo

Contents

Preface

I am grateful for the good company of those who have offered me opportunities to explore in detail the ideas raised in this book. I think of many groups, classes, and congregations who have engaged and challenged, but especially of the following: Clare Goddard and the Maddermarket Theatre in Norwich; Ben Quash and Nick Adams and the students of Fitzwilliam College, Cambridge; Michael Stagg and the clergy and people of his Deanery in Norwich; Wanda Standley and the students of Emmaus House, Norwich; Jo Bailey Wells and the community of Clare College, Cambridge; Stephen Barton and the Society for the Study of Christian Ethics; and Jeremy Begbie and Trevor Hart and the Institute for Theology, Imagination, and the Arts in St. Andrews. I am also grateful for the support of Graham James and David Atkinson in perceiving the connections between this project and the program of social and spiritual regeneration in which I was engaged in Norwich.

I am particularly grateful for those who have made this a better book than it would otherwise have been by reading and commenting on chapters and by offering expert advice. Ann Loades took the original idea seriously. Rick Simpson and Ben Quash offered early dialogue. Lynda Waterson and Rex Walford offered timely comments, especially on the theatrical dimensions of the argument. Jo Hartley and Philip Jones improved the chapter on human cloning considerably. David Warbrick, Mary Ellen Ashcroft, and Craig Hovey provided helpful comments on style. And Rodney Clapp and Rebecca Cooper at Brazos Press proved to be marvelous editors.

I am most grateful of all for those without whom there would have been no book. John Inge introduced me to the work of Keith Johnstone, at a time when Stanley Hauerwas was beginning to do for me what I hope this book may do for its readers. Jo Bailey Wells always knew that behind the sometimes desultory offers of her pusillanimous husband lay a yearning author seeking permission. And Ernie Ashcroft told me to cut out the excuses, sit down, and just write the thing. Here it is.

Introduction

Summary of the Argument

Improvisation in the theater is a practice through which actors seek to develop trust in themselves and one another in order that they may conduct unscripted dramas without fear. *Improvisation: The Drama of Christian Ethics* is a study of how the church may become a community of trust in order that it may faithfully encounter the unknown of the future without fear. It is a treatment of how the story and practices of the church shape and empower Christians with the uninhibited freedom sometimes experienced by theatrical improvisers. It is an account of the development of trust in self, church, and God. In the process it is a renarration of Christian ethics, not as the art of performing the Scriptures but as faithfully improvising on the Christian tradition.

Improvisation: The Drama of Christian Ethics is in three parts. In the first part I propose that improvisation is an appropriate mode in which to understand the nature and purpose of Christian ethics. In the second part I outline six practices that characterize improvisation in the theater and that I suggest might characterize Christian ethics also. In the third part I offer four examples of how these practices enable Christians and the church to engage with particularly significant contexts and issues.

In proposing that improvisation is a helpful way in which to understand the practice of Christian ethics, I take the argument in four stages. The first stage, chapter 1, questions the notion of "ethics" as a discrete discipline by showing through a sweeping historical narrative that what constitutes ethics has always been subject to the church's understanding of God and to its location in society more generally. Thus the rest of this volume, being concerned with ethics, will always have an eye to the imitation of God's action and the recognition of the social location of the church. The second stage, chapter 2, takes another broad sweep, this time across the contemporary field of Christian ethics. I distinguish between three strands, universal, subversive, and ecclesial, locating the present study in the third strand. I then maintain that an ecclesial ethic is properly characterized by a narrative understanding of doctrine. This leaves the third stage, chapter 3, with the burden of showing that, given that it portrays the action of God and the nature of human response, doctrine, particularly in an ethical vein, is inherently dramatic, rather than simply narrative, in character. Here I set my argument alongside those of others who have argued this point, and I outline the broad dimensions of the Christian drama. Finally I break new ground in proposing that even drama is too static an understanding of theological ethics. Ethics cannot be simply about rehearsing and repeating the same script and story over and over again, albeit on a fresh stage with new players. This does not do sufficient justice to the unfolding newness of each moment of creation. The Bible is not so much a script that the church learns and performs as it is a training school that shapes the habits and practices of a community. This community learns to take the right things for granted, and on the basis of this faithfulness, it trusts itself to improvise within its tradition. Improvisation means a community formed in the right habits trusting itself to embody its tradition in new and often challenging circumstances; and this is exactly what the church is called to do.

In outlining the practices of theatrical improvisers and showing how they inform and describe the discernment and practice of a Christian community, I develop six modes of activity. I begin in chapter 5 with the vital role in ethics of the formation of habits. Ethics is not about being clever in a crisis but about forming a character that does not realize it has been in a crisis until the "crisis" is over. It is just the same for improvisers in the theater. Improvisation is not about being spontaneous and witty in the moment, but about trusting oneself to do and say the obvious. The key to both ethics and improvisation is what the players regard as obvious, and thus the real issues in both lie in the imagination. In chapter 6 I reflect on status, a key notion in improvisation, and a neglected notion in Christian ethics. I suggest the benefits that consideration of status might make to writing on Christian ethics and offer humorous examples to demonstrate the significance and the universality of status transactions. In chapter 7 I describe perhaps the foundational notions in theatrical improvisation, those of accepting and blocking offers. I begin to suggest how these notions help to display the frustrations of much ethics in the contemporary context. Chapter 8 is a more theoretical chapter, less explicitly linked to specific practices in improvisation, but necessary to the argument because it explores the difference between gifts and givens, which is central to the subsequent chapter. In a sense, chapters 7 and 8 are introductory chapters to chapter 9, perhaps the key chapter in the book. In chapter 9 I outline the practice of overaccepting, in which a community fits a new action or concept into a larger narrative, into the greater drama of what God is doing in the world. Finally, in chapter 10, I introduce the second key practice, reincorporation. This is an eschatological practice in which discarded elements in the drama are woven back into the story, and it is particularly appropriate in relation to those whom Jesus' Jubilee came to restore.

By this stage the community of readers is perhaps yearning for worked examples of how these practices may shape their imagination and habits. In part 3 I have two aims in mind. The first aim is to show that the practices I commend, though they have not been given these names before, are not "original." I am not trying to commend "a new way of doing ethics," but to offer a coherent and suggestive series of practices that describe what the church's faithful social response has always been. And so I have taken two contexts in which particular authors have, like me, tried to show what faithful discipleship means under extreme pressure, and I have demonstrated how these authors' understanding of faithfulness is almost exactly the same as what I have portrayed, albeit without the explicit categories I am proposing. I begin with William Cavanaugh's remarkable discussion of the role of the Roman Catholic Church in Chile under the Pinochet regime. I chose this treatment because, after several years of outlining to individuals and groups the practices of improvisation and their significance for Christian ethics, the most common response is anxiety that I am advocating that the church capitulate to evil, or at least offer no robust response to it. Cavanaugh's book is exactly on this theme: how does the contemporary church engage with human evil? I have no intention in this chapter of providing a comprehensive, objectively balanced account of Chile in these years: I quote no other source, although I am aware that many Christians in Chile during this period saw events rather differently. My point is simply to show that a respected scholar, in a widely acclaimed treatment concerning this key context of the church's role in relation to political oppression, advocates a series of perceptions and proposals that resemble my own argument remarkably closely.

The second example is not so much about human sin as about flawed creation. It considers what it means to cope with acute mental and physical neediness. The chapter centers on the experience of the theologian Frances Young in bringing up a son who has multiple special needs. But partly because seeing the story entirely through the parent's eyes causes problems in relation to my understanding of status, and partly because a comparison of the issues of illness and disability seemed constructive, I have treated Margaret Spufford's account of her own and her daughter's severe illnesses alongside the story of Frances and Arthur Young. Again the principal aim here is not to shed new light on how Christians and the church engage with these distressing contexts, but simply to display how faithful treatments of these issues already follow the pattern of reflection to which this book seeks to give more systematic expression.

In the last two chapters I make constructive engagements with two further issues. Unlike the two previous, they do not threaten to destroy faith and/or the church: on the contrary they offer to take away frustrating limitations to human life and promise a flourishing future. One is the question of human cloning, which promises to overcome the limitations of the human body and bring a kind of salvation short of heaven. The other is the case of genetically modified foods, which promise to solve the world's food shortages at a stroke. The response to these issues in Christian circles has not been coherent, and the arguments used have in many cases not been theological ones. My treatments in these two chapters are an attempt both to use the practices proposed in this book to portray a theological response to these issues and meanwhile to test this book's proposals in two contexts of pressing public concern.

What This Book Is

As I have talked with individuals and groups about the relation of theological ethics to theatrical improvisation over the last ten years I have been aware of a variety of enthusiasms and anxieties evoked by the subject, some of which are central to the concern of this study, but many of which belong elsewhere. Many of these reactions concern the popular understanding of the term "improvisation" and the associations it provokes in people's imaginations. But there are a number of other concerns frequently expressed, and I have already referred to the misplaced anxiety that I am suggesting that the church has no response in the face of aggressive human evil. The purpose of this and the next section are to attempt to address some of these concerns so as to enable the community of readers to engage with the argument with an imagination characterized more by expectation than by suspicion.

This book is an essay in theological ethics. That is to say, it doubts that there is such a thing as an ethic to which anyone can subscribe, regardless of tradition. It sees the principal role of Christian ethics as describing how Christians have formed habits by maintaining a tradition over centuries, largely embodied in written texts and in key practices, particularly the practices of worship. Christian ethics is not about helping anyone act Christianly in a crisis, but about helping Christians embody their faith in the practices of discipleship all the time.

This is an essay in constructive Christian ethics. A whole generation of writers in Christian ethics has spent the last three decades establishing the principles outlined in the previous paragraph.[1] Much of this work has been in critical mode, exposing the internal flaws in more conventional modes of ethical writing and pointing out that these modes left much to be desired from the point of view of faithful Christian discipleship. While I touch on these debates in the first four chapters, the purpose of this book is not to go over those debates again. It is to describe constructively what Christian ethics might now look like, in an era where character, narrative, imagination, worship, nonviolence, and the voice of the excluded are taken seriously as themes that shape the discourse.[2]

This is a constructive essay that values the place of the imagination in ethics.[3] It assumes that essential to a notion of the kingdom of God is a perception that things might be different from how they are. In other words, when a community is in Christ, there are no "givens," no nonnegotiable facts about existence that one must simply accept, other than the great gift of the gospel.[4] To be a Christian is to see the gift of the gospel as one's only given. This is whence the church derives its power. It is not constrained by a conventional "realist" list of "givens"; it exists in a wonderful moment of possibility, in the Easter moment of resurrection, when all things are possible but not all things, on this side of the eschaton, have yet happened. Thus it is appropriate that the central section of the book has plenty of humor, because that humor should be a feature of the inbreaking kingdom. It is to inspire that sense of wonder and joy, that playful, spirited sense of possibility, and to inspire those practices that flow from it and renew it, that this book has been written.

This essay seeks to inspire the imagination of communities. It is assumed that a healthy community has a blend of thinkers and doers, of practitioners and reflectors. This is designed to be a book that brings together academic theologians, those in formal ministries, and those whose vocation is to serve the church in a more conventional career but who seek to do so in theologically informed ways. My hope is that the academy, the altar, and the marketplace will all find in this book a reason, an encouragement, and a method for exploring their theological imagination together. Hence I have carefully located my proposal within the contemporary academic discourse and used a minimum of jargon; but when justification for bolder claims is required, I have used the appropriate apparatus to support them. The use of both academic argument and accessible illustration is intended to draw Christians into conversation, to foster the discerning communities that the argument seeks to empower. The assumption of the argument—which is made explicit in chapter 13—is that the unit of Christian ethics, the "body" whose integrity and flourishing it seeks to promote, is not the individual or the world but the church. The body that matters is the body of Christ. The last thing this book is intended to make possible is the ability of the detached ironic observer to make pleasing patterns with the world's stories and assumptions in order to support a clever disengaged superiority. The retreat into the indulgently cerebral is a denial of the incarnation; theological reflection must always be in a spiraling dialogue with embodied community. This has been the context in which this book has taken shape. The only reason why the reflection on the author's contexts has not been materially incorporated into this volume is that plenty of such reflection has been published elsewhere and there comes a time when discussion of current lived communities of faith needs to stop out of respect for those communities' ability to live under God and not under the constant intrusive scrutiny of theologians.[5]

This essay seeks to explore how the Bible can shape the imagination of communities in ways that lead to fruitful corporate life. It stands, humbly, in the tradition of writers such as Hans Frei, David Kelsey, and George Lindbeck, who have sought to trace how the broadly narrative character of the Bible can shape the imagination of the reading community.[6] It may then be asked how I can justify using extrascriptural categories (the six practices of improvisation) in an essay that seeks to affirm the central place of the Bible in Christian ethics. I have two answers to this. The first is that I see these practices of improvisation as true to the narrative of Scripture, and I have accordingly sought to illustrate my argument from scriptural stories and church history at every stage. Overaccepting is at the heart of the incarnation and the resurrection; reincorporation is at the heart of the parousia and the kingdom of God; status transactions are all over narratives like the Joseph saga and Jesus' passion; forming habits is what Paul's letters are constantly appealing to his readers to do.

The second answer is that I see the biggest danger in the use of the Bible in ethics in the church is to make it some kind of Gnostic system of law or philosophy, which exists primarily in the mind of the believer and in the believer's personal life of devotion. The practices of improvisation I see as helpful because they foster a process of communal discernment and practice, and it is this, rather than written documents, that I see as the heart of the church's life. In other words I see the Bible as making the conversation that is Christian ethics possible, rather than concentrating on command and making conversation impossible.

Last, this essay seeks to inspire the imagination of communities in such a way that it renews their engagement with the pressing issues of the world around them. Some strands in theological ethics have attracted an unfortunate and unjustified label of being "sectarian." This volume takes for granted that interaction with all that is in God's world that has not yet recognized his sovereignty is a dimension of almost everything the church does—and the chapter on status makes clear that the church does not engage in this interaction with any sense of superiority or distaste. To withdraw from engagement with wider society on the grounds of the preservation of purity or dedication to holy living would not be in the spirit of the incarnation, in which Jesus, fully human, interacted with all kinds of people, the devoted, the hostile, and the indifferent. But meanwhile to advocate engagement without also clarifying the character and identity of the church that engages would not be in the spirit of the cross, which constantly reminds the Christian that following Jesus will in the end lead to conflict and suffering. This book is intended to inspire engagement, but also to sustain the church when that engagement is demanding.

What This Book Is Not

This book is not saying that Scripture and tradition count for nothing in ethics, or that improvising means spontaneous anarchic autonomy without regard to serious outcomes. That much should be abundantly clear already, but the popular perception of improvisation dies hard, so it is worth stating this denial explicitly. Christian ethics and theatrical improvisation are both about years of steeping in a tradition so that the body is so soaked in practices and perceptions that it trusts itself in community to do the obvious thing. This book sets out to be an imaginative, suggestive, and stimulating contribution, but not a revolutionary one. At the heart of its argument is the assumption that these practices have been true to the faithful discipleship of the church since the beginning.

This book is not an anthropological study in how human beings in specific contexts conduct certain forms of behavior that come under the general term improvisation. I make no claims for whether improvisation is a helpful term for understanding ethics in general. My claim is simply that its disciplines and practices resemble the disciplines and practices of Christian ethics sufficiently closely that a detailed treatment may be highly illuminating. It is for others to judge whether improvisation is a helpful category for ethics in general. My expectation is that, unless one is assuming that there is a tradition to which a community is endeavoring to be faithful, and unless there is a certain mischievous and subversive character to that tradition, improvisation will have little to offer. I take Christianity to be that kind of mischievous and subversive tradition.

Neither is this study a detailed exploration of the role of the theater in relation to Christian theology and ethics. When I use the term "theatrical improvisation" I do so to refer to the methods and traditions employed by actors when they improvise; I make no wider study of the theater, nor do I reflect in any serious detail on notions such as the stage, the audience, and the author in relation to either theater or ethics. Nonetheless there are some practices of the theater, such as rehearsal, that do seem germane to this study, and I refer to them in chapters 3 and 4.

Perhaps most importantly, this essay is not a consideration of musical improvisation. The analogy between the way improvisation may be seen in Christian doctrine and the way it is practiced by skilled instrumentalists in an orchestra or jazz quartet has been considered by a number of authors. I have nothing to add to their work, not just because of its thoroughness, but more importantly because I simply have no qualifications to do so—my grasp of musical practice being so limited.[7]

I confess a certain frustration that, when a constructive interest in improvisation is taken, attention often quickly focuses on preaching. Preaching is a vital aspect of worship, and is an important practice in the shaping of the church. But to focus on the preacher as the one who improvises on the scriptural text is to miss two significant dimensions that this study seeks to highlight. One is that improvisation is not primarily about words: the first two practices I note, forming habits and assessing status, are not primarily cerebral or verbal practices. The second is that improvisation is a corporate activity: preaching always presupposes a period of corporate discernment and embodiment, which in most church services lasts little longer than the time it takes for the preacher to return to the stall. This study considers that process of corporate discernment and embodiment as central to the mission and worship of the church.

This book is not intended as a comprehensive survey of the conventional pantheon of issues in Christian ethics. It does conclude with four studies of particular contexts and issues. The first two are intended as illustrations and the final two as worked examples, but there is no attempt to apply the theoretical exposition to the full range of issues habitually discussed in classrooms and home groups and consultation documents and textbooks. It will no doubt emerge that the methods advocated in this study work more straightforwardly for some "issues" than for others. There is no panacea for resolving tragic questions of what to do when whatever one does seems to be wrong. This book is not proposing a new and rigid system for treating all issues in ethics: it will be seen that the different practices are taken in a different order in each of the final four chapters, as appropriate to the issue in question. It needs to be remembered that this study is part of a more general movement that is trying to move the center of gravity in Christian ethics away from "issues" toward the formation of habitual assumptions and practices. Concentration on "issues" implies that the church and the world are swimming along together nicely, and that it is only when one or the other approaches some rocks (declaration of war, innovation in biotechnology) that enquiry needs to begin. I am assuming that such an easy coexistence can never be the perception of the Christian community—that the world (and the church) is riven by sin, abounding in fear, mistrust, injustice, inequality, unreconciled relationships, and unacknowledged grace, and altogether far from the glory and enjoyment of God for which it was made. Any engagement with "issues" can only be in the context of a more general response to this alienation from God and the kingdom, which the church exists to address.

And again, lest it not be obvious, this volume is under no illusions about the flawed character of the church itself. In every generation the church has confronted—or has been forced to confront—the fact that its own practice has sometimes been worse than—or indistinguishable from—that of those forces in society that have taken God's freedom not yet to believe. This generation is no different. And yet the gifts God has given for redemption—himself in his Son and the Spirit, the Scripture and the sacraments, the hope of the kingdom and the practices of mercy—are ever new, and salvation without recourse to them is no salvation at all. This essay is a consideration of how to use the gifts God has given for the church to participate in the salvation and the redemption of the world; but it knows how clumsy the church can be in using those gifts.

Ethics: The Practice of God and the Practices of the Church

Enough of loosening the muscles and clearing the throat: it is time to begin. As the community of readers ponders the chapters that are to follow, it may be helpful to bear in mind one insight from Mark's Gospel as a signature tune to accompany the words.

Mark's Gospel comes in two halves.[8] There is a description of Jesus' ministry, largely in Galilee, and his acclaim by some and rejection by others. And there is a passion narrative, beginning with the triumphal entry into Jerusalem. Each of these halves has a key parable early on, which shapes the readers' understanding of the events and characters that follow. In the first half of the Gospel the key parable is the sower (4:3–20). The sower parable tries to come to terms with why not everyone responds to the gospel with glee. Satan carries off some (the scribes and Pharisees); others are crippled by fear (the disciples); others simply love other things more than the gospel (Herod, the rich young man). How does God address the problem of human resistance to the gospel? He *overwhelms* the land with a superabundant harvest. He does not destroy but astonishes. In the second half of the Gospel the key parable is the tenants in the vineyard (12:1–12). This parable tries to come to terms with why Jesus is about to be killed by the very people he came to save. It places him in a long tradition of those who proclaimed God's sovereignty to Israel. It knows he will, like them, be rejected. How does God address this profound human wastefulness of his gifts? He stops giving more gifts but *uses the ones they have thrown away*. The stone that the builders rejected becomes the cornerstone.

These represent God's two primary ways of working in Mark's Gospel. In the incarnation he overwhelms humanity with the abundance of his grace. And in the resurrection he uses what humanity has rejected to save humanity. The first kind describes what in this book I call overaccepting. The second kind describes what in this book I call reincorporation. They are the two most significant practices in improvisation. If they are the way God works in his gospel, should they not be the principal ways in which the church seeks to imitate him? That is the thesis of this book.

PART ONE

Plowing

1

Ethics as Theology

Aristotle and the Early Church

This chapter tells the story of how Christian ethics came to be where it is today.

Aristotle saw humans as political beings.[1] He saw the city-state as the unit of corporate life. Human flourishing lay in the appropriate conduct of these corporate relationships. This is politics. Politics concerns the discovery of common goods that would not have been identifiable without the discussions between people who might otherwise think of themselves as strangers. Politics thus makes possible the art of resolving issues in ways that do not lead to violence. Nonetheless Aristotle regards violence as inevitable too, and the virtues he commends are ones that are particularly suited to the soldier.

There are four significant statements here, of which the early church found two straightforward to accommodate, two more difficult. It was straightforward, first, to share Aristotle's assumption that human flourishing is best understood corporately. Paul's proposals to the Corinthians are that they consider what will build up the church. His frustration with them is that the stories he has heard about them concern destructive activities that are bound to be very damaging to corporate life. The notion of *polis*, city, could thus with some ease be translated into the notion of *ekklesia*, assembly (or church).

More difficult, second, was the character of the city-state. Humans may well be political, but this was not to be, for Christians, an abiding city. The New Testament was based around two stories: the journey of Jesus and his companions to Jerusalem, bearing the cross, and the journey of Paul and his companions to Rome, bearing the gospel. The *ekklesia* was a tent not a castle: it was not built on abiding foundations. The people of God were a pilgrim people—traveling light, on the move. Jerusalem was no longer the focus of the Promised Land; its temple was no longer the place where sin was forgiven and grace restored. Israel had lived by spatial notions of home and exile. The church was to transform these into temporal notions of past atonement and future reunion.

For a people sharing a common journey, Aristotle's third conviction, that of virtue, was particularly appropriate. Virtue is a kind of power, the power of being good at something: a power that cannot be acquired overnight. Virtues are derived from repeated practices that a community continually performs because it regards them as central to its identity. Repeated practice nurtures skill, an excellence that derives from repeated performance. Skill develops habit, a disposition to use skills on occasions and in locations different from the times and places where the skill was developed. Habit develops instinct, a pattern of unconscious behavior that reveals a deep element of character. This is the language of virtue. The early church quickly developed key practices that became central to its identity. Chief among these were baptism and Eucharist. The virtues required for a pilgrim people were ones that could be derived from a correct understanding and performance of such practices. A community like the Corinthians who were not practicing the Eucharist faithfully had little prospect of developing the subsequent virtues of justice, temperance, and love.

Where the early church most decisively parted company with Aristotle was in his fourth assumption, that virtue was bound to be shaped by violence.[2] Pilate gave the crowd in the Praetorium a significant choice. They could take Barabbas, the man who offered a rapid solution through seizing control; or they could take Jesus, who claimed to be already a king. They chose Barabbas; but the early church chose Jesus. Thus the early Christians' paradigm of virtue was not the soldier embodying the love of power but the martyr embodying the power of love. To the powerful Roman Empire, citizens who would not take up arms to defend the state were more insidious than revolutionaries who took up arms to destroy it.

The emergence of the church exposed what Aristotle had taken for granted. Now the character of the church was to be transformed, as in the fourth century the Roman Emperor and, in due course, the whole empire embraced the formerly subversive Christians. This revolution gradually exposed what the early church had taken for granted. The early church believed that its own fragile and vulnerable state was deceptive. In fact Christ had conquered the powers by his death and resurrection and ruled as sovereign. They demonstrated this faith by maintaining nonviolence, the practice of confronting evil using only the weapons that Christ himself used. The early Christians also believed that they were a distinct people with a special vocation. Their form of life was dictated by no criterion other than faithfulness to Christ. This identity was expressed in baptism. They believed their common life and servant practice was at the heart of the gospel. They believed their calling was to show what kind of life was possible when communities lived in the light of God's providence, and they embodied this faith in their celebration of the Eucharist.

The Sources of a Reasonable and Useful Church

The new Christian empire challenged these three assumptions. It challenged the commitment to nonviolence. Loyalty to the empire became the test of loyalty to Christ. One could hardly be loyal to the empire if one was not prepared to fight on its behalf; and in any case the struggles of the empire were in the service of Christ. Thus whereas for the early church faith in God's sovereignty was expressed by nonviolence, for the church under the Christian empire faith in God's sovereignty required fighting God's battles.

Likewise the identity of the church was transformed.[3] Far from being an often-persecuted minority, it became the government. Baptism gradually ceased to be a statement of membership of another country and became an affirmation of citizenship of the empire. The church became the arbiter of truth and justice for all people, not just those who by commitment and conviction shared its faith. The church became invisible.

And the heart of the gospel shifted. From being located in the common life of a pilgrim people seeking to discern God's providence in their interactions with one another and the world, it came to be located in the imperial palace. Now that a Christian at last had the opportunity to exercise authority, the significant aspects of the New Testament seemed to be those that best informed the use of power. Thus the paradigm of the Christian moved from martyr to soldier or magistrate, and the beginning of Christian life moved from baptism to birth.

The Christian empire did not have long to develop these assumptions. The barbarian invasions and the breakdown of the Western empire took away the security offered by a single rule and a single faith. Christian life became a specialist pursuit, particularly associated with those in monastic communities and the ordained life, together with outstanding individuals, including Christian kings. Once again, the assumptions of a previous era were exposed. There was no longer the hope that one individual could unite Christendom under godly rule. The location of the gospel thus moved again, this time to the monastery. The conflict with the pagan and Muslim world meant that baptism was a statement of allegiance, and violence was a necessary resort to ensure survival. There was a deep sense of a precious civilization that had been lost: whether that world had been one in which the church had been faithful seemed not to be the key question.

The revival of the culture of western Europe that followed this turbulent period was based partly on the recovery of much of the classical heritage. The culture of the church was a mixture of the culture of the two previous eras. In some respects Christian life exuded the confidence of a powerful Christian ruler, a secure citizenship of an earthly kingdom, and a philosophical assurance that the fruits of human reason coalesced harmoniously with the gifts of divine revelation. In other respects Christian life seemed a precarious struggle against the pervasive enemies of war, famine, and disease, and consequently future judgment, promising heaven and threatening hell, proved the greatest stimulus to faithful living.[4]

The great conflicts within and between states and nations that erupted in the wake of the Reformation illustrated the rival notions of Christian life and the rival sociologies derived from them. The new world that emerged in western Europe in the seventeenth century once again exposed the assumptions of its predecessors. The two rival cultures of the Middle Ages, as I have described them—the secure and the precarious—shared an underlying sense of their place in history. They both understood that the classical period was a golden era, and that the more that could be recovered from it, the richer life would be. (They differed over the extent to which that was possible.) But now a new perception arose: progress. Scientific and philosophical developments encouraged the notion that the golden era might lie in the future, not the past. Salvation lay not in archaeology and theology but in biology and geology.

Religious wars appeared to have seriously dented the moral authority of Christianity.[5] But in any case the movement was away from maintaining authority in external institutions, seeking instead to locate it in the moral individual. The seeds of salvation were now regarded as lying within the self, in the moral law written on every heart; those seeds were no longer assumed to lie outside the self, in the possession of one institution, the church. The drama of the universe ceased to be God's unfathomable forces of life, death, and judgment, and the church's negotiation of them through the preaching of the biblical narrative and the ministration of the sacraments. Now the center of attention was the human individual, the new self, and the drama was humanity's struggle to know and command its environment.

When the center of gravity lay in the common life of the church, the Christian life consisted of faithful participation in the practices of that body in the light of the story of Israel and Jesus. When the center of gravity moved to the seat of political power, the Christian life was directed to ensuring that political power was governed by a greater authority. When the center of gravity was a lost and mourned golden era, a valid Christian life could be offered as a lone heroic gesture amid the encircling gloom. But when the whole notion of external authority and definitive practices was questioned, how could Christianity maintain a call on the new center of gravity—the choosing individual?

Many denied that anything had changed. It was still possible to argue that the center of gravity was political power. After all, the church remained visible at or near the center of government in many western nations. But for those who realized that the church's feast was over, there were two ways of ensuring that Christianity maintained a place at the table. One way was to show that Christian faith was reasonable. Thus there was much work in historical and archaeological veins to demonstrate that the story told in the Bible was plausible and broadly (or wholly) true. Meanwhile there began to be work in a more psychological vein designed to show that religious experience was often genuine, and may well correspond to the philosophical claims of the church. The other way was to demonstrate that Christianity was useful. It became common to show how the historical Jesus embodied and espoused the virtues most highly valued by contemporary society; the church could be seen as a community of ordered love promoting a society of sustainable peace. In short, whether or not Christianity was true, it certainly made people behave better. In an industrializing society where the ability of the urban poor to organize themselves was ever increasing, this argument proved very attractive to many of those in power.

These two strategies for securing the abiding relevance of Christianity, reasonableness and utility, share some assumptions. They share a sense that the convictions of the early church are largely unhelpful for informing ethical debate today. An ethic that is based on God's sovereignty, on the affirmation of the distinct identity of the church, of the significance of its practices of baptism and Eucharist—these convictions are seldom introduced into contemporary ethical discussion. If the center of ethics is the choosing individual, the theories that will prove reasonable and useful are those that make no distinction between persons and treat circumstances and issues regardless of the identities and characters of the people facing them, regardless of notions of overarching providence or everlasting destiny, regardless of the habitual activities of those involved. In this form of argument there may be a valid place for Christianity, as a system and tradition of thought that advocates certain values, but there is little or no place for the church—for the church, like all corporate institutions, seems to represent the tradition of external authority, which has been rejected by contemporary ethical thinking.

The two strategies do, however, differ in a way similar to the way I have described the difference between the Middle Ages and the modern era. The former looked back to restore a lost security, whereas the latter looked forward to establish a new possibility. The claim that Christianity is reasonable is based largely on the reliability of its historical evidence. It is thus principally a retrospective argument. It corresponds with the conviction that ethics is an intrinsic matter, that is, actions are inherently right or wrong in themselves. This intrinsic view of ethics accords with the notion that a natural law, or law of created order, has been established, and the moral life is simply a matter of identifying it and sticking to it. Even when all theological reference is removed from the description of natural law, there is still a strong retrospective force at work. The sense is that there *is* a proper state of things, which *has always been so*, and that departing from it will violate, infringe, or unbalance this proper state.

By contrast the claim that Christianity is useful is not so much an appeal to the past as a commendation for the future. It is principally a prospective argument. It corresponds with the conviction that ethics is an extrinsic matter, that is, that actions are not necessarily right or wrong in themselves, but they should be judged by the likelihood of their bringing about desirable outcomes. This extrinsic view of ethics accords with the assumption that the person acting is the center of the moral universe, and that there is no agreed moral good other than the free activity of each individual so long as it does not infringe on the free activity of another individual. It is the task of individuals to take their destiny in their own hands. The future is a land of opportunity that can be secured by appropriate action in particular circumstances.

These two approaches, the intrinsic (or deontological) and the extrinsic (or consequential), are the two principal forms of ethical argument today. They are the contemporary "establishment," the norm in reference to which any other approach must define itself. The former could be called "ethics for anyone," since it sees the individual as a universal category, the principles of whose actions could apply to anyone, anywhere, at any time. The latter could be called "ethics for everyone," since it has a more democratic impulse, looking for outcomes that suit the most people in the most circumstances.

These are not the only approaches. They rest on the assumption that ethics is "for anyone and everyone," that the same principles and procedures apply to all people in all situations. But as the modern era gives way to the postmodern, a growing number of voices point out the suppressed power relations that underlie these approaches. The ideology of "ethics for everybody" is challenged by the conviction of "ethics for the excluded." Feminist ethics, for example, points out the way conventional approaches frequently confirm the marginalization of women. Other voices speak with and for people excluded by race, class, or sexual orientation. Some of these advocates are modernists, as concerned for individual expression as the conventional approaches—they simply want individual liberty to be extended more justly. They accept the notion of ethics for anyone and everyone, but they want to see equality established so this ethics can take effect. Others regard the excluded group rather as the early Christians saw the church—as a minority community whose practices offer a rival model to the patterns of mainstream society. Environmental ethics extends the representation of the voiceless to the animal, vegetable, and mineral order. Sometimes these and other ethical issues are pursued by particular interest groups as single-issue questions. This represents a loss of confidence in the just conduct of the legislative process; it bypasses party politics in an effort to focus justice on particular questions isolated from all other considerations. It thus recalls some of the cultural breakdown that followed the demise of the western Roman Empire.

Recovering the Resources of Church History for Ethics

The foregoing account has told the story of Christian ethics in six broad eras. For the ease of the narrative (I make no broader claim) I have called these eras early church, Christian empire, decay of empire, Middle Ages, modern, and postmodern. Each of the eras has its own characteristics and assumptions about the nature of the Christian life. Each era emerges from and overlaps with its predecessor. The contemporary scene in Christian ethics is made up of remnants of all the previous eras. There are those who are guided by the modern need to make Christianity reasonable and useful, as a discipline that seeks understanding that suits all people in all situations. There are those who seek to rescue some cause of righteousness amid the chaos of contemporary life. There are some who seek an ethic for rulers, perceiving the church's role as guiding the ethical conduct of government. And there are those who concentrate on faithfulness and common life, whether as the early church understood it or in a new quasi church of marginalized values.

The approach advocated in this book seeks to learn from all of these developments. With the emerging postmodern era, it acknowledges the difficulty of doing "ethics for everybody." It recognizes the tendency of overarching systems to marginalize particular groups. With the modern era, it understands the tension between the Christian tradition and the prevalent emphasis on the thinking individual as the subject of ethical reflection. With the medieval period, it takes seriously the notion of judgment and the precarious characteristics of the Christian life. With the era of the decay of Empire it values the place of exceptional lives of holiness as signs of hope. With the Constantinian period it accepts the need for the church to recognize its political power. But the era with which it has most in common is that of the early church.

In common with the early church this book's approach seeks first to understand ethics specifically for Christians, rather than more generally "for everybody." It restores baptism, rather than birth, as the entry point to the body in question. Because of this it attends to Aristotle's notion of virtue. This is by way of recognizing that ethics is about making good people who live faithfully, rather than about guiding actions so that any person can act rightly. Ethics is about forming lives of commitment, rather than informing lives without commitment. In common with the early church this approach seeks also to understand the common life of the church, its internal "politics," and its relationships with all who are not its members as the heart of God's concern. It restores the Eucharist not just as a sacrament sealing salvation, but also as a practice forming the habits and instincts of the common life of the body. By attention to the regular details of life, it emphasizes that the approach to apparent crises of decision lies in attending to the regular habits and practices already embodied by the community. Dependence on God's providence is a demonstration of faith that, in Jesus and the Holy Spirit, the Father has already given the church all it needs to cope with any crisis that might come along. The church practices that faith by the mode of discernment it adopts—that is the subject of this book. By learning from the early church's practice of nonviolence, this approach insists that the practices of peace—conversation, negotiation, arbitration, reconciliation, celebration—are always involved in the discernment of truth. Thus, though the approach reasserts the church's identity, it can never be one that isolates itself from the rest of society. By being and working with the poorest and most vulnerable, by talking and negotiating with the most powerful and influential, and by seeking to bring all to understand and embrace the Christian faith, the church maintains conversation and seeks to practice nonviolence.

Most of all this approach learns from the early church because it stresses that ethics is theological. Ethics is not about using power, restoring former glory, or fulfilling individual freedom: it is about imitating God, following Christ, being formed by the Spirit to become friends with God. Baptism marks the entry to Christian life because it is the sacrament that enacts entry to new life through Christ's death and resurrection. The Eucharist characterizes the common life because it enacts the way peace and daily bread come through Christ's broken body. Nonviolence is significant because it enacts the way God in Christ chose to save the world and it affirms the victory of the cross. God has broken his life open that we might become his friends by using the gifts he has given us. Ethics considers the best use of these gifts. The way a community discerns the use of God's saving gifts is the subject of this book.

2

Theology as Narrative

Three Strands

There are three broad strands in contemporary writing on Christian ethics. One we might call "universal." The universal approach is principally concerned with finding common ground. Its focus is questions and dilemmas in the public sphere. These include the beginning and end of life, the beginning and conduct of war, the appropriate balance between nature and technology, and issues of global concern such as climate change and the distribution of wealth. It is not generally innovative methodologically. It is usually happy to work with the conventional deontological and consequential categories in seeking to find common cause with nonreligious approaches for the treatment and resolution of issues of public concern. As far as it seeks to articulate a specific Christian contribution to these debates, it is generally guided by the modern need to make Christianity reasonable and useful, as a discipline that seeks understanding that suits all people in all situations. This might be termed "ethics for anybody."[1]

A second strand we might call "subversive." The subversive approaches begin in an attitude of rebellion. On closer inspection, the rebellion is perhaps not so much against the idea that there can be a universal ethic. The point at issue is that the universal ethic tends to be dictated by the powerful, and thus is not truly universal at all, but just a minority view spoken with a loud and influential voice. Beneath this loud and influential voice lies a threat of violence. Such violence is plausible because if a view truly is universal, dissent may quickly seem irrational and reprehensible, and in need of swift correction. Subversive ethics protests at the way the "mainstream" account suppresses alternative voices, excluded for reasons of gender, race, or other social or environmental location, and seeks to make those voices heard, thereby questioning the apparent consensus.

The positive agenda that follows from making these voices heard is more diverse. (One is conscious of Kin Hubbard's observation, "It's going to be fun to watch and see how long the meek can keep the earth after they inherit it.") Some see the church as a way of restoring an inclusive society where no voices are suppressed. This is the more optimistic view. Such people sometimes look to recover and attend to neglected parts of church history. They may for example find periods or places where women's ministry was accepted and valued, where different races were harmoniously incorporated into one fellowship, or where a healthy relationship between human beings and the rest of creation flourished. Others conclude less hopefully that the church will always be wedded to the powerful, that there will never be an inclusive society, and that faithfulness lies in appealing to a new quasi church of marginalized values. This might be called "ethics for the excluded."[2]

A third strand, which we might call "ecclesial," seeks to articulate a distinctive theological ethic. This theological ethic has significant similarities and differences with the previous two approaches. It seeks dialogue with other traditions, but not in the way the "universal" approach does. It perceives that the universal approach does less than justice to the particularity of the Christian tradition. Ecclesial ethics is concerned with the liberating power of Christianity, but not quite in the way the "subversive" approach is. It considers that liberation lies in identifying the particularity of the tradition, rather than in overcoming or ignoring it. It also assumes that if the church is to be faithful, it must always be the church of the poor. The much-quoted saying "The poor are always with you" means not ". . . and therefore you can ignore them," but ". . . and therefore you are always with the poor." The subversive approach is stronger on particularity than the universal strand, but has an anthropology that the ecclesial approach sees as still too much wedded to individual autonomy or self-expression. Ecclesial ethics considers that liberation lies not specifically with the articulation and expression of experience but with the traditions and practices of the church and the character and acts of God. This might be called "ethics for the church." This study pursues this third approach.

At this stage I am concerned to point out that each kind of ethics—universal, subversive, and ecclesial—presupposes a story. I shall now outline what that claim means.

Underlying Narratives in Christian Ethics

The story presupposed by the universal approach is the most difficult to identify, because it is the least self-conscious. But that makes its identification and description all the more important. It is difficult to identify because what I am calling the universal approach covers a considerable variety of methods, each with its own first principles. The proponents of these methods have tended to be rather more conscious of the ways in which their method differed from other methods than they have of the ways in which all of the methods made common assumptions. Indeed, it is perhaps only when the voices of those who have experienced being excluded from the story have made themselves heard that universal ethics has begun to appear as a story at all, and not simply a right and natural order inhabited by competing perceptions.

The simplest way to explore some of these methods is to notice the elements of the Christian faith each method takes to be foundational. A variety of models present themselves, of which five may be mentioned here. One model of theology takes its notion of theology to begin with reflection on and study of sacred *texts*—notably, the books of the Bible. These texts are taken to be distillations of wisdom beyond that reachable by unaided human reflection. They are considered, together and separately, as revelation. The purpose of theology is to provide an exegesis of these sacred texts. Another model of theology is to locate the foundational substance behind the texts in the *events* the texts describe. This approach sees sacred events as central, and the texts as one means, perhaps the best but certainly not the only, of getting to the sacred events. Theology is principally concerned with establishing the history of these vital events. A third model of theology sees truth as lying beyond texts and even events, and instead in a logical system of interlocking *doctrines* describing the person and activity of the sacred being, God. Dogmatic inquiry and reflection thus exist to distill ordered and plausible truth from a range of sources, including text, event, and practice. Sometimes nontheological discourse is given a higher status in this inquiry, and the object is to produce a *philosophical* system rather than a dogmatic one.

With the turn to the subject associated with the Enlightenment, it has become more common for theology to be considered as the study of sacred *experience*—not necessarily of sacred characters long ago, but particularly of the range of experience accessible to the contemporary heart and mind. And this is the point at which the narrative character of the universal approach begins to emerge. For it quickly appears that some people's experience seems to count for more than others'. If an experience is related that questions, challenges, or contradicts the accepted wisdom, it can be very difficult for that experience to get a hearing. What is revealed is the social structure of knowledge. A whole series of implicit power relations emerges. There are unspoken rules governing who gets to decide if something is legitimate, valuable, or true. And this discovery is where subversive ethics begins.

Subversive ethics constantly highlights the power relations at work in theological and other discourse. The winners have written not just the history, but the theology too. So, to take the most common example, men have constructed a theology of a male God: this has underwritten a patriarchal social structure and inhibited women's freedom, experience, voices, ministries, lives.[3] To take a similarly oft-quoted example, the intimate link between Christianity, commerce, and "civilization" in the scramble for Africa contrived, in many cases, to leave faith in the hearts of the conquered and land in the hands of the conqueror.[4] In another sphere, reflection on the experience of faith among the poorest residents of Latin American countries has enabled many to articulate that their principal encounter with God takes place not in the pietist quietism commended by some of their church leaders but in the active attempt to take control of their own economic and social destiny.[5] Again, a suitable reading of the creation story has given permission to an ideology of domination over the nonhuman creation that has left the two-thirds world and its rain forests and marginal lands reeling from the rampaging demands of the rich countries' consumers.[6]

In each case the widespread experience of the "excluded" has been that their experience seems to be part of a different story from the prevailing theological and social narrative. The rival notions of theology as exegesis of sacred texts, history of sacred events, formation of a dogmatic or philosophical system, or reflection on sacred experience seem, in the light of these rival and excluded stories, to have rather more significant agreements than differences. Universal ethics presupposes that there is one story, but masks that story in the assumption that it is everybody's story. Subversive ethics, by beginning with the experience of exclusion and oppression, points out that this (by no means universal) ideology has an implicit story; that this story is an instrument of domination; and that in fact there are numerous rival stories, representing a host of suppressed parties. Sometimes subversive ethics can take a "modern" turn and substitute a new metanarrative for the one it has supplanted—assuming, for example, that Marx's story of class struggle defines the Latin American context. More often, subversive ethics takes a postmodern turn and rejoices in the many liberated narratives and previously forgotten histories, whether they are compatible with one another or not. The notion of coherence can become secondary to the emphasis on the authentic and legitimate voicing of the experience of oppression.

This therefore is the perception of many in the theological world: that the denial of narrative and the emphasis on propositional truth is an acquiescence in an oppressive system of power relations; that any form of overarching metanarrative is likely to be a covert form of oppression by other means; and that the discovery, permission, and affirmation of previously suppressed stories is an imperative that supersedes the quest for a single, coherent expression of truth. What therefore might it mean to talk of narrative in ecclesial terms?

Ecclesial Ethics and Its Discontents

Ecclesial ethics is ethics for the church. Each of the previous definitions of theology had an understanding of the location of the discipline. Some saw that location in a particular text; some in a particular sequence of events, described by the text; some in a particular order of doctrinal or philosophical thought. A counterview saw theology residing in human experience, particularly in the experience of oppression and exclusion. Ecclesial ethics has its own definition of theology. It sees the key location of theology as being in the practices of the church. This is only secondarily about a sacred text, sequence of events, or set of doctrines; it is primarily about the formation, development, and renewal of a sacred *people*. It is this people, the sacred community, that is the center of ethical reflection. This is what God wants as his witness in his world and as companion in the kingdom. This is what Jesus came into the world to embody and gave his life to make possible. This is what the Bible was written to encourage and guide, and this is what theologians are called to resource and challenge. The sacred community is the touchstone of virtue. That which builds it up and enables it to be faithful is good and right and true; that which attempts to bypass it or contrives to render it invisible or undermines it from within is dubious, misguided, or dangerous.

The story presupposed by ecclesial ethics is as follows: Israel was called to be a priestly kingdom and a holy nation. Being holy meant being distinctive and being like God. Being priestly meant that other nations would benefit from the "ministry" of Israel so long as Israel retained its distinctiveness. God then gave Israel everything it needed to be holy and priestly. It had the law to guarantee God's promise and reveal God's heart. It had the land in which to grow and flourish. It had, in due time, a king to provide unity under God and leadership in God's ways. And it had the temple to enshrine its covenant with God and to restore that relationship whenever the people went astray. Land, king, and temple were lost in the exile, and each was restored only in parody. Though the people returned to the Lord, they were ruled by foreigners. Though there were sometimes kings, there was no return to the tradition of David. Though there was a new temple, there was no ark of the covenant at the heart of it. But during the exile the people's sense of what constituted the covenant was renewed, and this renewal provided the space in which God did a new thing for and with his people.

Jesus embodied that renewed covenant and redefined land, king, and temple. He called to him a renewed people, with continuities going back before the exile (twelve apostles representing the twelve tribes) but also with resonances of a people returning from exile (the incorporation of outcasts, the unclean, tax collectors, and women). He directed the people's attention to an eschatological horizon beyond the land dominated by the Romans. He pointed out that the second temple had not brought reconciliation with God and spoke of his body as a new temple. The resultant conflict was played out on his body, in his passion and death. Through his resurrection and the sending of the Spirit, his disciples realized that a new and definitive reconciliation had taken place. Meanwhile, the notion of his "body" had changed. Now it was they who, in the practices of forming their common life—incorporating newcomers, maintaining the community, deliberating over its good order, and restoring it when it faced the setbacks of external persecution and internal dissent or weakness—it was they who, in these practices, were now his body. They were a royal priesthood and a holy nation. They had a vocation to imitate God in Christ and to offer their distinctive life as a gift to the world. And they, too, found that God gave them everything they needed to follow him. Paul's journey to Rome echoed Jesus' journey to Jerusalem. As Jesus' journey focused the hopes of Israel, so Paul's journey opened those hopes out to the whole world.

The centuries that followed brought periodic persecution, and this, together with the desire to incorporate the maximum number of newcomers into its fellowship, made the offer of increasing involvement in the government of the empire from the early fourth century very attractive. However, the price of this was to make the church largely invisible. The journey to "universal" ethics names these ways in which the church became invisible. The location of theology and ethics ceased to be the sacred community, the holy people, and became a host of other things. The journey of St. Antony symbolizes this change.[7] The conversion of

the Roman emperor meant that one battle had been won, but another
had been lost. Antony left Alexandria, the great city of antique culture,
to set up his cell in the Egyptian desert as the first of the Desert Fathers.
The battleground was no longer on the boundary of church and world.
It was now in the human heart, between flesh and spirit.

Three temptations have misled the church ever since the time of St.
Antony. The first is to see the principal location of theology as the world,
or "society"—the political whole. By making the church invisible this
approach gives up on God's primary mode of working in the world. It
also opens the church's heart to further temptations. Christians may
begin to confuse the church and the world, trying to make the world the
church, or treating it as if it were. If Christians do not have a distinctive
community, they will seek prominent positions amongst the powerful
in the world. They may well regard it as their responsibility, rather than
God's, to make the world come out right, to usher in the kingdom. They
will therefore need to form a different set of allies, and find themselves
with a different set of enemies. This is the danger of "universal" ethics.
And this is before it even starts to coerce those who disagree.[8]

A second, contrasting, temptation often corresponds with a very
negative, even dualist, view of the status of creation. The temptation
is to assume that because the sacred community is the key location of
theology, because God's principal way of working in the world is through
the church, then God has no purpose for the rest of his creation. This is
putting the holiness of the community prior to the holiness of God. The
church may be the principal way in which God works in the world, but
it is by no means the only one. The church needs to be alive to all the
ways in which God works in the world, not to confine itself to just one,
albeit the principal one. Sectarianism is usually regarded as one way
in which the church makes a problem for the world. The nature of this
alleged problem is twofold. The existence of groups who emphasize their
separateness weakens liberal democracy and makes conflict more likely.
In the particular case of Christian separateness, the world is furthermore
deprived of the (perhaps ambiguous) advantage of the church's ministry,
and of a healthy place in the church's theological scheme. But this is
to see the issue the wrong way around. Sectarianism is not primarily
a problem for the world, although it can present dilemmas for liberal
democracies. Sectarianism is, on the contrary, primarily a problem for
the church. It is a problem because a church that is cutting itself off
largely or entirely from its surrounding society is thereby depriving
itself of many of the ways in which God's grace is made plain in the
world through the Holy Spirit. God is still giving the church all it needs
to follow him, but the church is denying itself access to many of these
gifts. It is like the third slave who buries his talent in the hillside—and

it can expect the same reward. This temptation is much discussed and feared by social commentators—but is in fact relatively rarely adopted. It remains a temptation nonetheless.[9]

A third, more subtle, temptation can thrive under the guise of either of the previous two. It is to perceive that in the knowledge of certain key pieces of information, not universally available, one has a unique power—power, for example, to be intimate with God and to live with him eternally. This perception of a secret knowledge is known as Gnosticism. The name "Gnosticism" is a term associated with a heresy of the second century. But the Enlightenment's turn to the subject and the contemporary desire to secure individual security and fulfillment provide fertile soil for a looser use of the term "Gnostic." For the Gnostic, the spiritual quest is an inherently individual matter. The location of theology, if such a term can still be used, lies in the heart and mind of each discrete individual. Human community is secondary, and is valuable only to encourage, resource, or stimulate the individual experience. Other people are more likely to be an obstacle than to be a requirement of fulfillment. Gnosticism consistently bypasses the need for human community and establishes communion with God on grounds that do not require the conversations and compromises and habits of regular contact with other people.

Within the second, "sectarian" temptation Gnosticism underwrites a sense of superiority over the faithless, perhaps evil, world. The church becomes a group of people who each have a special knowledge, or an access to a special experience, that the world cannot have. While contact with the world might extend the number of people who may discover that knowledge or experience, it carries the perpetual risk of sullying or diminishing the knowledge or experience by sharing it with those who would not respect it or even seek to undermine it. The first, "universal" temptation is a more common place to find it. Gnosticism tends to exist as an emphasis on personal piety, perhaps together with an emphasis on doctrinal purity. Thus Christians may engage in the most damaging public practices while still assuming that thinking "the right things" about salvation or having a "close personal relationship" with God ensures that righteousness remains with them.

A church whose members believe that the true location of theology lies in their own private knowledge and experience is desperately vulnerable. It is defenseless against an ideology that calls them to corporate commitment and sacrifice. So long as that ideology makes no demands on their doctrinal purity or individual experience it can persuade Christians to perform ghastly injustices and cruelties without realizing their error.[10] Such tragedies have taken place countless times in recent decades, from Auschwitz to Kigali, from Santiago to the Pentagon. The individual simply is not strong enough to carry the full weight of theological liberation—to become the church. Gnosticism delivers the church into captivity—into exile. What is needed is an understanding of the church that is not so committed to the universal or the individual that the church becomes invisible, but is meanwhile not so committed to the visibility of the church that it seeks to make the world invisible (at least to the church). What is needed is for the church to be restored as the primary location of theological and ethical enquiry.

This then is the story that ecclesial ethics presupposes, the "narrative" that lies behind narrative ethics; and these are the temptations the telling of this story is designed to avoid. Four elements coalesce to make this distinctive ecclesial ethic. The *church*, the sacred community, is understood as the focus of God's purposes for the world, the witness of his grace, and the earnest of the destiny he has prepared for all of creation—friendship with God. The unit of ethics is neither the universal world nor the isolated individual but the particular church. The *narrative* I have outlined above is the way the church remembers its identity, recognizing that the failures and blind alleys are as significant as the saintly lives and golden eras. This narrative paints tiny human lives, plans, and histories into the awesome canvas of God's everlasting providence. It slips earnest efforts and ignoble failures into the pocket of God's original creation and final fulfillment. It embraces the tyranny of the pointless present with the everlasting arms of sacred memory and saving hope. The Christian story places Christ at the center of meaning and delivers humanity from the agony of meaninglessness, transforming the unavoidable fate of our mortal folly into the glorious destiny of his unending joy. Confidence in this story gives the church the resources to engage with other and rival stories. The center of the church's life is the *practices* through which the church is formed, extended, and restored. Through reading Scripture, baptizing, sharing communion, seeking God's forgiveness, being reconciled with one another, interceding, making peace, the church incorporates its tradition and offers a priestly ministry to the world. The church constantly reflects on the way it performs these practices, seeking always to be shaped into the life of Christ by carrying them out faithfully. Narrative and practices form *witnesses*—disciples who embody the church's life in prayer and service. These witnesses are the church's truth claim—it has no purchase on truth that is detached from the transformation of lives and communities brought about by its narrative and practices. Individuals are not the location of theological reflection, but they can be the symbols and narrative and sacramental transformation. Their changed lives embody the hope of the community. They are the most visible face of the church, the most public ambassadors of God.[11]

Saints and Heroes

A number of questions may still remain. How do these ecclesial witnesses differ from Gnostic individuals? How does the particularity of the church's narrative issue in lives of witness? What criteria define the faithfulness of that witness? Is Christianity about great individuals or about good communities? The answer to these questions lies in a significant distinction that summarizes the argument of this chapter. The distinction lies in a subtle difference between antique and theological wisdom.

Aristotle sought to inspire his readers to be heroes. The virtues he commends are noble ones, and the lives he advocates are ones of effort and attention. His followers will, if faithful, be capable of making decisive interventions that swing the course of a battle, or a debate, or a long cultural struggle. Without them, all might be lost. They are formed in the virtues required to negotiate an awesome role: they are prepared to be the center of the story. They stand out from the crowd, they form friendships only with others of similar stature. They are self-sufficient and resilient amid setbacks. The definitive icon of virtue is the soldier, who is prepared to risk death for the sake of a higher good. The noblest death is death in battle, for battle offers the greatest danger, thus requiring the greatest courage.

Today's readers tend to have difficulty reading Aristotle. But they find him difficult not because he places the hero at the center of the story: they take for granted that the story is about them. Neither do they particularly balk at the underlying assumption of violence—the emblematic role of the soldier: for they assume that in a world of limited goods, there is bound to be conflict at some stage so that good may prevail. No, what today's readers find most difficult about Aristotle is his assumption that, though everyone would want to be a hero, very few people will be, and that so being requires a Herculean effort of discipline and will. Today's readers object to such elitism. Democracy flattens out such distinctions. It dictates that everyone has the "right" to be a hero, and it shouldn't be restricted to those with aptitude, effort, and skill. Because everyone can be a hero, the most mundane of activities and commitments and achievements may be regarded as heroic. The exception is the hero that makes a beautiful gesture abstracted from story—who forms a human bridge to help passengers escape a sinking ship, or rescues a child from the flames. Anyone can be a hero by making a spontaneous gesture. The point is not that these activities are highly regarded, but that everyone must have the right to be regarded as the center of his or her own story.

Aquinas did not seek to inspire his readers to be heroes. The virtues he commends are not those that enable his readers to make decisive interventions in the heat of battle or the height of controversy. The virtues he proposes are those that enable Christians to follow Christ. They are not called to be heroes. They are called to be saints. The word "hero" does not appear in the New Testament. The word "saint" occurs sixty-four times. What is the difference between a hero and a saint? Five differences present themselves.

To start with, there is a significant difference between the kind of story that is told about heroes and the kind of story that is told about saints. The hero always makes a decisive intervention at a moment when things are looking like they could all go badly wrong. The hero steps up and makes everything turn out right. In other words, the hero is always at the center of the story. By contrast, the saint is not necessarily a crucial character. The saint may be almost invisible, easily missed, quickly forgotten. The hero's story is always about the hero. The saint is always at the periphery of a story that is really about God.

Next comes the question of why the story is told. The hero's story is always told to celebrate the virtues of the hero. The hero's strength, courage, wisdom, or great timing: such are the qualities on which the hero's decisive intervention rests. By contrast the saint may well not have any great qualities. The saint may not be strong, brave, clever, or opportunistic. But the saint is faithful. The story of the hero is told to rejoice in valor. The story of the saint is told to celebrate faith.

Third, there is what the story takes for granted. The definitive heroic icon is the soldier, who is prepared to risk death for the sake of a higher good. The noblest death is death in battle, for battle offers the greatest danger, thus requiring the greatest courage. The story assumes that in a world of limited resources, there is bound to be conflict at some stage so that good may prevail. But saints assume a very different story. They do not need to learn how to fight over competing goods, because Christ has fought for and secured the true good, and the goods that matter now are not limited or in short supply. Love, joy, peace, faithfulness, gentleness—these do not rise or fall with the stock market. The saint's story does not presuppose scarcity; it does not require the perpetuation of violence. Whereas the icon of heroism is the soldier, the icon of sanctity is the martyr. The soldier faces death in battle; the martyr faces death by not going to battle. The soldier's heroism is its own reward: it makes sense in any language that respects nobility and aspires to greatness. The martyr's sanctity makes no sense unless rewarded by God: it has no place in any story except that of Christ's redeeming sacrifice and the martyr's heavenly crown.

Fourth, there is what happens when the story goes wrong. The hero is at the center of the story. It is the hero's decisive intervention that makes the story come out right. Without the hero all would be lost. So if the hero makes a mistake, if the hero bungles or exposes a serious flaw—it is a disaster, a catastrophe, probably fatal for the story and, if it is a big story, possibly pretty serious for life as we know it. By contrast, the saint expects to fail. If the saint's failures are honest ones, they merely highlight the wonder of God's greater victory. If the saint's failures are less admirable ones, they open out the cycle of repentance, forgiveness, reconciliation, and restoration that is what Christians call a new creation. A hero fears failure, flees mistakes, and knows no repentance: the saint knows that light only comes through cracks, that beauty is as much (if not more) about restoration as about creation.

Finally, the hero stands alone against the world. The story of the hero shows how he or she stands out from the community by the excellence of his or her virtue, the decisiveness of his or her intervention, or their simple right to have his or her story told. The story of God tells how he expects a response from his disciples that they cannot give on their own: they depend not only on him but on one another for resources that can sustain faithful lives, and they discover that their dependence on one another is not a handicap but is central to their witness. Of those sixty-four references to saints in the New Testament, every one is in the plural. Saints are never alone. They assume, demand, require community—a special kind of community, the communion of saints. Heroes have learned to depend on themselves; saints learn to depend on God and on the community of faith. The church is God's new language, and it speaks not of a country fit for heroes to live in but of a commonwealth of saints.

That is why, if theological ethics is to tell a story that continues to be about God, it must concentrate on the narrative and practice of the church and the witness of the saints.[12]

3

Narrative as Drama

I began by telling a story that displayed how ethics arises from theological reflection on context. I went on to show how all theological reflection presupposes a narrative and to commend a particular narrative and a particular mode of theological reflection. It is my purpose now to demonstrate that narrative is appropriately subsumed under the more comprehensive and appropriate designation of drama.

As I noted in the previous chapter, one understanding of theology describes it as a discipline that studies sacred texts. Were that to be my understanding also, the category of narrative would be an appropriate genre in which to proceed. The Bible is the key sacred text, and the Bible tells a long, loose, but still coherent story, upon which the nonnarrative passages are dependent and to which they give enrichment. Another view of theology is to see it as the consideration of sacred events, the significant moments and sequences behind the texts. This too lends itself to narrative interpretation—the notion of "salvation history." But my argument rests elsewhere. I take the principal location of theological enquiry to be the community of faith.

If the community of faith is the primary subject of theological ethics, narrative becomes an inadequate category for interpretation. In my previous chapter I criticized what I described as the "Gnostic" temptation. This is the temptation to regard the interactions with other disciples that make up the routines and practices of community as either tiresome interruptions of the seamless individual experience or unnecessary trappings of the pure doctrinal knowledge that are often taken to be the heart of Christian identity. The reason why a narrative understanding of theology is inadequate to describe the life of the community of faith is that it remains open to such a Gnostic interpretation. The narrative—notwithstanding its many blind alleys, false prophets, unresolved tensions, and inconsistent outcomes—may still become a "secret knowledge." Such a treatment is flawed because it can be a "secret" that the church perceives itself to have as a means of making itself superior to the world (as a talisman of salvation); and it is misguided in that it can be a "knowledge" that inhibits embodiment and becomes a substitute for action.

Theological ethics requires the written text, but is not limited to the written word. It assumes interpretation, but can never be just a verbal matter, written or spoken. It inevitably involves the organization of interpretation and its structuring into doctrine, but this exercise must always be a support to something else, not an end in itself. That something else is the embodiment of the text, the events it describes, its interpretation and systematic construal in the practices and performance of the community. This is a dynamic, spiraling process of constant repetition, reinterpretation, transfer, and restoration of meaning, of things never being the same again and other things being rediscovered, ever new. It is what happens when words leave the page, when thoughts leave the mind, when actions ripple through other lives and cause further actions and further thoughts. It is what happens when narrative becomes drama.[1]

Von Balthasar and Theo-Drama

The theologian who has given most consideration to the notion of theology as drama is Hans Urs von Balthasar. He searches for a genre that does justice to the dialogue between God and humanity, to the interaction between the finite freedom of humanity and the infinite freedom of God, and to the way those dialogues are played out through the reception and rejection of the Word. He proposes an understanding of salvation as a drama of divine recklessness and human caution.[2]

Von Balthasar charts a similar journey to that which I made in the last chapter, but on a much grander scale. In the second volume of his *Theo-Drama*, he makes a distinction between three perspectives from which a person may regard a story. Following Hegel's outline in his *Aesthetics: Lectures on Fine Art*, von Balthasar describes the way the dramatic perspective differs from the epic and the lyric.[3] The *epic* point of view is that of the person who has not witnessed the events, but has carefully gathered up all the appropriate information, and has been concerned that his or her own judgments and presuppositions should not unduly influence the account. The skill of the storyteller in weaving a host of disparate details into a comprehensive, coherent, and plausible narrative is as much valued in epic as the ability to offer the detached, objective maturity of the observer. The *lyric* perspective accepts that a profound narrative is almost bound to have a significant impact on the storyteller. If the observer is genuinely close enough to see events as they unfold, he or she will probably have a deep personal investment in their outcome, or will at least have found that the story has far-reaching resonances with aspects of the observer's own character and experience. The fact that the narrator is so close to or almost becomes part of the story makes the narrative all the more compelling as the listener disentangles the subjective from the more objective aspects of the account. The *dramatic* perspective synthesizes the strengths of the epic and lyric dimensions. Like the lyric, it does justice to the role of the subject, the way that events arise from the hearts and minds and actions of people, rather than from impersonal external forces. Like the epic, it perceives an object that has reason and validity beyond the subjectivity of the involved observer.[4]

An illustration will further explain von Balthasar's (and Hegel's) three perspectives, and how drama emerges from the dialectic between epic and dramatic. During the Israeli destruction of Jenin in the West Bank in April 2002 I was in Tunisia, sitting down to supper with a friend in her house in a suburb of Tunis. During supper my friend's sister telephoned from England. She said she had seen on the British television news a report of an attack by local Muslim extremists on a synagogue in Jerba, a hundred miles south of Tunis. My friend reported this at the table with some concern. For her, it highlighted the aspects of life in Tunisia that she had struggled with, despite her conversion to Islam, throughout the forty years since she had begun to live in the country, and it raised painful issues of identity. My friend's seventeen-year-old granddaughter was at table with us. She had no concerns about her identity. Though her mother was both Tunisian and British, her father was Tunisian, and she herself had spent her whole life in Tunisia. She did not grasp what had happened until the story of the events in Jerba was related a second time in Arabic. Then her eyes turned to fire, her shoulders stiffened, and her cheeks warmed. "They do it to us," she said, hotly (referring to the coalition she perceived between the current military policy of the state of Israel and, more vaguely, global institutions influenced by leaders who are Jewish). "Why shouldn't we do it to them?" My friend looked at me plaintively, and in consternation. "Islam needs a reformation, but it can only come from the inside—not from people like me. But I am part of this world now, it is my religion too—and I must share in that reformation somehow."

In the language of von Balthasar, my friend's sister and the BBC news aspired to an epic perspective. Their concern was to be detached, objective, factual, dispassionate, thorough, coherent, and mature. My friend's granddaughter embodied the lyric mode. Her passionate response was anything but detached, but the real action was taking place in her own heart, in the realm of her own limited experience. Though clearly not responsible for the events in Jerba, nor the victim of the events in Jenin that triggered them, nor indeed having ever personally experienced the suffering she described, she nonetheless talked the language of "we," with the passion of a participant. Yet she was not a participant, nor did the event stir her to any particular active response. My friend, in contrast, displayed the dramatic dimension. My tension, as her guest, was in watching her feel involved in all the different points of view, yet try to maintain her identity, her integrity, her own ability to tell a coherent story. While the news from Britain demanded thought, and my friend's granddaughter's reaction demanded feeling, my friend's predicament demanded involvement, dialogue, response. As she was embraced by the story, one could not help but enter the story with her. This was not just a story, nor was it, by contrast, a story primarily about her: but it was a story in progress, in which she saw herself as a participant, albeit not a central one. Her perception of the events in Jerba quickly moved her to action—not just a reaction, but a life quest involving identity and sacrifice. The point at issue here is not the appropriateness of her response but its genuineness, its imaginative participation, and its effect on the observer.

Von Balthasar points out that the epic perspective is inadequate as a mode of theological discourse. It talks of key events as finished and completed. The Eucharist becomes a memorial of an event, rather than an event in itself. God is a third person subject, and individual action is always governed by a deeper force, above and beyond the particular agent. Epic can see it all from the perspective of a disinterested observer. It tells a story that draws out the significance of events for a wider, perhaps universal context. In this sense, the epic perspective is neither possible nor desirable. It is not possible because reality is much more contingent, and perception much less detachable, than the epic point of view assumes. Epic tells a story, but not a story that resembles the world as it is, nor the world that is part of God's story. It ignores the absurdity of a detached account of God, as if one had a broader view than God has. It is not desirable because judgments involved in detached perception tend not to provoke or inspire appropriate involvement. I keep a cartoon in my study of a bevy of psychiatrists gathering on a harbor wall, in deep discussion. Out in the bay is a drowning man, waving and hollering to them. The caption says, "So we're agreed, then: it's probably a cry for help." This is the undesirable mode of the epic perspective.

Von Balthasar is equally clear when it comes to the shortcomings of the lyric mode. For lyric, reality is not so much total objectivity, but intimate subjectivity. Experience and expression are the key, and objective fact and reality are secondary. Lyric lends itself to a spirituality that imaginatively engages with past events, that speaks with Christ on the cross, touches his wounds, and experiences the Eucharist as a living sacrifice of power and passion. Heart speaks to heart, not head to head. But, like the epic perspective, the lyric mode is inadequate in its perception of the world and in its apprehension of God. In relation to the world it is exaggerated in its perception of the self-importance of what is, in the end, a creature. In relation to God, it mirrors Greek mythology in dragging God into the world's process of suffering. The story of incarnation, death, and resurrection is not primarily an event in the believer's heart. It is more dramatic than that.

Von Balthasar's notion of drama brings together the internal intentions and dispositions of acting characters with the external events and deeds of the story. Thus he synthesizes the subjectivity of lyric with the objectivity of epic. The apostolic witness is one whose life and faith speaks to believer (lyric) and unbeliever (epic), and whose experience of God's prior action becomes part of the testimony. The authors of the New Testament write as apostolic witnesses in this dramatic mode. Mark writes in the wake of the women's ironic silence as they leave the empty tomb with the good news. Paul writes as one who has been met on the Damascus road and assumes that others will likewise be met on their journeys. As other authors have pointed out, drama offers a new way for theology to engage with time. Lyric ignores time by reverting to atemporal subjectivity, while epic strives to overcome the contingency of time through imposing an artificial coherence. Drama celebrates and embraces an open and social future.[5]

The theo-dramatic expanse of history is explored over five volumes. It is a drama of infinite (divine) versus finite (human) freedom. The Father is the author of the drama, the Son the actor, and the Spirit the director. The main characters are God, who is responsible for the play, humanity, which is endowed with and condemned to freedom, and the mediator, Jesus Christ, who is the true character, and a model for the others. Israel, the nations, the Christian individual, and the angels and demonic powers all take their places among the dramatis personae. The following passage summarizes God's role in the drama:

The Father . . . could not involve himself more profoundly than by [sending the Son and the Spirit]. . . . The Son dedicates himself to the world's salvation just as eternally as the Father does; from before all time, he pledges himself to carry out the world plan, through his cross, for the good . . . of the world. And even after accomplishing his earthly mission, when he seems to "wait" for the end . . . he fills this period of waiting with his kingly . . . and even bellicose . . . activity. Thus, having overcome the last enemy, he acts as Judge, subsequently to hand the kingdom over to his Father. As for the Spirit, the incorruptible "witness" who registers all things objectively, he is also the "love of God poured forth" . . . throughout the entire drama; he is profoundly involved from within, right to the very end, and "with sighs too deep for words" he moves the tangled drama on toward its solution, "the glorious freedom of the children of God."[6]

In this spirit von Balthasar notes René Girard's portrayal of the way Jesus unmasks the use of sacrifice as redemptive violence. While pointing out that it was sin, rather than just sin's consequences, that Jesus took on himself and overcame, von Balthasar nonetheless commends Girard's project as "the most dramatic" in contemporary soteriology and theology generally.[7]

The conclusion of the drama is that the cross "completes the world's incorporation into the divine life."[8] Through the ascension, heaven's gates are perpetually open, and the Christian lives in heaven as much as on earth. "The world is a gift, a gift presented by the Father to the Son, and by the Son to the Father, and by the Spirit to them both. It is a gift to the Trinity because . . . each of the divine persons, in a way that is their own, has enabled the world to have some part in the wondrous exchange of the inner-divine life."[9]

Reconsidering von Balthasar

A number of commentators have criticized von Balthasar's execution of his grand project. Perhaps the most common observation is that his treatment is almost too much about God. That is, the theo-drama is an event too much within the divine life. Humanity's role amongst the dramatis personae is relatively insignificant. Likewise when he comes to describe the church, von Balthasar is too prone to revert to the language of perfection and ideal types. Even when he meditates on the descent to hell, he falls into mythological language, departing from the drama of time. In short he cannot quite maintain the dramatic tension of balancing epic and lyric: anxious about modernity's tendency to question, to doubt, and to debate, he lapses into epic mode and the perception of a predetermined narrative.[10] The underlying implication is that open-ended, undetermined time is the enemy of the theo-drama, rather than its friend. The present tense, the time and place where the theo-drama is worked out in ordinary and extraordinary ways before watching eyes, the time and place where the church strives to embody this drama, somehow disappears.

It will have become apparent to the reader that there are significant similarities between von Balthasar's notion of epic and my description in the last chapter of the aspirations of "universal" ethics. There are corresponding similarities between von Balthasar's understanding of lyric and my description of some of the commitments of "subversive" ethics. What I described as the "Gnostic" temptation can be seen, in the light of the foregoing treatment of von Balthasar, as the temptation to avoid the vicissitudes of time by reverting to inner lyric experience or overarching epic truth. What is needed is a truly dramatic theological ethic, one that incorporates von Balthasar's commitment to a synthesis of lyric and epic, while genuinely embracing time as a friend, and therefore reinstating the practices of the church and the significance of the present. This is what I now seek to describe.

In a highly suggestive essay, Tom Wright explores what it means to regard the Bible as authoritative. He seeks to explain how a story, specifically this story, has "a shape and goal that must be observed and to which appropriate response must be made." He explores this suggestion as follows:

> Suppose there exists a Shakespeare play whose fifth act had been lost. The first four acts provide, let us suppose, such a wealth of characterization, such a crescendo of excitement within the plot, that it is generally agreed the play ought to be staged. Nevertheless, it is felt inappropriate actually to write a fifth act once and for all. . . . Better, it might be felt, to give the key parts to highly trained, sensitive, and experienced Shakespearian actors, who would immerse themselves in the first four acts, and in the language and culture of Shakespeare and his time, *and who would then be told to work out a fifth act for themselves.*
>
> . . . The "authority" of the first four acts would not consist in an implicit command that the actors should repeat the earlier parts of the play over and over again. It would consist in the fact of an as yet unfinished drama, which contained its own impetus, its own forward movement, which demanded to be concluded in the proper manner but which required of the actors a responsible entering in to the story as it stood, in order first to understand how the threads could appropriately be drawn together, and then to put that understanding into effect by speaking and acting with both *innovation* and *consistency.*
>
> . . . Among the detailed moves available within this model, . . . is the possibility of seeing the five acts as follows: (1) Creation; (2) Fall; (3) Israel;

(4) Jesus. The New Testament would then form the first scene in the fifth act, giving hints as well (Rom 8; 1 Cor 15; parts of the Apocalypse) of how the play is supposed to end. The church would then live under the "authority" of the extant story, being required to offer something between an improvisation and an actual performance of the final act.[11]

I believe the proposal that God's story, like Shakespeare's stories, is a five-act play is immensely promising, and I shall shortly outline what I see as the potential of this model. But before doing so I will point out four points of disagreement with Wright's suggestion.

The first is that I sense it is wrong to put the church at the end of the story. It is not the church's role to make the story end well. The story is not an enigma that God has left the church to resolve. The church lies within the story, rather than at the end of it. In this sense von Balthasar is right—the story is fundamentally about God. Von Balthasar may over-emphasize the degree to which the story is about the intra-Trinitarian relations, but nonetheless the story begins and ends in God. To see the church as the conclusion of the story, or as the company charged with bringing the right conclusion out of the story, is too "lyric." The story ends when and how God wants it to, whether the church has "guessed right" or "performed faithfully" or not.

The second point, following on from the first, is that Wright's model insufficiently distinguishes the church from the eschaton. The reason the church is not at the end of the story is that God brings the story to an end. The eschaton has been criticized for being an "epic" doctrine. Apocalyptic speculation lends itself to the Gnostic temptation of a secret knowledge that tries to circumvent the contingencies of community and the open-endedness of time through the assurance of a guaranteed ending. But eschatology and apocalyptic are not necessarily the same thing.[12] Eschatology seeks to show the sovereignty of God in the outcome of his creation. It does not have to speculate about timings, events, or portents. It simply states that the God who began the story and transformed the story will end the story as he sees fit. Act Five must be his final act, the eschaton.

The third disagreement is that Jesus should be in the middle of the story. Jesus embodied the true relationship with God for which the world was made; he embodied the ultimate covenant to the world to which God committed himself. He was the point to which the creation of the world pointed forward, and he is the point to which the end of the world, as final conclusion and as purposeful telos, points back. It makes no sense to distinguish the New Testament from Jesus, since the New Testament was written to attest to Jesus. Jesus must take his place in Act Three.

The fourth point of engagement is the separation of creation and fall into Acts One and Two. This hardly seems justified on the scriptural treatment given to these inaugural events. It also presupposes that the fall is an act of God. One may be concerned to ensure God's sovereignty over all events, good and bad, and one may even, in the light of Easter, see the fall as that happy sin of Adam that allowed so great a redemption. But it is surely more helpful to see the fall as human misconstrual of God's created gift of freedom, and thus to see it as part of Act One. Thus the first act, like the following three, contains both glory and horror.

A Five-Act Play

What emerges after these four amendments to Tom Wright's model is a revised version of the five-act play. Act One is creation, Act Two is Israel, Act Three is Jesus, Act Four is the church, and Act Five is the eschaton. This is a truly theo-dramatic model. It avoids being too "epic" by offering a genuine spirit of openness, tentativeness, and contingency in the fourth act. There is no question of another epic tendency, dispensationalism. The principles and the narrative of the first act continue through the three that follow; the covenant of the second act is alive and significant in the third and fourth; the theme of the third is the key to understanding all the others; and the character of the fourth ("the holy city") is at least partly preserved, though transformed, in the fifth. The role of the fourth act balances the need for a genuinely human dimension to the drama, with the need for a genuinely divine shape. If the fifth act is explored too fully the drama becomes too epic; if it is ignored, the drama becomes too lyric. It is in preserving the delicate balance of this fivefold shape that the genuine theo-drama of the five-act play unfolds. I shall now outline the dimensions of each act in turn.

The first act is creation. The drama of this act is that there was too much love in the Trinity for God to keep it to himself. The world is not the center of the story: God is. Things do not have to be the way they are—they exist because God chose for them to be. He is the creator and he is surrounded by his creatures. His creatures do not exist for themselves, but have a purpose for him. He made them this way because he wanted one like each of them. Their chief purpose is to glorify him and enjoy him forever. And yet these creatures use their freedom ill. They choose, but have lost the art of making good choices. God pours out just as much love as before, but so little is returned, so much creative, playful, joyful energy is wasted. The mystery of why God bothered to make the world is compounded by why he continued to bother to love his creatures when they turned away—and is rivaled by the mystery of why his creatures do not bother, cannot be bothered, in return. Here is the drama of creation, of how God came to turn his infinite freedom into a covenant, and how humanity comes to turn its finite freedom into a prison.

The second act is Israel. God longed to be in true relationship with his creation through that part of creation that apprehended his glory—humankind. The prologue to Genesis describes how this failed in Adam and failed again at Babel. So God called Abraham, and Abraham followed. The rest of the Old Testament is a love story, in which Israel strives with God, unable to live with him and unable to live without him. Here we find what vocation and covenant mean. God will not leave Israel alone: therein lies a promise and a warning. Israel exists for God and for the salvation of the nations. Here is the drama, the wrestling of the story: can Israel find the forms of life that honor her call to be holy? How will God woo or wrest Israel back when Israel strays? How far is too far to stray? Will God save the nations another way? Is there an epic destiny underlying the lyric experience of slavery and exile?

The third act is Jesus. This is the definitive act, at the center of the drama, in which God reveals his character: the author enters the drama. In him all the fullness of God was pleased to dwell. There is constantly a lyric level of human encounter, of intimacy and betrayal, of challenge and confrontation. But there is also an epic dimension of the magnetism of Jerusalem, the inevitability of the passion, the inability of the grave to keep Jesus down. Here the drama is at its most stark. Is God totally vulnerable, or has he kept something back? Will God's people understand, comprehend, and follow him, or will they seek to overcome, stand over, obliterate, and annihilate him? Will their rejection of him cause God's rejection of them? If he overcomes death, what will he not do?

Christians are in act four, the church. Israel thought it was in a three act play, creation—Israel—Messiah, and the shock was that when Jesus came he neither restored political authority nor did he bring the story to an end.[13] Instead, he inaugurated Act Four. In this act, the church is given all it needs to continue to be his body in the world. It receives the Holy Spirit and is clothed with power and authority. It is given the Scripture, made up of the apostolic witness of those who seek to report, while being drawn into, the drama. It is given baptism, a lyric way in which to incorporate people into an epic drama. It is given the Eucharist, a regular event in which the body of Christ meets the embodied Christ, in a drama of encounter, reconciliation, and commission. It is given a host of other practices to form and sustain its life. Will those gifts prove to be enough? Will the church seek solace elsewhere? Will the ways God speaks and acts beyond the church prove more vivid than the ways his voice is heard and his deeds are perceived within? Will rival churches parody these practices, will the lyric of the human predicament or the epic of alternative narratives prevail? This is the intense drama of the present moment, of every moment in the church's history.

Still to come is Act Five, the end (or eschaton). This is a frightening thing for those who have built up power and resources, but for those who have nothing to lose it is unbounded joy. The timing of the end is not known, but that it will come when God chooses is certain. The drama of that time may yield some shocks—as the secrets of all hearts are revealed. But in God's revelation there will be no shocks, only surprises. For the God who will then be fully revealed will not be different in character from the God who revealed himself in Act Three. The face on the cross is the face on the throne. Again, the lyric desire for personal comfort and assurance is as strong as the epic desire to know times, seasons, and portents. But the drama of the eschaton is the drama of how God transforms the poverty of nature by the riches of grace, of how he turns fallenness and striving and pain into communion and gladness and joy by no other power but the power of the cross.

There are two kinds of mistakes that can easily be made about this five-act drama. These two mistakes hint at a substantial, if by no means comprehensive, description of sin. The first, lyric, mistake is to think one is in a one-act play rather than a five-act play. The world—if by that broad designation is meant all that has taken God's freedom not yet to believe—thinks it is in a one-act play. In a one-act play, all meanings must be established before the curtain comes down. This life is all there is: heritage has no logical value other than insofar as it contributes to fulfillment in this life. All achievements, all results, all outcomes must be celebrated and resolved before the final whistle. The myth of human fulfillment, the stretching of human capacity to its utmost and the filling up of the resultant space with experience and reward, means everything must be squeezed into the unforgiving span of a single life. The five-act drama, in its epic dimensions, means that Christians are spared such a crisis. They are not called to be effective or successful, but to be faithful. Faithfulness is but effectiveness measured against a much longer timescale: since Act Three has happened and Act Five is to follow, Christians can afford to fail, because they trust in Christ's victory and in God's ultimate sovereignty. Their faithful failures point all the more to their faith in their story and its author.

The second mistake is to get the wrong act. This is still a lyric step, since it generally overemphasizes one's own role in the drama. If one assumes one is in Act One, one places oneself, rather than God, in the role of creator. There have been no significant events before one's appearance in the drama. There is no experience to learn from, no story to join, no drama to enter. This is the desire for independence, to be a self-made individual. No one else's rules have validity: everything must be discovered, named, assessed for oneself. Similar is the assumption that one is at the end of the story. This is as much the case in the church, thinking it is in Act Five, as in the world, taking itself to be near the end of a one-act play. On the great debating points of church order, people talk as if Jesus and the early church lived an eternity ago, and that they set everything in stone. But what if Jesus lives today, and the church still has thousands or millions of years ahead of it? Perhaps we are the early church, still haggling over the details, and rightly so. On nuclear weapons people similarly assume that they are near the end of the story. Blowing up the world would indeed be terrible. But the five-act drama proclaims that humanity has already, in Act Three, done the most terrible thing possible by crucifying the Lord of glory. And a proper understanding of God's sovereignty recognizes that he could well have another world, in all the myriad complexity of this one, all ready and prepared, on hand to replace this one with should he ever sense the need. Humans are not the creators, nor the finishers, of God's story.

Similar mistakes lie within Acts Two and Three. The mistake of assuming one is in Act Two is to behave as though the Messiah had not yet come. Yes, one is a member of a special people, called by God; but no, God has not yet revealed the definitive way in which he encounters his people and in which he moves in the world. Thus one can be moved to sacrifice others, or oneself, in order to change things, rather than recognize that Christ has made the sacrifice instead. This tendency is particularly common on questions of peace and war. God is on our side, yet the other side appears to be winning, or at least posing an intolerable threat: therefore, so that God's will may prevail, we must destroy the other side, or at least teach them a lesson. The fact that the Messiah *has* come, and *has* shown how God addresses conflict, and *has* shown that we should concentrate on the abundance we can share rather than the scarcity that will be fought over—this fact tends to be ignored. These are the assumptions of Act Two.

If the context is taken to be Act Three, it is easy to confuse one's own role with that of Jesus. Everything one does then has decisive significance for the world—and even for God. This is the tendency I described in the previous chapter of seeking to be a hero rather than a saint. The roles of the Christ and the disciples are paradigmatically displayed in the story of the feeding of the five thousand. The disciples find the food, distribute it, and clean up afterward: but it is the Christ who transforms the poverty of their resources by the riches of his grace and gives his people everything they need. To take on the role of Jesus, rather than enjoy being a disciple, is to assume one lives in Act Three. This point of view is always fashionable—everyone likes to think they live in significant times. But the shape of the five-act play reminds the church that it does not live in particularly significant times. The most important things have already happened. The Messiah has come, has been put to death, has been raised; and the Spirit has come. This is a great liberation for the church. It leaves Christians free, in faith, to make honest mistakes.

Baptism takes the Christian from a one-act play to a five-act play. In baptism, Christians are taken into a drama, where God has created them and others for a purpose, where Israel has answered a call and pursued a vocation, where Jesus has become one like them and has conquered sin and death, where the Spirit has empowered the church to follow Christ, and where God will end the drama when he sees fit. Christians find their character by becoming a character in God's story. They move from trying to realize all meaning in their own lives to receiving the heritage of faith and the hope of glory. They move from fearing their fate to singing of their destiny. For this is the effect of God's story: it transforms fate into destiny.

4

Drama as Improvisation

Ethics presupposes context, and an understanding of context presupposes narrative; yet if context is to be understood as genuinely communal, and ethics as genuinely interactive, then that narrative must be understood as drama. Such is my argument so far. If the Christian story is drama, then ethics, the embodiment of that story, is appropriately regarded as performance.

Performance

Nicholas Lash develops this notion of performance in an essay entitled "Performing the Scriptures."[1] Taken together, he argues, the texts of the New Testament "tell the story" of Jesus and the early communities of believers. It is the life and practices of the believing community that are the fundamental form of the *Christian* interpretation of Scripture. The performance of Scripture is the life of the church. Lash goes on to argue

> that Christian practice, as interpretative action, consists in the *performance* of texts which are construed as "rendering," bearing witness to, one whose words and deeds, discourse and suffering, "rendered" the truth of God in human history. The performance of the New Testament enacts the conviction that these texts are most appropriately read as the story of Jesus, the story of everyone else, and the story of God.[2]

59

Lash illustrates this by pointing to American society, whose life, activity, and organization are the enactment of the American constitution. Thus the Scriptures are the "constitution" of the church, and Christian ethics concerns their enactment. In the performance of a play there must always be an element of creativity that enables the performers to make the text a living event. Lash describes the Eucharist as the best illustration of the interpretative performance that is the whole of the Christian life. Praise, confession, and petition enact the meanings they embody. The story is told in order that it may be performed when the participants depart in peace: "the quality of our *humanity* will be the criterion of the adequacy of our performance."[3]

Times and circumstances change, however, and there is no final or definitive interpretation of either constitution or Scripture. This is a problem for Lash. He is concerned that the finality of God's self-disclosure in Christ should not be impeded. He concludes that those performing the text should continue to understand the question to which this text sought to provide an answer. If the text ascribed unsurpassable significance to the life and death of this one man, then appropriate performance should do the same. The story is told differently: but it must continue to be the same story.

What remains unclear from the ethical implications of Lash's conclusion is what the Christian community is to do when it faces circumstances in which it is not clear how the story is to be performed. Christian ethics cannot, like *King Lear,* be read off the page of the text: Christians do not have "parts" in the drama, with "lines" pre-prepared and learned by heart. Frances Young hints at this issue in the last chapter of her book *The Art of Performance.*[4] She talks of the practice of cadenzas in concertos. The performer of a cadenza keeps to the style and themes of the concerto, but also shows virtuosity and inspiration in adapting and continuing in keeping with the setting and form. However Young's vision of performance is very limited—considering only the hermeneutical skills needed by the preacher and teacher. What of the skills needed by the Christian community as a whole?

Walter Brueggemann discusses in some detail the notion of biblical faith as drama.[5] He notes several dimensions of drama that make the metaphor attractive. Drama must sustain both the constancy and the development of character, so that the third act is consistent with the first, without being a simple repetition. One is told all one needs to know about the characters by what happens to them on stage.[6] There is a settled script—yet one that can be rendered in a variety of ways. He describes our life as "a collage of dramas, in which we cope with significant others, in which we struggle for constancy and freedom, and in which we find ourselves endlessly scripted but seeking to act gracefully and freely, to work the script

in a new way."[7] Drama teaches us that we need other characters to play
with and against: the biblical drama teaches us that God is "a genuinely
other character who takes a decisive role in the drama," and that we are
"others" to God.[8]

Like Young, Brueggemann limits his perspective to that of the preacher
and teacher.[9] Brueggemann's view is incomplete because it does not incorporate the activity of a *community* of interpretation, and because it does
not offer ways in which such a community might face ethical practice in
the future. There is insufficient attention to the sense of open-endedness
of the drama. It is not just a question of repeating the same script, albeit
in different ways: Brueggemann's account needs an extra dimension.

Kevin Vanhoozer extends the notion of performance into his understanding of speech-act theory.[10] Just as plays are written to be performed, the
Bible is written to animate "creative fidelity" in its performance.[11] Scripture
is divine action, an event longing to be given form in time and space. It
is a communicative act of God, in which he invites the reader to enter
the story. Performance is the way the church responds to this communicative act. Christians become "apprentices" to the Bible.[12] Vanhoozer's
treatment helps in underlining the communicative dimension to the
drama, but more is required if one is to appreciate the nature of the
extra dimension added to a text by dramatic performance. It is still too
restricted to words, and too likely to see drama as primarily a means of
transmitting an inherently verbal message. "Dramatic action" is as Ivan
Khovacs points out, by contrast, "to do with what happens in the spaces
between the words," and not principally about delivering a propositional
"message" via cognitive faculties. "We would do ourselves a disservice if
we understood the incommunicative, affective engagement in the drama
as merely a back door entry into the sobriety of cognition."[13]

Shannon Craigo-Snell is alone of the authors I have surveyed in her
incorporation of the genuinely embodied and communal character of
performance, and thus of interpretation. "Theatrical performance, like
Christian practice, has a script, is communal, is done in dialogue with
society, employs a variety of methods and of media, and is embodied."[14]
"A theater company is a group of people striving together towards an
experience of the sublime. The individuals have different roles and func-
tions, yet each is a part of the communal process of interpretation." The
church is similar, and must likewise "balance between internal community and external connection, between integrity and pertinence."[15]
Craigo-Snell expands on the ways the church performs scripture: "When
we read or sing the Psalms together, we perform them. When we enact
scenes from the life of Jesus, breaking bread and washing feet, we are
performing. When we obey a direct commandment, we are, in some
sense, performing that commandment."[16]

Craigo-Snell highlights the ways in which "Scripture, like script, is both complete and incomplete." Both script and Scripture inherently move toward greater fulfillment in the event of performance.

> The very structure of a script contains an incompleteness that is an invitation for our embodied and active interpretation, an invitation to create an event that is more than a script alone can be. . . .
>
> Acting out of their relationship with Scripture, Christian communities shout and dance, they get happy and they mourn together, they bake casseroles and sing hymns and comfort one another and open soup kitchens and raise money for the homeless. If Christian interpretation is really like theatrical performance interpretation, then these events and activities are not merely the results of an understanding that comes from interpretation: they are part of the interpretative process.
>
> . . . Our understanding of Scripture comes to fullness with our performance of it. . . . I may encounter God in the story of Jesus ministering to the poor and outcast, yet my encounter is far more intimate if I place myself in that story and struggle in solidarity with the oppressed.[17]

What Craigo-Snell is talking about, her central analogy, as Khovacs points out, is the process of rehearsal. Rehearsal is the theatrical moment when roles are tried and tested, interactions practiced and perfected, words are filled with action and the silences between them filled with significance, when text is given body, voice, and character, where mistakes are not disastrous but instead become ways to discovering deeper meaning.

Thus to sum up the argument of the chapter so far, the notion of performance has much to offer a dramatic reading of theology. Performance does justice to the embodied, communal way in which the church tries to involve itself in the life enjoined by the Scripture while remaining faithful to the character of God that emerges from the biblical witness. However, the notion of discipleship as the performance of a script has significant drawbacks, and I shall briefly highlight four of them.

Problems with Performance

One problem arises from the expectation that the script provides a comprehensive version of life, in which all eventualities and questions meet their appropriate forms of engagement and resolution. This expectation is quite clearly an inappropriate one. The script does not provide all the answers. Life throws up circumstances that the gospel seems not to cover. If performance of a script is regarded as the paradigmatic form of discipleship, a great deal of disappointment or doublethink is likely to result. It cannot simply be a matter of performing the same story in new circumstances. The story must make some allowance for the new circumstances.

Another problem with the notion of performance is that it gives the impression that the Bible encompasses the whole of the church's narrative. But that is not the case. The script may not change significantly in character, but it is not finished. There is more to the Christian story than the pages of the Bible disclose. Too much talk of performing the story can encourage the common perception that the two thousand years that lie between the end of the New Testament and the present day are of no theological significance. If disciples are indeed performing a story, they are performing a story that is getting longer all the while it is being performed.

An attendant drawback is that the idea of a script suggests the re-creation of a golden era. It suggests that there was a time when the characters did get it right, when Israel was holy and faithful to God, when the disciples heard Jesus' words and straightaway put them into action—and that the task of the church is to reenact that righteousness, to conjure up once more the glorious days of intimate fellowship. There are indeed scriptural portrayals of ideal followers, of Daniel who withstood all oppression, of Bartimaeus who tossed aside his cloak and followed, of the early believers who had all things in common. But these accounts are greatly outnumbered by stories of fragility and failure, of the golden calf, of more than daily manna collected, of the disciples who fled Gethsemane, and of Ananias and Sapphira withholding their wealth. Discipleship is not simply a matter of replicating Scripture, but of being moved to learn from others' mistakes, and to tell a truthful story that reflects the truth the Bible displays.

A fourth shortcoming that performance interpretations risk is that the notion of script can militate against genuine engagement with the world. This can arise out of any of the three weaknesses already named. A comprehensive story needs no dialogue partner. A complete story leaves no significant theological place for the present tense, for new discoveries and God's revelation in surprising places. An orientation toward a golden era is likely to make any contemporary performance feel like a hopeless failure. Craigo-Snell is alive to these concerns, and she stresses that performance is sensitive to the world beyond the stage—but she does not elaborate on how that interaction takes place and how it is necessitated by the notion of performance. Neither do any of the authors treated in the foregoing discussion.

These drawbacks can encourage the church to follow predictable courses. Sometimes it lives in the past, aspiring to a world of scriptural purity. It easily loses the playfulness of rehearsal and becomes paralyzed by the fear of making a mistake. Nostalgia for a time when most people declared the truth of Scripture with their lips and showed forth its blessings in their lives tends to dwell less on the time of the early church than on a half-recalled folk memory of sepia spirituality.

Just as common is to see the shortcomings of performing the script and take them as a reason to dismiss the script as a guide for life. A heavy emphasis on the more arcane aspects of Scripture encourages the conclusion that it is the fruit of a bygone era. New circumstances need new modes of understanding, and tradition has no role other than a source of stories and an encouragement to virtue. In some hands, the very notion of binding tradition is seen as a curtailment of freedom. When freedom is understood as the flinging-off of constraints, the performance of any script other than one's own is bound to seem like an imposition. More often, such a rejection of the script comes as a reaction after the sadness of a failed performance. The difficulty of finding answers, or the harshness of carrying them out, can easily provoke the wholesale dismissal of the notion of performing a script.

A third course is to seek to translate the script into contemporary motifs. This is generally done in an effort to save the notion of tradition in the face of the tendency to dismiss the script altogether. What invariably happens is that the narrative character of the drama gets lost. In its place comes a number of abstractions, sometimes taken to be a middle course between scriptural witness and secular experience or wisdom. These can easily result in the focus of the drama moving away from the church, its practices, and its interaction with the world, and moving instead toward either the faceless forces of social formation, such as markets, arms, and communication systems, or the privatized interiority of personal decision-making. In either case, the church becomes invisible and the Scripture a curiosity.

The nineteenth-century essayist J. A. Froude described his experience of modernity in these terms: "Thus all round us, the intellectual lightships had broken from their moorings, and it was then a new and trying experience. The present generation which has grown up in an open spiritual ocean, which has got used to it and has learned to swim for itself, will never know what it was to find the lights all drifting, the compasses all awry, and nothing left to steer by except the stars." These words continue to offer a profound description of the moral experience of many contemporary Christians. Many people long for old certainties, Froude's "moorings." Sometimes the moorings are identified with the security of a world bounded and permeated by Scripture, a golden era when faithful Christians performed the unambiguous script. In the absence of secure moorings, there is all the more need for "stars"—inspirational, charismatic figures, who bring the scriptural world to life.

The longing is for the epic security of the anchor and the lyric intensity of the stars. But instead they find that they are alone and bewildered, free from the moorings that generations ago provided a structure to life; and moreover the sea is rough, and refuge is hard to find.

Improvisation

How can the church continue to be faithful without the reassurance of the script? This is the central question that pervades my whole inquiry. I have considered performance, but that, while allowing for the "spaces between the words," is still tied to the script. I have glanced at rehearsal, but that, while offering a still looser form, continues to presuppose a fixed script. It is not that the text of Scripture is not, or should not be, fixed. It is that there is a dimension of Christian life that requires more than repetition, more even than interpretation—but not so much as origination, or creation de novo. That dimension, the key to abiding faithfulness, is improvisation. Gerard Loughlin explains concisely what this means.

> When a person enters the scriptural story he or she does so by entering the Church's performance of that story: he or she is baptised into a biblical and ecclesial drama. It is not so much being written into a book as taking part in a play, a play that has to be improvised on the spot. As Rowan Williams puts it, people are "invited to 'create' themselves in finding a place within this drama—an improvisation in the theater workshop, but one that purports to be about a comprehensive truth affecting one's identity and future."[18]

My contention here is that the notion of improvisation, as understood and practiced in the theater, meets all the concerns that the notion of performance was intended to fulfill, without the drawbacks of the notion of performance that I have highlighted in this chapter. When improvisers are trained to work in the theater, they are schooled in a tradition so thoroughly that they learn to act from habit in ways appropriate to the circumstance. This is exactly the goal of theological ethics. I shall now explore some of the advantages of seeing the task of Christian ethics as improvisation.

Improvisation is inevitable. When Christians, whether scholars in a colloquium or parishioners in a house group, whether bishops in retreat house or aid workers in a field station, gather together and try to discern God's hand in events and his will for their future practice, they are improvising, whether they are aware of it or not. They—almost invariably—accord authority to Scripture, and generally to some other forms of discernment, perhaps tradition, or reason, or experience, or something similar. These provide the boundaries of their performance, their stage, as it were. And on this stage they strive to enact a faithful drama. Whether debating the use of language in theological discourse or considering whether to resign a job because of misgivings about one's boss's integrity; whether seeking a harmonious breakthrough in church order or considering appropriate models for development work in the face of famine: each of these is a stimulus to faithful improvisation, fresh embodiment of the grace and truth of the scriptural witness. In each case, improvisation is the only term that adequately describes the desire to cherish a tradition without being locked in the past.

Improvisation is scriptural. I shall defend this claim in later chapters, but for the moment it is necessary only to note that it is true to the earliest traditions of the church. The Acts of the Apostles describes how the good news of Jesus Christ spread throughout the eastern Mediterranean, while remaining rooted in and identified with Jerusalem. The missionary impulse inevitably came into tension with the identity of what began as a Jewish movement. When the disciples met at the Council of Jerusalem, they had to find a way of maintaining the particularity of God's call to Israel in the new context of the Gentile mission. This demonstrates improvisation at the beginnings of the church—the constant need to find ways of staying faithful in constantly changing circumstances and environments. Indeed, Jeremy Begbie describes the whole of the Acts of the Apostles as "a stream of new, unpredictable, improvisations."[19]

Improvisation is ecclesial. As I shall show in later chapters, it incorporates key practices of the church. It is, in a way that corresponds to Craigo-Snell's notion of rehearsal and performance, a form of hermeneutics. It is concerned with how a text and a tradition are realized by a community in new circumstances. It creates new examples, new aspects of the narrative in the course of its drama, and thus contributes to the hermeneutical spiral of action, reflection, and new encounter with text and tradition. Improvisation is concerned with discernment. It is about hearing God speak through renewed practice and attending to the Spirit through trained listening. It is corporate, since it is concerned with a group of people acting and reflecting like a theatrical company. It is concerned with engaging with the world.

Some Misconceptions

Before moving any further, I shall pause to address the principal and most common anxieties evoked by the use of the term "improvisation."

I take each of these concerns as unfounded, since they are all based on misunderstandings of the principles or practice of the discipline.

One misapprehension is that improvisation is about being original. This is a misapprehension for two reasons, one concerning the nature of theatrical improvisation, the other concerning the nature of the Christian drama. In terms of theatrical improvisation, every actor must learn to avoid trying to be original. Few things paralyze action more than one actor refusing to engage unless he or she is able to do so in an original way. The only way it is possible to keep the drama going is to be obvious. This takes training and courage, as I shall show in later chapters. If theatrical improvisation has a notion of sin, then trying to be original is high on the list. When we turn to the nature of the Christian drama, it is easy to see why. For if one takes up the notion of the Christian drama as a five-act play, as I described in the previous chapter, the role of improvisation becomes clear. To be original is to sin by supposing oneself to be in either the first or the last act. Either one assumes one is at creation, and one is in the position of originating all things; or one is at the end, ensuring that all things come out right. In short, one is living in a one-act play, and one is oneself the center of the drama—a hero, to use the term introduced in chapter 2. If Christians live in the fourth act of a five-act play, they have permission to improvise—as saints. They have no need to make everything come right, nor have they need to correct perceived shortcomings in any of the previous three acts. They simply use the resources of the first three acts, and what they anticipate of the final act, and faithfully play with the circumstances in which they find themselves. It is those who live in a one-act play—the "world," all who have taken the freedom of God's patience not yet to believe—who should be more likely to find themselves paralyzed by the need to be original. The church has no reason to be paralyzed: it has permission to be obvious.

Being obvious is thus a demonstration of faith, an embodiment of discipleship. Being obvious means trusting that God will do what only God can do, and thus having the freedom to do what only the disciple can do. Being obvious means trusting that the practices of discipleship, shaped by the Holy Spirit, are enough—there is no need for a "second blessing," whether in the form of further revelation or in a flash of spontaneous insight or inspiration at a moment of crisis. The community of disciples that has been formed in the habits of the Christian story has all its attention on the surprises God will bring. It is not racked with anxiety about what inspired thing it must now do.

Another, similar misconception is that improvisation is about being clever or witty. From this perspective, improvisation is not for the common person, but for the elite, whose innate talent and quick reflexes place them in a different drama from the blundering and ordinary majority. Once again, this rests on a misunderstanding of theatrical improvisation and an incorrect reading of the Christian drama. Improvisation is not about outstandingly gifted individuals who can conjure rapid-fire gags from a standing start. It is about nurturing a group of people to have such trust in one another that they have a high level of common understanding and take the same things for granted. Then they can relax, and the audience, if there is one, can enter the apparently telepathic communication that emerges between them. It is this relaxed state, the apparent effortlessness that is sensed when people genuinely and gleefully cooperate with one another, that provides the fascination and joy in improvisation—rather than the witty repartee. The theological issue is similar to that in the case of originality. The church in Act Four can relax, because the important work has already been done. To be a saint does not require one to have outstanding gifts or talents. All it requires is that one employ all the resources of the church's tradition—the first three acts—rather than create them for oneself, and that one long for all the glory of the church's destiny—the fifth act—rather than assuming one must achieve it oneself. In the present, fourth act, one must seek in all ways to cooperate with the other members of the company, the communion of saints, rather than try to stand out from them as an isolated hero.

The last two concerns might be described as those of an "epic" observer concerned that improvisation might become too "lyric." One is the common fear that improvisation is probably or potentially demonic. This fear arises from a deep-seated fear of the unconscious. There is no doubt that improvisation engages the unconscious, and particularly the collective unconscious, in a way not normally associated with Christian ethics or hermeneutics. For the improviser, the unconscious is not to be feared as a dark realm of dangerous instinct and forbidden desire. It is instead to be trusted as a gift of God that can, like all other aspects of the baptized person, be transformed and conformed to the service of God. It is an aspect that has been neglected or mistrusted in most accounts of the moral life. It is open, as are other aspects of the person, to self-deception and sin, to a failure of the Christian imagination; but the practices of the church, reconciliation, penitence, sharing peace and admonition, are there to safeguard the unconscious as much as any other aspect. By articulating the unconscious, improvisation opens the Christian community up to grace: it does not bury its unknown gift, but trades with it, and thus comes to know it, and to trust God to forgive and heal it when necessary.

The other common "lyric" assumption is that improvisation is trivial and self-indulgent. This is perhaps because it is associated with humor and the ephemeral, and also because it can create intensely committed communities that seem united by no substantial goal, only the formal means of interacting. I suspect this is a characteristic epic perception. Underlying it is the assumption that Christian ethics is an intensely serious, somewhat earnest, and decidedly difficult discipline, weighing matters of daunting substance, and only to be entered reverently, soberly, and after serious thought. In this perspective improvisation sounds suspiciously like a joke, an artifice—an insult. Such a view risks being more solemn than God. Throughout the Christian drama there is joy and playfulness that arise in human and divine communion. It is inherent in Act One—the play of creation, the desire for Adam not to be alone. It is there in Act Two—the dance of David before the Lord, the irony and humor of a host of narratives. It is there in Act Three, as a company of disciples are found, follow, consistently and then definitively lose the plot, only to be found new roles again in a restored company. And it is there in Act Five, as vindicated victims take their seat at the banqueting table and their place in the heavenly choir. So why not in Act Four? The church can afford to concentrate on details, because God has given her time to follow him. Taking time for the trivial is therefore a sign of faith, not foolishness. The church can afford to take the risk of the humorous and ephemeral, because the joke is God's and the laughter is divine.

Free from the paralysis of being original, the pressure to be clever, the fear of the unconscious, and the demand to be solemn, the church can faithfully follow its Lord by improvising in the fourth act. Happy to be obvious, relaxed, open to the unconscious, and playful, improvising transforms the Bible from a script that needs performing into a manual that trains disciples to take the right things for granted. No longer need Christian communities anxiously glance over their shoulder, lest they make a terrible mistake that betrays their performance of the script. Instead they can trust the practices and patterns of their common life and have confidence that God joins their faithful improvisation.

It is not necessary to be too precise about defining the stage, players, and audience. After all, both the tradition of improvisation and the Christian story are as interested in disrupting any static notions of this kind as they are in upholding them. For example, God may be regarded as the audience—but he involves himself in the drama. He may be regarded as the key player, as for von Balthasar, but he undoubtedly allows his creation to play a full part. He could be described as the stage, the one who defines what is possible in the drama—but in the third act he transforms what is possible in the drama. Likewise the church may be regarded as the actor—yet it must not take itself to be the central actor in a one-act play. The church may also be regarded as the audience, lauding and magnifying God's unique acts. Or the church may be seen as the stage on which God's quest for the world's response of love is performed. And, in turn, the world may be the audience for the church's witness, or the unwitting actor in a divine drama, or the stage on which God and the church improvise their performance. Each may respectively be seen as any of the three (stage, players, and audience), or all, at different times. These reversals and interplays of expectation and custom are the stuff of improvisation.

My treatment will, however, remain true to some customs. In particular it will follow three features characteristic of most theatrical improvisation: the use of games, the prevalence of humor, and the sense of an implicit but always surprising narrative. My proposal comes in six stages and begins with the character of the improvising community.[20]

PART TWO

Planting

5

Forming Habits

The Operating Theater and the Lecture Theater

"The battle of Waterloo was won on the playing fields of Eton."[1] The Duke of Wellington's famous reflection on the climax of the Napoleonic wars was not a statement of personal modesty. It was a recognition that success in battle depends on the character of one's soldiers. It was a statement that Britain had institutions that formed people with the kind of virtues that could survive and even thrive in the demanding circumstances of war.

The argument of this chapter is that the moral life is more about Eton than it is about Waterloo. Eton and Waterloo represent two distinct aspects of the moral life. Eton represents the long period of preparation. Waterloo represents the tiny episode of implementation—the moment of decision, or "situation."

Contemporary ethics seems to offer a series of baffling dilemmas. The moral life seems to be an impossible negotiation of hopeless quandaries. Why is this? The reason is that it has become conventional to study Waterloo without studying Eton—in practice, to study Waterloo as if there were no Eton. Ethics has become the study of the battlefield without much recognition of the training ground. This has happened because ethics has come to be understood as the study of what is right always, everywhere, and for everybody. In other words, ethics considers what all people have in common, not the areas where they differ. It concentrates on the general, not the particular. In the case of the Duke of Wellington's observation, Waterloo is perceived to be what people have in common—a battle is a battle. Eton is considered to be an area where they differ—the French education system was different from the British.

To put the matter in more conventional terms, ethics has become the study of right and wrong actions—because actions are considered to be common to all people always and everywhere. The focus of ethics has come to rest on the choice that an individual in a situation faces between one action and another. The great debates in ethics are perceived to be between those who believe some actions are inherently right and others inherently wrong and those who judge actions by the relative desirability of their likely consequences. Ethics is seldom perceived to be about the people doing the actions, because these people's characters are inevitably varied.

But this is where the Duke of Wellington's remark is so significant. He says that one cannot understand Waterloo without understanding Eton. In fact, what went on at Eton was more important than what went on at Waterloo. At Eton, people were trained to shoulder the kind of responsibility they were later to encounter at Waterloo. The real decisions that took place at Waterloo, decisions that shaped the future of European history, had been taken many years earlier. The Duke of Wellington is saying that ethics is about people, not about actions. The heart of ethics lies in the formation of character. Once out in the "battlefield," it is too late. The following story illustrates his point.

One day in the 1950s, in an Edinburgh hospital, a child died tragically on an operating table. Later that week, two friends were talking over the sad events. One of the friends expressed sympathy for the surgeon involved, since he had encountered an unexpected complication. The other, a colleague of the surgeon, strongly disagreed, in these words:

> I think the man is to blame. If anybody had handed me ether instead of chloroform I would have known from the weight it was the wrong thing. You see, I know the man well. We were students together at Aberdeen, and he could have become one of the finest surgeons in Europe if only he had given his mind to it. But he didn't. He was more interested in golf. So he just used to do enough work to pass his examinations and no more. And that is how he has lived his life—just enough to get through, but no more; so he has never picked up those seemingly peripheral bits of knowledge that can one day be crucial. The other day in that theater a bit of "peripheral" knowledge was crucial and he didn't have it. But it wasn't the other day that he failed—it was thirty-nine years ago, when he only gave himself half-heartedly to medicine.[2]

The Duke of Wellington's observation about a Belgian field applies equally well to the Edinburgh operating table. Just as the battle of Waterloo was won on the playing fields of Eton, so the battle for the sick child's life was lost on the golf course. An athlete trains for months for a marathon race, and no amount of enthusiasm on the day can make up for deficiencies in preparation. A student studies for years for an exam: again, no amount of thought on the day can make up for deficiencies in preparation. A doctor studies and trains and practices for years to excel in surgery: no amount of goodwill on the day can make up for deficiencies in preparation.

Ethics is not primarily about the operating theater: it is about the lecture theater, the training field, the practice hall, the library, the tutorial, the mentoring session. There are two times—one, the time of moral effort, the other, the time of moral habit. The time for moral effort is the time of formation and training. This is "Eton." Training requires commitment, discipline, faithfulness, study, apprenticeship, practice, cooperation, observation, reflection—in short, moral effort. The point of this effort is to form skills and habits—habits that mean people take the right things for granted and skills that give them ability to do the things they take for granted. The time for moral habit is the "moment of decision." This is "Waterloo," or "the operating room." Waterloo and the operating room separate those whose instincts have been appropriately formed from those whose character is inadequately prepared. In every moral "situation," the real decisions are ones that have been taken some time before. To live well requires both effort and habit. There is a place for both. But no amount of effort at the moment of decision will make up for effort neglected in the time of formation.

The moral life should not be experienced as an agony of impossible choice. Instead, it should be a matter of habit and instinct. Learning to live well is about gaining the right habits and instincts, rather than making the right choices. If one has the right assumptions and instincts and habits, many of the things others might experience as crises of choice will pass without one being aware of them. Meanwhile, if one has not developed such habits, decisions that do arise are likely to be insoluble. In the story of the surgeon, the moment of moral effort came in the student's commitment to his studies in the face of the lure of the golf course. If the commitment had been sufficient at the time of formation, habit and instinct in the operating room would have meant that a moment of crisis would have passed without anyone being aware of it. As it was, the patient died. By putting all the emphasis on the operating room, contemporary ethics makes the moral life seem like an agony of impossible choice. For those living in a disconnected present tense, guessing about an unknown future, considering of value only those things that they share with all people everywhere and always, this may well be so. But contemporary ethics neglects the only time from which liberation from this paralysis can come—the past. For it is only moral effort and formation in the past that can offer freedom from impossible moral effort in the present.

The parable of the wise and foolish bridesmaids portrays preparation as readiness for judgment.[3] The foolish bridesmaids are hopelessly unprepared for the bridegroom's coming. They have no lamp oil. At the moment of decision, they have no resources to inform their judgment. For the wise bridesmaids, by contrast, preparation is all. The real decisive moment came long before the bridegroom arrived. Like the surgeon on the golf course, the foolish bridesmaids were faced with impossible moral effort in the present. Only careful preparation could spare them from what the Lord's Prayer calls the *peirasmos*, the time of trial too great to endure.

Imagination and Formation

Forming the right kinds of instincts is really about developing the imagination. It is through the imagination that one aspires or desires, perseveres or reveres, envies or sympathizes. One may distinguish two kinds of imagination, rather as one may distinguish between habit and effort. There is the imagination that one uses in one's ordinary perception of the world. This "ordinary" imagination enables one to take for granted those things that one needs to be able to rely on. But there is also the imagination that is inventive and revolutionary, perceiving objects as symbols of things beyond themselves. This latter, "creative" dimension is described by one Christian philosopher as the ability "to see simultaneously what is and what might yet be for the best, to engage at the same time the most creative of human passions, and consequently to lure into action and to sustain commitment."[4]

This ability "to see simultaneously what is and what might yet be" is the creative force of training in how to live well—otherwise known as moral formation. The pain and care of schooling in a tradition is about learning to see the ambiguity of the world truthfully, yet maintaining hope. The practice of the moral life, meanwhile, is not so much about being creative or clever as it is about taking the right things for granted. Thus what I am here calling the "creative" imagination corresponds to what I earlier called moral effort. This is what moral training is about. Meanwhile what I am here calling the "ordinary" imagination corresponds to what I earlier called habit. When one comes to a moment of crisis, one depends on the habits one has already formed.

Imagination, in this twofold sense, is a key element in the moral life. It is important to stress this because imagination tends to be perceived as the opposite of morality. Imagination tends to be associated with spontaneity and originality, while morality is assumed to be about worthy but dull things like fulfilling expectations and maintaining trust. It is much better to recognize that both imagination and morality are concerned with describing the world in which people perceive themselves to live and act, helping communities form practices consistent with life in such a world.

I have argued that there are two stages in the moral life. There is the stage of the moral situation, the stage that requires the ordinary imagination to respond from habit and instinct. And there is the prior stage of moral formation, the stage that requires the creative imagination to form character through moral effort. I have suggested that this stage of moral formation is vital and has been neglected in conventional ethics, because it attends to aspects where people differ, rather than to aspects that they have in common.

It is worth noting the political implications of this argument. When the crisis of ethics, the time for acute moral effort, is understood to be the moment of decision, and when ethics itself is understood as the balancing of moral principles so as to adjudicate tricky cases of conscience, the result is implicitly socially conservative. It is conservative because it assumes that the status quo is broadly satisfactory—so satisfactory that one need only agonize over its anomalies. In such a view, sometimes known as "quandary ethics," the majority of life, run by habit, is rudely interrupted from time to time by quandaries, which require concerted moral effort to resolve. The view I have been propounding sees things the other way around. Moral effort and the creative imagination are concentrated in the time of preparation, the formation of character; the "moment," if it comes, is to be addressed by habits already formed. In other words, the majority of life, run by moral effort, is occasionally interrupted by crises, which are resolved by habit. Crises are not a perpetual threat to equilibrium: on the contrary, one anticipates that threats to one's integrity will inevitably arise, and therefore sets about forming a character with habits in place to deal with those threats.

When the politics of this argument are made explicit, it becomes clear why theologians have a stake in its outcome. For the church can never be satisfied with the view that all is generally well and is only occasionally interrupted by crises. The Christian understanding of sin is that the world has fallen from this state of well-being. The world is in a perpetual state of crisis interrupted by moments of well-being—the actions of God: Father, Son, and Holy Spirit. There is no place for the complacency that says all is well or the despair that says all is lost. There is instead a balance between the concentrated effort of our drawing near to God and the surprising grace of his drawing near to us. In this argument I am suggesting that the categories of effort and habit may find theological partners in the categories of discipleship and grace. If Christians have learned to take the right things for granted (discipleship), they will more readily experience God's ways with them and the world (grace).

The church's faith is that, in story, sacrament, and Spirit, God has given his people all that they need to live with him. The church's creative energies are largely concerned with preparing its members to be able to respond by habit to unforeseeable turns of events. It is not the church's role to speculate on what the future may hold. The church's task is to be prepared for whatever the future may bring. It prepares through discipleship to be open to grace.

Back in the 1930s at the huge Roman Catholic seminary at Ushaw near Durham there was a man studying for the priesthood named Gerald Culkin. One day he read a play by Anton Chekhov and was so thrilled with it that he went out and bought *Teach Yourself Russian*. Each night when his studies were finished he left the other students playing billiards and went to his room on his own to learn the language. By the time he was ordained he could read it fairly well. Soon afterward the Second World War started and Gerald went to Beirut as an army chaplain. He met lots of Russians there, but couldn't make himself understood with his *Teach Yourself* way of speaking. Eventually he learned to speak real Russian with them.

Gerald was moved to Egypt and spent a lot of time comforting the wounded and dying. After a particularly heavy battle, with many injured, he came back to his tent exhausted, to be told that there was one more man to see. The man was in a desperate state, and Gerald could see that he didn't have long. Gerald spoke to him in English, but got no response. So he tried with his few words of French, and his fewer words of Italian, German, Spanish, even Arabic. Gerald was on the point of giving up when the dying man, on his stretcher, slowly and painfully made the sign of the cross in the Orthodox manner. Gerald suddenly realized that the man was Russian. In the last hour of the man's life he was able to hear a few words of confession, give absolution, and help the man through the Lord's Prayer. He held the man's hand until he died.

One can picture Gerald coming out of the tent and recalling all those nights at the seminary in Ushaw, all those times he was tempted to give up learning Russian and instead have a game of billiards or a chat with the others. And in retrospect it is clear that all that effort had been a time of preparation; perhaps his whole life had been a time of preparation: and it had all been worth it just for this last hour with the dying man.[5] Moral effort, for Gerald, lay in choosing Russian over billiards: when the crisis came, he acted from habit.

Gerald Culkin's story illustrates all the themes of this chapter. The time for creative imagination, moral effort, and discipleship was at Ushaw. The time for ordinary imagination, habit, and grace was in Egypt. The great majority of life is spent in preparation: this is where the emphasis in Christian ethics needs to be. And the experience of grace in the moment of crisis, of decision—the "situation"—came not through being clever or inspired in the moment, but through falling back on something he had once worked hard at and now took for granted.

Alongside this account of the formation of mental resourcefulness may be placed a corresponding portrayal of the development of physical reflexes. Together the two narratives may illustrate Christian formation in word and sacrament, thought and action. This story, a fictional account, illustrates the balance between the long, slow, disciplined practice of the creative imagination and the sudden, shocking necessity of habitual action. John Irving's novel *A Prayer for Owen Meany* has a similar structure to the story of Gerald Culkin. The novel describes the childhood and adolescence of two boys in 1950s New England. Their amusing adventures are scattered across the first half of the book, but the atmosphere becomes more somber as their country goes to war in Southeast Asia and they try everything they know to avoid the Vietnam draft. Throughout the story, they keep coming back to the same school basketball court to practice, over and over, what they call "The Shot"—the same old basketball maneuver. The significance of this habit—a habit that becomes a ritual—becomes clear as the novel comes to its conclusion, set in an airport. A berserk teenager, his life scarred by the social consequences of the war, sets about an appalling revenge. He prepares explosives to massacre a crowd of Vietnamese orphan children. In the dramatic climax to the story, Owen is able to use this long-honed basketball maneuver for an unanticipated purpose: to catch a grenade, thus saving the children and thwarting the boy's murderous purpose. The rescue costs Owen Meany his life.[6]

These two stories, of Gerald Culkin and Owen Meany, differ in a significant way from the story of the surgeon. The difference is that neither Gerald nor Owen could have known the circumstance for which they were preparing. While the surgeon's crisis came in the course of his regular duties, both Gerald and Owen (through war in each case) found themselves in situations that were as drastic as they were unforeseen. And yet both discovered in the crisis that they were able to do by habit all that was required. Discipline and training had provided them with the skills to engage the unexpected.

The two stories, of Gerald and Owen, both conclude with moments of genius. But, as is often said, those who are called geniuses attribute their status to 99 percent perspiration, 1 percent inspiration. Most of the Christian life is faithful preparation for an unknown test. Their actions, particularly Owen's leap, seemed spontaneous. But what is spontaneity but the result of years of experiments?

Relaxed Awareness

The stories of Wellington's Waterloo and the surgeon's ether, or Gerald's last rites and Owen's shot, together with the categories of habit and effort, creative and ordinary imagination, grace and discipleship, all have a bearing on the practice of theatrical improvisation. For it, too, is perceived to be about spontaneity, but is in fact about years of experiments. It, too, is about long preparation before following instinct. It, too, is about being ready to face the unknown. This state of readiness, the alertness that comes from years of disciplined preparation, is the condition to which improvisers aspire. Jacques Lecoq, one of the leading practitioners in using improvisation as a way of preparing a script for performance, uses the term *la disponibilité*.[7] *La disponibilité* is a condition of relaxed awareness. In this state of awareness the actor senses no need to impose an order on the outside world or on the imagination; there is openness to both receiving and giving. The actor is at one with the whole context: self, other actors, audience, theater space. It is like the condition of athletes at the height of their form and fitness, but added to that is an awareness of others and an openness to the unknown. The improviser in this state of readiness has at hand all the skills of the trade that the following chapters will explore. There is trust and respect for oneself and the other actors. There is alertness and attention. There is fitness and engagement. There is an understanding of narrative—of what is an end and what is a beginning of a scene or story. There is an ability to keep the narrative going and to explore a situation. There is a willingness to reintroduce discarded material. There is an aptitude for altering and playing with status roles, for relating to others, remembering, sustaining, and developing character, and sensing the shape of a story.

The last thirty years have seen a revival of the understanding of virtue in Christian ethics. Many writers make a similar journey to that made in this chapter. They refer back to Aristotle and Thomas Aquinas and speak of the various skills or potentialities that are needed, practiced, and nurtured in the Christian life. Jacques Lecoq's notion of *la disponibilité* and the description I have given of the way the "ordinary" imagination works in the habit of taking the right things for granted both concern skill. Skill is the faculty of a person who has undergone disciplined training. Another word for moral skill is virtue. Virtue ethics has become a shorthand term for all the writers in the field who have grown tired of the conventional emphasis on decision and the neglect of the character of the person or "agent" making the decision. The emphasis on virtue in Christian ethics has shifted attention from the deed to the doer. It is the agent who matters, more than the action: ethics is about forming the life of the agent more than it is about judging the appropriateness of the action.

A person with skills of this kind has gained them through years of training. Such a player will not strive too hard to be original. The prison of originality arises from a misunderstanding of the nature of spontaneity, rather as the prison of quandary ethics arises from a misconception of the moral life.

Perhaps the most widely respected writer on theatrical improvisation, Keith Johnstone, speaks of spontaneity in words that are equally relevant to ethics:

> The improviser has to realise that the more obvious he is, the more original he appears. . . . People trying to be original always arrive at the same boring old answers. Ask people to give you an original idea and see the chaos it throws them into. If they said the first thing that came into their head, there'd be no problem.
>
> An artist who is inspired is being *obvious*. He's not making any decisions, he's not weighing up one idea against another. . . . How else could Dostoyevsky have dictated one novel in the morning and one in the afternoon for three weeks in order to fulfil his contracts?[8]

Experienced improvisers know that if they have attained a state of relaxed awareness, they can trust themselves to be obvious. It is not too difficult to draw an analogy between this state of relaxed awareness and the Christian experience of contemplative prayer. In the popular imagination, prayer is something one resorts to in a time of crisis. To the Christian disciple, by contrast, prayer can either be moral training in the disciplines of listening to God, or it can be an experience of the grace of "being obvious" in God's presence. The former is the prayer of effort, the latter the prayer of habit. The aim of the former is to make the latter a matter of instinct—an unself-conscious activity that becomes "second nature." The practices and disciplines of Christian discipleship aim to give the Christian this same state of relaxed awareness, so that they have the freedom—indeed, the skill—to "be obvious" in what might otherwise seem an anxious crisis. Those with that relaxed awareness, who take the right things for granted, are what the church calls saints.

How is it done? How does the church produce saints? How do Christians learn the right habits and come to take the right things for granted? What are the repeated practices that train the moral imagination? An ethic that transfers attention from action to agent, from decision to training, from quandary to character, from what it is right for all to do to what is good for some to be, must answer these questions in detail.

For Christians the principal practice by which the moral imagination is formed, the principal form of discipleship training, is worship. Worship is the time when the conventional rules of the fallen world are suspended, when God is at last addressed as Lord, when time and heart and voice and posture are directed toward knowing God and making him known, toward experiencing the glorious liberty of being his child, when need and expectation are focused on their true source, when all desires are known and no secrets are hid, when attention moves from what is to what might yet be. Each aspect of worship represents a vital dimension of moral formation.

How Worship Forms Character

When Christians gather together to worship, whether two or three or two or three thousand, they are quickly reminded or become aware that they are in the presence of God.[9] The ability to name the presence of God develops skills that stand in the tradition stretching from wrestling Jacob to the broken bread of the Emmaus road. By naming the presence of God the community develops the skill of wonder, the virtue of humility, and the notion of God's glory and faithfulness, in a tradition that stretches from the pillar of cloud to the Great Commission. At much the same time they become aware of the presence of one another. By committing themselves to meet regularly together Christians practice the skills of politics, the nonviolent resolution of conflicting goods in corporate life, the virtue of constancy, and the notion of the body of Christ. More gradually, they become aware of those who are not gathering together—those who are absent. This is how the community develops the practices of pastoral care and evangelism, the skill of memory for those missing, the virtue of love for the lost, and the notion of the communion of saints.

When Christians listen for God's word in Scripture, they learn to listen for God's word in every conversation. They develop the skill of storytelling, of finding their place and role in the story, of recognizing beginnings and endings, of seeing the author at work; and also the skill of listening, of realizing how much there is to discover, of fitting their own small story into the larger story of God. They practice the virtue of prophetic hope, the conviction that God has acted before to save his people and will act again to set them free. They learn the notions of revelation, of truth, of communal discernment, of authority, history, and tradition.

When Christians intercede together, thus putting themselves in place of others before God, Christians develop the skill of distinguishing pain from sin, suffering from evil, need from want. They practice the virtues of patience and persistence—and of prudence, for they learn only to request what they can cope with receiving. They learn the notions of providence and the kingdom of God, and what it means to have an advocate before the Father.

When Christians come naked and humble before God in baptism, they learn to come naked and humble before God in death. They develop the skill of naming their own sin, of identifying their participation in human and global fear and finitude, of handing that sin over in penitence, of spiritual disciplines of preparation such as frequent prayer, knowledge of Scripture, and fasting. They practice the virtue of courage, in anticipating their own death, and faith, in committing themselves to the one who judges justly. They learn the notions of adoption by the Father, justification through the Son, new birth in the Spirit, liberation from slavery, the resurrection of the body, and vocation to a life of prayer and service. They realize that salvation is a gift to be received, not a reward to be earned.

By having to share the peace before sharing the bread, Christians learn that reconciliation is as necessary to their lives as their daily bread. They develop the skills of admonition and truth-telling, of not letting the sun go down on their anger, of forgiveness and working at relationships. They practice the virtues of mercy and forbearance, of humility and honesty, of patience and courage. They learn the notion of forgiveness, of the body and its members, of the ultimate unity of grace and truth.

By sharing bread with one another around the Lord's Table, Christians learn to live in peace with those with whom they share other tables—breakfast, shop-floor, office, checkout. They develop the skills of distribution, of the poor sharing their bread with the rich, and the rich with the poor. They develop the skills of equality, of the valued place of differently abled, differently gendered and oriented people, those of assorted races and classes and medical, criminal, and social histories. They develop the practices of giving and receiving, of handing over the firstfruits of labor and receiving back the firstfruits of the resurrection. They develop the skills of participating in the life of heaven, in realizing their simple actions anticipate God's eternal destiny. They practice the virtues of justice, generosity, and hope. They learn the notions of regular dependence on God's abiding providence, of the coming kingdom, of sacrifice and holiness.

Finally, when Christians are sent back out into the world they learn what it means to be salt and light, to be distinct yet among. They develop the practices of service and partnership, of seeking out the ways of God in the most benighted corners of the world. They learn the disciplines and techniques of cooperating with people of very different principles and stories, of resolving conflict without violence and standing beside the weak and afflicted. They practice the virtues of justice, peacemaking, temperance, and love. They learn the notions of mission, proclamation, incarnation, and kingdom.

Thus in worship Christians seek in the power of the Spirit to be conformed to the image of Christ—to act like him, think like him, be like him. There is a folktale that offers a parable of this endeavour. Once there was a rich man. He met and fell in love with a young maiden. She was lovely in form, and lovelier still in character. He rejoiced when he saw her. Yet he grieved also. For he knew that he was not like her. His face was hideous and his heart was cruel. He considered how he could win her hand.

Eventually he hit upon a plan. He went to see a mask maker. He said, "Make me a mask that I shall become handsome. Then, perhaps, I may win the love of this noble young woman." The mask maker did as he was bid. The man was transformed into a handsome figure. He tried hard to summon a character to match. It was sufficient to win the heart and hand of the fair maiden, and they were married. Ten years of increasing happiness followed. But the man knew he was carrying a secret. He sensed that true love could not be founded on deceit. He had to know if his wife really loved him, if she loved the man behind the mask. So one day, with a heavy heart and trembling hand, he knocked a second time on the mask maker's door. "It is time to remove the mask," he said. He walked slowly and anxiously back to his home. He greeted his wife.

To his astonishment, she made no comment, nor showed any untoward reaction. There was no scream, no horror, no revulsion. He searched for a mirror. He looked—and saw no ugliness but a face as handsome as the mask, a face so different from his original face. He was amazed and overjoyed—but bewildered and confused. He ran back to the mask maker to find some kind of explanation. The mask maker said, "You have changed. You loved a beautiful person. You have become beautiful too. You have become beautiful through loving her. You become like the face of the one whom you love."

This is what Christians seek to do in worship. They spend time in the presence of the one whom they love. They hope thereby to become like him. Worship is a habit, but like all good habits, one that comes about through moral effort. The creative work lies in the preparation. The moment of worship is like the "moment" of decision. It is the time for instinct and habit, a time of being obvious and ordinary—so long as one has formed the right instincts and habits, and learned to regard the right things as obvious and ordinary.

Formation and Games

Worship is like a game. It has its own rules, customs, and etiquette. It suspends normal patterns of thought and behavior. It takes place in its own controlled space and time. It is undertaken for its own sake, for no other purpose. But it can nonetheless have widespread benefits in forming, training, and developing its participants. In this respect it is like the "playing fields of Eton"—the place of other games, with other benefits, but likewise undertaken for their own sake. The benefits of worship, which I have described above, are not necessarily helpful in this world. But they offer training for entering another world, the kingdom of God. Heaven is the time when the game becomes reality. This is what it means for the kingdom to break in.

It may sound disrespectful to describe worship as a game. But this would be a misunderstanding of the purpose of games. Games are, for example, a very helpful form of training. A game lasts for a short time. It is understood to be a suspension of conventional rules. It is a project, rather than a life's endeavor. It is thus relatively safe. Because it is safe, one has the freedom to experiment, make mistakes, and discover hidden gifts and talents. By playing a game over and over again one may develop habits and establish skills. One may also perceive analogies with situations in conventional life to which those skills and talents may be transferred and applied. One may quickly see that games are a well-attested method of training for all kinds of practices, and that worship is a game that trains us for heaven.

Theatrical improvisation is all about games. Games are both training and performance—both preparation and "situation." Improvisation thus inspires us to see the whole of life as a game and—far from that being trivial—to imagine the whole of life as worship. This chapter has been about getting ready. The next chapters are about playing. They are full of games, games that illustrate, identify, inspire, train, test, and tease. Many are amusing, some hilarious. But they are not trivial. Training for worship, training for discipleship is vital—in many ways it is worship, it is discipleship. Training in improvisation is an analogy for worship and discipleship—an analogy at times so close it becomes the real thing. These improvisation games are best played by actors with *la disponibilité*—by people of alertness, ready to play. In just the same way, worship is best enjoyed by a community of character—by disciples of holiness, ready to pray.

6

Assessing Status

Status and Human Interaction

The great cry of liberation theology is a cry for theology to take seriously its context. Liberation theologians insist that theology begins with action in context, and that the second step is reflection on that action. It is a challenge to all the characteristics of theology—the who, what, when, where, why, and how. The who is different—theology is done by the poor, not just by the leisured, educated classes. The where is different—theology is done amid the urban and rural barrios and shantytowns of South America, not just in the comfort of European universities. The what, when, and how are different—theology is critical reflection on action that is already in progress, not just abstract speculation on ideas. It is done by suffering communities rather than by privileged individuals. It reflects on present realities, not past events. It engages with real relations of power, not idealized notions of service. The why is different—theology is done not to understand the world, but to change it.

This turn toward context is a significant step in uniting ethics and theology. But the insight that comes from theatrical improvisation takes us a step further. It points out that context is an issue not just when there is a notable difference in wealth, education, class, privilege, working pattern, or living conditions. Context is an issue in any and every interaction between two or more people. And this is not a static context of environmental situation or conventional social role. It is not something that people accept because of who they *are*. It is something that people choose in the way they *do*—the way they relate to a given other. Do they act and speak in a way that assumes superiority or inferiority, dominance or submission? This is the choice that improvisers call status. Status informs *every single interaction between people*—no casual movement or gesture is without significance. There are no innocent remarks or meaningless pauses.[1]

Status interactions are the ways people try to maneuver conversations and interplays into forms that reaffirm their preferred mode of relationship. Behind every status interaction is an implicit incipient story, and in many ways status names the negotiation over what kind of story this might become. Consider two strangers approaching one another from opposite ends of a long corridor. A host of small gestures and movements establish status from some distance away, so that passing may take place with appropriate posture and respect. High-status players warn others that it is not worth the risk of coming near. Low-status players advise that it is not worth the bother. It is important to note that both modes are forms of defense. Most people are "status specialists"—they feel comfortable with their accustomed status, but naked and vulnerable when forced into the "wrong" status.

Compare three teachers. One was well-liked, but could not keep control of the class. He frequently touched his face, often blinked, tended to twitch and laugh nervously, invariably arrived breathless and late for class and apologized for doing so, and regularly started sentences with a short "Er" as if he were interrupting the pupils' concentration. Another was widely disliked, but had no trouble keeping discipline, and had no need to resort to punishments or threats. He sat nervelessly still. He paused before each reply or pronouncement, and sometimes interjected a long "Er" before he spoke. His head remained still while he spoke, and he never touched his face. He often used pupils' names when he spoke to them. A third teacher was genuinely loved. He seldom punished, but still kept the attention and interest of the class. He smiled easily, walked tall, but was always relaxed. The atmosphere in the class could be lively and humorous—but then suddenly calm and thoughtful. The first teacher was a low-status player. The second, a compulsive high-status player. The third, a status expert who could raise and lower his own status at will.

Status is a seesaw. If people bring themselves up, they bring the other person down. If they bring themselves down, they bring the other person up. Note the following interaction (I have highlighted the status transactions in brackets):

A: What do you like to read, when you get the time? [Raises B, by suggesting B is busy and thus high status.]

B: More recently I have generally gone for the later works of Tolstoy. [Raises self, by accepting shortage of time, choosing author of notoriously lengthy books, and implying a wide knowledge of his and other works.]

A: Ah! I remember *War and Peace* vividly from my childhood. [Raises self and crushes B by suggesting B's high culture was already assimilated by A in childhood.] My parents let me stay up to watch the series on television. [Crushes self and raises B once more.]

Once actors have become thoroughly familiar with status, such that it becomes automatic, they can adapt to complex situations effortlessly. Instinct takes over and everything seems easy. This is aptly demonstrated as follows:

> If someone starts a scene by saying "Ah, another sinner! What's it to be, the lake of fire or the river of excrement?" then you can't "think" fast enough to know how to react. You have to understand that the scene is in Hell. . . . If you know what status you're playing the answers come automatically.
> "Well?"
> "Excrement," you say, playing high status, without doing anything you experience as "thinking" at all, but you speak in a cold voice, and you look around as if Hell was less impressive than you'd been led to believe. If you're playing low status you say "Whichever you think best, Sir," or whatever. Again with no hesitation, with eyes full of terror, or wonder.[2]

Choosing Status

Thus the first dimension of status is to realize that status transactions characterize every interaction between two or more people: they are a part of every relationship, however fleeting, impersonal, or superficial. But the next dimension emerges when one discovers that status is not given or bestowed by another, but chosen by oneself. Even more significant is to appreciate that one kind of status is neither "better," nor more admirable, nor more worthy than another. Christian communities that, at least tacitly, assume that meekness and servility are fine aspirations can be slow to appreciate this. But a crucial breakthrough in improvisation comes when actors realize that high and low status are simply alternative methods for getting one's way—for arranging a social interaction along lines that one can subtly control and manipulate. At first acquaintance, it is commonly assumed that high status is much more powerful than low status. Thus one might assume that life is a battle for status, and that all the winnings go to the most high-status player. The following illustrations show that this is far from the case.

There are two siblings. One, A, lives in the apartment of the other, B. B comes downstairs in the morning and asks if there are any letters. Finding them, he sees they have been opened. If A plays high status, the scene goes something like this:

B: Why did you open my letter?
A: Is it open?
B: You always open my letters.
A: I don't know who did it.
B: No one else has been here!

Extreme conflict, perhaps violence, ensues. If A plays low status, it is a very different story.

B: Did you open my letter?
A: Yes.
B: [Stopping the attack] Yes?
A: Yes.
B: Well, what did you do it for?
A: I wanted to see what was inside.
B: [Stalled again] How dare you open my letters?
A: You're right to be angry.
B: I told you never to open my letters.
A: I always do it.
B: You do?[3]

B seems paralyzed by A's reaction. Unless A raises status, B cannot become angry. It proves impossible for B to punish someone who is determined to apologize and prepared to be humiliated. Meanwhile A experiences extraordinary joy, exhilarated to be controlling B like a puppet.[4] A certain amount of reflection on one's own experience may bear this out. It is remarkably difficult to sustain righteous anger against a person who makes no effort to suggest they are in any sense in the right. If the person then suggests that they abhor their own behavior, and that they are, or were, not in full control of their own actions, they are making themselves so low-status that it disarms the person seeking a conventional pattern of trial, punishment, and reconciliation. This is how young children learn to adopt a particular status that suits them—a status that can stay with them for a lifetime. High status brings certain rewards, but assumes jealousy, envy, and regular conflict. Low status is a way of avoiding conflict and punishment, but at the cost of regular humiliation. Later on in years, people can find it hard to "break the habits of a lifetime" when it comes to the status they habitually play.[5]

Status and Conventional Relationships

The next stage is to introduce a conventional relationship and to witness the difference between the status people are and the status they play. This is the most fascinating dynamic in status interactions. It concentrates on the distinction between person and role. It is generally known as Master-Servant. A common experience of this kind of status transaction is that of customer–shop assistant. The expectation is that the customer calls the tune and the assistant plays it. But the servant often knows best. I once joined a friend who was going into a superior high-street outfitter. "Do you sell those little pieces of plastic you insert into a shirt to stiffen the collar?" my friend asked. The assistant, hardly glancing up, proffered a handful, and said, "We don't sell them, sir, we give them away." On another occasion I complimented a butcher on his display of meat and asked if there was any he particularly recommended. "It's all recommended, sir, otherwise we wouldn't sell it," he retorted. A friend once went into an ecclesiastical furnishings outlet. "I'm looking for one of those collapsible lecterns that you can fold away after the service," he said. "I think you'll find our lecterns don't collapse, sir: it will be a legilium you'll be looking for," came the reply. In each case the "servant" raises their status above the master by virtue of their extensive expertise in their particular field, but deflects any note of hostility in the corresponding lowering of the "master's" status by the use of superficially accommodating language. The servile language masks a high-status response, and prevents it from seeming aggressive. These details provide the fascination in such interplays. The most famous master-servant relations are ones where the servant has all the power, but will lose it the very moment that either party acknowledges it is so—thus Sir Humphrey Appleby and Prime Minister James Hacker, Jeeves and Wooster, or perhaps Tony Blair and George W. Bush. The seesawing and constant reversals of status provide the dynamism.

The story of Harry illustrates the significance of status and the fascination of the interplay of status roles. Harry's story was related to me by a friend called Robin.[6] While studying for the Lutheran ministry, Robin was placed in a parish in Akron, Ohio. Harry was a member of Robin's placement parish. The pastoral staff of the parish went to see him at home once a week. They generally brought a tape of the Sunday service, a weekly bulletin, and the sacrament. It tended to be the last role handed out at the staff meeting. The time came for Robin to discover why.

When Robin first called on Harry, she got a shock. Harry lived in a run-down white clapboard house. He was a big person, sitting in an overstuffed armchair with an oxygen tank beside it. His legs were virtually useless. The house was pervaded by a smell of must, urine, and dirt. It was repulsive. Nonetheless, Robin went a second time, and gradually Harry came to trust that she would return regularly. As he realized he was not going to be rejected by her, he began to talk more about himself and the way he saw things. Yet he seldom said much about his debilitating physical condition, or the squalor in which he was living.

One day Harry said to Robin, "It's time for you to have a look in the cellar." Reluctantly, and somewhat uneasily, Robin walked to the cellar door. She carefully opened it and looked into the darkness. "Go down the steps!" Harry insisted, realizing her hesitancy. To Robin's astonishment, she saw a large and imposing weaver's loom set up in the basement. There were piles of old clothes and torn strips of cloth. Robin stared in amazement. After trying for some time without success to relate the creativity of what she saw to the dirt and smell of the man she knew, she came back up the stairs, totally bemused.

Harry instructed Robin to bring him a pile of rugs from the kitchen. He took them from her and put them down in front of him, and began to tell the story of his life. He explained that he took in any old clothes that nobody wanted, and scraps of cloth from the rubbish heap. He then wove them into something new. The something new was the pile of rag rugs she had found stacked in his kitchen. He then gave what he had made to people who needed a rug. Why did he do it? Because, he said, he felt he was like the old clothes and the waste cloth. He was on the rubbish heap of life—alienated from his friends and his family, unable to work, unable even to breathe properly. He gave Robin his finest rug. Some weeks later, she conducted his funeral.

The time came for her to return to her seminary and complete her studies. At one tutorial she shared Harry's story with a group of her colleagues. After the session, a fellow student touched Robin's arm, took her to one side, and said, "Harry was my uncle." The student was in tears, for she realized that she had lost her chance of reconciliation with him. She had thought of Harry as a pariah but she could now see he was a saint. Robin retrieved her precious rug, which Harry had given her, and gave it to her fellow student. Even after his death, Harry's ministry was transforming the lives of people whom he touched. As Robin told me the story she added, finally, "I am still moved by his witness."

Robin begins the story in an ambivalent status: she is called to be a Lutheran minister, a profession that requires good character, education, training, and discipline, and generally is associated with having a number of skills. It therefore carries considerable status, as a role.

But she is only a humble trainee, so, in relation to her colleagues in the parish, she is of low status. When she takes on the task of going to visit Harry, it appears initially that this confirms her low status: it is a task that inevitably falls to the most low-status of the staff team, being so undesirable. As her visits become regular, her status gradually increases, as her colleagues' curiosity is aroused. Harry is, initially, of very low status—being a recipient of the rag rugs, Robin becomes his student, his pupil. Returning to the seminary, Robin the trainee of the staff and the student of Harry becomes a teacher, showing Harry's niece where the kingdom is truly to be found. The reason the story is so affecting is largely due to the extraordinary range and number of twists of status that continue throughout, the fact that every relationship subverts expectations of status, and the fact that status roles are constantly subverted and transformed.

Similar factors are at work in a number of Old Testament narratives. For example, the tension in the Joseph story begins when he is one of the youngest of Jacob's sons, yet the eldest son of the favored wife, and recipient of his father's gift. He seems outrageously high-status in reporting his dreams to his brothers, and this high status leads to conflict. He then has a second status tension, as the lowly slave who yet resists his master's wife's advances. Yet again he is the lowly prisoner who alone can decipher the lofty pharaoh's dream. The revelation scene with his brothers is a confirmation of the status-reversal from the original conflict. Likewise Samson's story is one of high status proclaimed and subverted, and of a deeply ironic conclusion that, blind, imprisoned, mocked, and exiled, he achieved more than in his days of glory. When Jael drives a tent peg through the head of the Sisera after his defeat at the hands of Deborah and Barak, the narrator of the book of Judges rejoices, not so much at the violence of the act, but at the status reversal that allows a woman with no force of an army behind her to bring down the mightiest of Israel's enemies. The story of Ruth is a narrative of how a very low-status person, through a mixture of loyalty, determination, and guile, was transformed into an ancestor of the great King David. In each case a mixture of conventional status roles and adopted status plays lead the characters to remarkable twists and turns of high-status impotence and low-status subversion.

Status and Space

The first stage in understanding status is to recognize that status transactions are inherent in every relationship. The second is to see that people make choices in their use of language and gesture about whether to play high or low status. The third is to appreciate that "high" and "low" are not moral designations, or even measurements of relative power: they are simply alternative strategies for getting one's way. The fourth is to begin to enjoy the dynamics of status interactions displayed in the affirmation and subversion of a conventional relationship. The fifth and last dimension to perceive is the significance of the use of space.

A typical corporate example of space interactions is a beach. A group of people sit on a beach. The next group to arrive will generally sit some distance away. If they were to sit close to the first group, they would have to choose either to be friendly, which might cause them anxiety, or not to be friendly, which would cause the first group anxiety. As more and more groups arrive, the definition of "close" shrinks. Personal space is established not by distance but by body posture—turning toward one's own group, staring at the sky, or covering one's face with a book. Churchgoers are familiar with the way these dynamics work in the way a church building fills up before an act of worship. Worshipers tend to scatter across the space available, making a number of status statements as they do so. One of the differences from a beach is that attending worship is generally a habitual activity, and the choice of seat is often a regular one. Thus people will adopt a status toward others who are usually there, but not on this occasion. It is quite common for one half of the building to be practically empty, for example on a holiday weekend, "because the people who sit there are away." The regulars continue to sit in relation to where others would normally be. Another typical example, this time concerning individuals, is a long sidewalk. When two strangers approach one another from opposite directions, decisions about who will move aside are made a hundred yards before the moment comes. Here is a description of what takes place:

> The two people scan each other for signs of status, and then the lower one moves aside. If they think they're equal, both move aside, but the position nearest the wall is actually the strongest. If each person believes himself to be dominant . . . they stop face to face, and do a sideways dance, while muttering confused apologies. . . . I remember doing [this dance] in a shop doorway with a man who took me by my upper arms and moved me gently out of his path. It still rankles. Old people who don't want to give way, and who cling to the status they used to have, will walk along the street hugging the wall, "not noticing" anyone who approaches them.[7]

These five dimensions of status each have significant implications for the church and its understanding of its ethical task and its relationship with wider society.

Status and the Church

The first dimension is to recognize that status transactions are inherent in every relationship. This is true on both an individual and a corporate level. The politics of local church life is, like the life of any organization, filled with status interactions. Consider the moment at which a date for a future meeting is arranged. One person gets out a tiny diary. Another gets out an enormous diary. Another gets out an electronic diary, which takes some while to warm up. A fourth does not carry a diary, but makes all arrangements through a personal secretary at the office. A fifth does not have a diary, because he considers that he can remember such special events as would break his routine. A sixth has left her diary at home. Then dates are suggested. One person explains his unavailability in terms of all his upcoming dental appointments and driving lessons. Another is out of the country for the next month. A third says he will need to consult his partner. A fourth says she could make the suggested time, but she would be an hour late. A fifth says he could make any time—he is completely flexible. A sixth says she must be getting away, but not to worry, just go ahead and she will try to fit in and let the others know. And then the moment comes when a date is set. Whose absence is insignificant, and whose is decisive?

This is a common experience of organizational life, not least of local church life. It highlights the underlying prevalence of status transactions in every conversation and encounter. But status interactions are similarly ubiquitous in the relationship of the local church corporately to the community it serves. How do the size, age, and design of the church building compare to other buildings in the community? Are the doors open, closed, or locked? Is the faith and activity of the church broadcast by notice board or kept a secret? What is the principal way in which the church encounters local people—through knocking on doors or written leaflets (the salesperson or mail-order company), prearranged meetings between representatives of organizations with common interests (the businessperson), or the availability of a designated representative at advertised hours for particular services (the professional person)? Does the local church believe it speaks for "all people of goodwill" in the community, or does it assume that its voice will probably be a minority view on most issues? Does it expect to lead, join, or follow? Does it call its leader pastor, minister, or priest, and what social standing does it expect its leader to have in the community? These are all questions of status.

Similar questions arise when the corporate context changes from local to national. Does the denomination consider itself to speak for truth, which needs no defense, or for a group of beleaguered believers, whose interests need upholding? Does the denomination consider itself part of government, concerned with the balance of power and the benefit of all? Or does it presume that it will always be with the marginalized and oppressed, and therefore never at the castle, always at the gate? Where does the denomination locate its national center of operations, and in what kind of premises? How does it institute and regard its leaders? How does it hope or assume non-Christians will regard these leaders? Will that esteem be earned, and if so, how—or can it be taken for granted? These are all questions of status.

I trust I have said enough to have established the significance for the church of my first two claims, that status transactions are inherent in every relationship, and that individuals and groups make choices in their use of language and gesture about whether to play high or low status. These claims apply on local and national scales, in regard to internal and external relations. I move on now to my remaining three claims about status, beginning with the last of them.

The use of space is highly significant in status transactions. This is because, when the security of distance is removed, status differences have to be recognized and negotiated. Some descriptions of the difference between church and world use spatial language. Terms like "inside" and "outside" are used, for example in Cyprian's famous words, "Outside the church there is no salvation."[8] The language of territory is central to the Bible. Abraham travels to the Promised Land; Joseph and his family travel to Egypt; Moses and the children of Israel travel back; Daniel and Esther find themselves in exile; Ezra and Nehemiah lead the people back; Jesus inaugurates a kingdom, but "not of this world." Does the church find itself in exile, on foreign territory? Or is this God's world, the church's home? Does the notion of Christendom imply a boundary, within which the church has sway, or at least influence, and outside which is missionary territory? And, if so, where is that boundary? How does the church spread itself on the "beach" of its contemporary environment? How does it meet other bodies on the "sidewalk"—does it step aside, hold close to the wall, "do a sideways dance, while muttering confused apologies"? Or is the church more like the older person who walks along the street hugging the wall, "not noticing" anyone who approaches them, clinging to the status they used to have? Is there a lingering expectation that others will step aside, not questioning such venerable status? And what is the church's instinctive posture—the open stance of the high-status player, or the fearful crouch of the one anticipating attack?

Michel de Certeau offers an extended discussion of the interplay of space and time in what I am calling status transactions. De Certeau makes a distinction between "strategies" and "tactics."

I call a *strategy* the calculation (or manipulation) of power relationships that becomes possible as soon as a subject with will and power (a business, an army, a city, a scientific institution) can be isolated. It postulates a *place* that can be delimited as its own and serve as a base from which relations with an *exteriority* composed of targets and threats (customers or competitors, enemies, the country surrounding the city, objectives and objects of research, etc.) can be managed. As in management, every "strategic" rationalization seeks first of all to distinguish its "own" place, that is, the place of its own power and will, from an "environment." . . . It is also the typical attitude of modern science, politics, and military strategy.

De Certeau regards this establishment of a "proper," a "break between a place appropriated as one's own and its other" as *"a triumph of place over time,"* and "a mastery of places through sight." He perceives that a certain kind of knowledge is "sustained and determined by the power to provide oneself with one's own place," giving scientific and military examples of autonomous cities, "neutral" or "independent" institutions, and laboratories pursuing "disinterested" research. By contrast with a strategy, he goes on,

> a *tactic* is a calculated action determined by the absence of a proper locus. No delimitation of an exteriority, then, provides it with the condition necessary for autonomy. The space of a tactic is the space of the other. Thus it must play on and with a terrain imposed on it and organized by the law of a foreign power. It does not have the means to *keep to itself*, at a distance, in a position of withdrawal, foresight, and self-collection. . . . It does not, therefore, have the options of planning general strategy and viewing the adversary as a whole within a distinct, visible, and objectifiable space. It operates in isolated actions, blow by blow. It takes advantage of "opportunities" and depends on them, being without any base where it could stockpile its winnings, build up its own position, and plan raids. What it wins it cannot keep. . . . It must vigilantly make use of the cracks that particular conjunctions open in the surveillance of the proprietary powers. It poaches in them. It creates surprises in them. It can be where it is least expected. It is a guileful ruse.

In short, "a tactic is an art of the weak." The key difference is that strategies seek to reduce temporal relations to spatial ones, pinning their hopes on the resistance that the establishment of place offers to the erosion of time; tactics, by contrast, rely on skilled use of time, through rapidity, rhythm, pertinent intervention, and delay. De Certeau also suggests that whereas strategies rely on grammar, tactics use the arts of rhetoric to subvert the dominance of strategic forces.[9] An illustration of a tactic is the French tradition of *la perruque* (the wig). *La perruque* is the tactic of appearing to be working for one's employer, while in fact doing one's own work—writing a college essay on the office computer, scanning the Internet for one's holiday flights while officially seeking new customers, borrowing a carpenter's lathe to make a small table for one's living room. It is not pilfering because nothing of material value is stolen. It is not absenteeism because the employee is officially still at work. The worker

> actually diverts time (not goods, since he uses only scraps) from the factory for work that is free, creative, and precisely not directed towards profit. . . . Into the institution to be served are thus insinuated styles of social exchange, technical invention, and moral resistance, that is, an economy of the *"gift"* (generosities for which one expects a return), an aesthetics of *"tricks"* (artists' operations) and an ethics of *tenacity* (countless ways of refusing to accord the established order the status of a law, a meaning, or a fatality).[10]

The Hidden Transcript

Moving from the use of space to the affirmation and subversion of conventional relationships brings us to the work of James C. Scott. Scott insists that politics is not just about openly declared dominance and revolt, but also more significantly about the "disguised, low-profile, undeclared" resistance of subordinate groups.[11] There is a whole world of "infrapolitics" between quiescence and revolt. In a distinction that echoes de Certeau's description of strategies and tactics, and Johnstone's notion of high and low status, Scott separates the "public transcript" from the "hidden transcript." The public transcript is "the *self*-portrait of dominant elites as they would have themselves seen."[12] It is

> the public performance required of those subject to elaborate and system- atic forms of social subordination: the worker to the boss, the tenant or sharecropper to the landlord, the serf to the lord, the slave to the master, the untouchable to the Brahmin, a member of a subject race to one of the dominant race. With rare, but significant exceptions the public per- formance of the subordinate will, out of prudence, fear, and the desire to curry favour, be shaped to appeal to the expectations of the powerful. . . . The dominant never control the stage absolutely, but their wishes normally prevail. In the short run, it is in the interest of the subordinate to produce a more or less credible performance, speaking the lines and making the gestures he knows are expected of him.[13]

As we saw in the discussion of status, so here the point is that a face-value reading of the public transcript may tell rather less than the whole story. The deference and consent that seem universal may only be a tactic, a preliminary form of subversion. One must see instead the hidden transcript, which

> consists of those offstage speeches, gestures and practices that confirm, contradict or inflect what appears in the public transcript. . . . [It] is produced for a different audience and under different constraints of power than the public transcript. . . . [T]hese are the forms that political struggle takes when frontal assaults are precluded by the realities of power. . . . [T]he aggregation of thousands upon thousands of such "petty" acts of resistance have dramatic economic and political effects. Poaching and squatting on a large scale can restructure the control of property. Peasant tax evasion on a large scale has brought about crises of appropriation that threaten the state. Massive desertion by serf or peasant conscripts has helped bring down more than one ancien regime. Under the appropriate conditions, the accumulation of petty acts can, rather like snowflakes on a steep mountainside, set off an avalanche.[14]

Just as for Johnstone every interaction involves a status transaction, so for Scott politics lies in the negotiation and interplay between the public and the hidden transcript. Just as for Johnstone it is vital to remember that high and low status are not designations of moral approval or disapproval, so for Scott it is important to note that "power relations are not, alas, so straightforward that we can call what is said in power-laden contexts false and what is said off-stage true. Nor can we simplistically describe the former as a realm of necessity and the latter as a realm of freedom."[15] The point is that status is a significant construal of power, and that just as a habitual fascination of improvisation is the affirmation and subversion of a conventional relationship, so in politics that conventional relationship is frequently realized as one of dominance and (at least apparent) subordination.

Status as a Moral Category

The one claim about status that remains to be illustrated is that "high" and "low" are not moral designations, or even measurements of relative power: they are simply alternative strategies for getting one's way. Of all the claims about status, this seems to be the one that those schooled in a theological frame of mind find it most difficult to grasp. There are good reasons for this. One of the most significant forms of dramatic tension in the Gospels is between Jesus as servant, slave, and crucified outcast and Jesus as Messiah, Lord, and Son of God. On the one hand the wind and seas obey him; on the other, though he saves others, he cannot save himself. Perhaps the most poignant moments in the Gospels come when these two portrayals coincide. On the road to Caesarea Philippi, no sooner has Peter acknowledged the Christ than that same Christ announces he is to be put to death.[16] When he is shown the tomb of his friend Lazarus, whom he has the power to raise, Jesus weeps.[17] When he is anointed at Bethany, Jesus points out the irony that the one person who honored his messiahship did so in a way that anticipated his burial.[18] At the Last Supper, Jesus takes water and a towel, and concludes by saying, "If I, your Lord and Teacher, have washed your feet, you also ought to wash one another's feet."[19] At the cross, at the very moment of Jesus' humiliating and shameful death, the centurion declares, "Truly this man was the Son of God!"[20] Paul summarizes the reversal in status in the hymn of Christ's glory:

Let the same mind be in you that was in Christ Jesus,
who, though he was in the form of God,
did not regard equality with God
as something to be exploited,
but emptied himself,
taking the form of a slave,
being born in human likeness.
And being found in human form,
he humbled himself
and became obedient to the point of death—
even death on a cross.

Therefore God also highly exalted him
and gave him the name
that is above every name,
so that at the name of Jesus
every knee should bend,
in heaven and on earth and under the earth,
and every tongue should confess
that Jesus Christ is Lord,
to the glory of God the Father.[21]

The implications of the New Testament witness on status are not transparent. There is a clear rejection of high status for high status's sake: "whoever wishes to become great among you must be your servant, and whoever wishes to be first among you must be slave of all."[22] But there is no explicit rejection here of high-status roles such as leadership and greatness. Meanwhile when low-status circumstances are thrust upon the disciple, they are to be celebrated in a high-status manner:

Rejoice insofar as you are sharing Christ's sufferings, so that you may also be glad and shout for joy when his glory is revealed. If you are reviled for the name of Christ, you are blessed, because the spirit of glory, which is the Spirit of God, is resting on you. . . . [And] if any of you suffers as a Christian, do not consider it a disgrace, but glorify God because you bear this name.[23]

Thus the tension that runs through Christ's life must likewise run through the heart of the disciple. In the language of improvisation, the disciple should not assume that being a Christian means being low status, for it is perfectly possible to play the role of servant in a high-status manner, as several earlier examples have shown. Neither should the disciple assume that following Jesus means they have automatic access to high status, for the New Testament constantly reminds Christians not only of how God unseats the proud, but also of how suffering accompanies faith. Instead, the disciple must learn, like Jesus, to be an expert status player. Discipleship involves a constant questioning, teasing, and subversion of status, both high and low. For the New Testament is all about status, but its message is that, in God's reign, status is far from static.

7

Accepting and Blocking

Saying "Yes"

"There are people who prefer to say 'Yes,' and there are people who prefer to say 'No.' Those who say 'Yes' are rewarded by the adventures they have, and those who say 'No' are rewarded by the safety they attain."[1] Improvisation begins when a community of people resolve to find ways of "saying 'Yes.'" Communities generally find three kinds of reasons why they prefer instead to "say 'No.'" They tend to see "saying 'Yes'" as impossible, improper, or dangerous.

Improvising seems dangerous because it requires participants to make use of their unconscious. Much of the fear about improvisation derives from a fear of the unconscious, and a suspicion that unconscious thoughts and desires are generally sinful. Such a fear suggests that the future and the self—particularly the self in a group—are dangerous. A simple verbal improvisation game called "Word at a Time" illustrates this sense of danger, this fear of engaging with the unconscious.

The game begins with the actors sitting in a circle. One actor says a single word. This becomes the first word of a story. The actor next in the circle follows immediately with a second word, the next actor says a third, and so on as quickly as possible until the story is considered complete. Adverbs are disallowed in order to keep up the pace and avoid delaying tactics. Inexperienced actors invariably try to control the story. But this only succeeds in ruining it. Every person who adds a word

103

has an incipient story in mind, and thus an idea of what word might follow. But each time he or she must instantly wipe that idea out of the mind—or else he or she will be paralyzed. If the players relax, cease to worry about being "obvious," remain highly attentive, and simply say whatever comes to mind, they will find the story seems to take on a life of its own, guided "by some outside force."[2]

The reason improvisation seems impossible to inexperienced players is that instinctively they spend most of their time trying to avoid being dangerous. The story constantly threatens to become obscene, psychotic, or unoriginal. These all represent danger. Thus there is a constant, irresistible temptation to "kill" the story. This can be done reactively by saying "Stop" or remaining silent; or proactively by trying to control its future, insisting on being clever or original, or closing it abruptly whenever its direction threatens danger.

This is why the formation of the Christian community in practices that form habits and instincts, described in chapter 5, is the first stage in improvisation. A community that is terrified of the danger lurking in its unconscious will be paralyzed when it comes to facing the unknown future. A community that trusts the practices it has inherited and allows them to shape its unconscious should be much more confident when facing the unknown.

In the last chapter a distinction was made between two kinds of imagination. One kind is the creative imagination, the kind that requires effort and originality. The other kind is the practical imagination, which simply requires the following of old habits in new circumstances—the ability to be "obvious." Most Christian ethics sees the future as a problem. It is a problem in much the same way that playing Word at a Time is a problem. Playing Word at a Time is a problem because either it is dangerous or it is impossible. The sense of danger corresponds to deontological ethics. It is a dangerous game, and the future is dangerous, because it is almost certain that at some stage one will behave "improperly." The sense of impossibility corresponds to consequential ethics. It is an impossible game, and the future is impossible, because it is almost certain that one will fail to control the story, to make it come out right.

The mistake made by both conventional forms of ethics in relation to the future (and to the game) is that they each assume that the future will throw up situations that will challenge their creative imaginations. Decisions will need to be made for which the resources are not readily available. The game Word at a Time shows why this is a mistake. Players who fall back on their own creativity and rely on their own originality in shaping a world ruin the game. Instead players have to use their practical imaginations. The middle of the game—the moment of decision—is no time for trying to be clever or original. Participants have to trust their own characters—characters that have been formed by the time the game begins.

At this point it is worth acknowledging a sense that may be lingering that the whole game of Word at a Time is improper, that rather than face its dangers and difficulties it would be better not to play at all. There are, after all, people who prefer to say "No," and they are doubtless rewarded by the safety they attain. But the parable of the talents (Matt. 25:14–30) is a warning to any considering withdrawing from the game because it seems difficult or dangerous. The third slave, the one who had received the one talent, said, "Master, I knew that you were a harsh man . . . so I was afraid, and I went and hid your talent in the ground." The master was not impressed. The slave had been given all he needed, and his hiding of the talent indicated a lack of faith. This parable is all about proving trustworthy in a few things, before being put in charge of many things. In just the same way games like Word at a Time are trial runs for Christian discipleship, apparently trivial tests to assess readiness for greater trials ahead.

Word at a Time, though a simple game, illustrates the skills that are necessary for keeping the story going. Keeping the story going may be dangerous but it need not be difficult. The key to keeping the story going is for disciples to remember that the story does not belong to them. The story is not just *their* story. The originality is already there in the story: the decisive elements in the story have already been performed. The church cannot do anything so bad that it could pervert the whole story. The creative imagination is thus engaged in forming Christians to be the kind of people who have the courage to keep the story going, even when it looks dangerous or when it threatens to reveal uncomfortable parts of themselves. Belief in God's sovereignty affirms that the story *will* keep going whether Christians are part of it or not. But the vocation of each Christian is to continue to be part of the story, to embody the story from the moment of baptism, regardless of the cost.

The Language of Improvisation

Three technical terms may assist in exploring what it means to say "Yes." The first is the term "offer." Anything an actor does may be regarded as an offer. An offer may be a speech, a facial expression or gesture, or an action—even an attempt to remain silent or still. Any of these things may be treated as an invitation to respond, and thus be treated as an offer. Thus in the game Word at a Time, each word is both a response to an offer and immediately an offer in itself. Offers are not to be regarded as good or bad in themselves: the key is what you do with them.

The second term is "accept." An actor accepts an offer by any response that maintains the premise of the action that constituted that offer. Imagine a child in the playground puts two fingers together and points them toward another child, and then clicks another finger and says, "Bang! You're dead." This is an offer. The second child then has the opportunity to respond to that offer. If the child is prepared to accept the offer, she will conventionally do so by yelping a strangled cry and falling over in a crumpled heap, for this maintains the premise of the first child's offer. To do this requires the same skills of the second child that are required to play the game Word at a Time. The second child must be willing and able to wipe from her mind any thoughts she herself had of actively controlling the outcome of the narrative, and resist the inclination to a passive refusal, such as "I'm not playing anymore."

The third term is "block." Imagine once again that the first child acts a shot and says, "Bang! You're dead." The simplest form of block would be to say, "I'm not playing anymore." But there are more subtle ways. If the second child were actively to refuse to accept the offer and fall down, but were instead to remain standing and say, "Bang! *You're* dead, not me," then this would also be a block. Blocking prevents the action from developing. It undermines one's partner's premise. It may be amusing to watch, but it kills the story. It happens when one actor is overwhelmed by the danger or difficulty of keeping the story going. Accepting sees the future as an opportunity—blocking sees the future as a problem. All sorts of possibilities are ruled out by blocking. Imagine once again that the first child shoots and says, "Bang! You're dead." This time the second child accepts the offer. Now the second child may begin to explore the afterlife of the dead soldier, and perhaps reappear to the first soldier as a ghost or angel. But this only becomes possible if the original death, the first offer, is accepted. Now the story can really develop, as the first child may be introduced to other angels, fall in love with one of them, have to choose whether to die in order to be united with the beloved, and so on.

What would it be like to be committed never to block, always to accept? What would it be like to be surrounded by people who are committed to the practice of accepting all offers? The interactions in such a community seem telepathic. It looks like everything has already been arranged. There is no such thing as an accident or an interruption. Everything becomes an offer that can be accepted.

> The actor who will accept anything that happens seems supernatural;
> it's the most marvellous thing about improvisation: you are suddenly in
> contact with people who are unbounded, whose imagination seems to

function without limit. . . . People with dull lives often think that their lives are dull by chance. In reality everyone chooses more or less what kind of events will happen to them by their conscious patterns of blocking and yielding.[3]

The story of the two trappers in Alaska illustrates what it might mean to accept all offers. Once upon a time there were two trappers in a hut all winter in Alaska. They made an arrangement whereby one of them should do the cooking until the other one found the food too disgusting, and then the other would take it over. Well, one had been cooking for a very long time and had got fed up because the other one never complained, so he thought he would serve up something truly terrible. He made a pie out of moose turds. Well, the other one sat in front of the pie and took a mouthful. For a moment he almost spat: then he said, "Moose turd pie! But good!" So the first one had to go on cooking.[4]

The delight of the story is that one would think that, regardless of whether cooking is regarded as high- or low-status, the cook was nonetheless the one with the power. But it turns out that the ability to accept all offers, to enjoy even moose turd pie, gives the second trapper all the power he could wish for.

One helpful accepting game is called "Group-Yes." The group has no leaders, and members say "Yes" to every suggestion. If they cannot say "Yes" with genuine enthusiasm they must leave the group and sit quietly at the side. Reflections on this game are valuable in understanding both the joy of and resistance to accepting all offers.

> I remind everyone that the game is an investigation of what the group wants, and that only if the players are honest will it give accurate feedback. Some exceedingly cooperative but "clever" students wreck the game every time. They intend to unite the group, but their "clever" suggestions are out of step, and suddenly they're alone. This rather shocking feedback trains them to be obvious, rather than "clever." . . . The exhilaration attached to playing Group-Yes can give the students insights into how negative their habitual interactions are.[5]

The exhilaration of perceiving what it might mean to be in the practice of accepting all offers is generally followed by anxiety. The anxiety assesses the sheer depth of the evil that is in the world and thus anticipates the range of occasions when it must be essential to block. It is important to look closely at some of the assumptions that lie behind the view that blocking is possible and necessary, let alone desirable. These assumptions concern violence and power.

Questions about Blocking

Blocking may seem to be the simplest way to keep one's hands clean—not to get involved in anything dangerous or improper. But as the discussion of the parable of the talents showed, it goes much further than that. Accepting offers is a practice that builds community by acknowledging, encouraging, and accommodating the other. It recognizes the dependence of all parties concerned upon one another. It requires the sharing of space and implies a continuing conversation about how to go on doing so. It shares time and assumes only the kind of outcomes that can benefit the other. It is not a competition that is about winning and losing.

Blocking undermines the other. It refuses to share space and time. It denies outcomes from which all can benefit. It assumes rivalry and enacts conflict in which there cannot be two winners, and most often all are losers. It is at least subtly, and sometimes overtly, aggressive. It presumes violence. The times when the church is tempted to block are exactly the times when it is called to deny itself, take up its cross, and follow Christ. For this response, the way of the cross, was Christ's engagement with evil, and his temptations to block were at least as strong as those of the church.

The choice of blocking can therefore be either passive or active. It is either a choice to shut oneself away and keep oneself unsullied by the world, or it is a choice to take up arms. These are theological choices. The passive choice represents a denial of the goodness of God's creation. It represents a refusal to engage with the complex realities of Christian discipleship. It reflects a denial of the redemption of all created things in Christ's resurrection. It speaks of an absence of hope. It forgets that it is not what goes into a person that defiles, but what comes out of a person. It presumes that abundant life can grow in a heaven of one's own making—and it assumes that heaven has walls, locks, and barricades.

The active choice is the choice of violence. This choice makes significant assumptions about God's power and about the church's power. The assumption it makes about God is that he has not already acted, that Christ has not already decisively defeated evil in his life, death, and resurrection. Thus the church acts as if it were Israel, in Act Two of the great drama, waiting for God to rend the heavens and come down, and in the meantime striving to secure his kingdom by all means possible. And sometimes the church acts as if it were in Act Five, taking upon itself the task of judgment, and assigning to itself the responsibility to impose the kingdom.

The assumption that active blocking makes about the church is that the church has the power to block, violently, should it choose to oppose the offers it deems to be evil. This is highly unlikely. And even if it were possible, would it be desirable? In order to secure such power the church would have to accommodate itself to the owners of such power. This would involve commitments that might prove just as unacceptable as being powerless in war. Blocking one evil might well involve accepting another. The one who lives by the sword dies by the sword. This demonstrates that questions of status underlie questions of accepting and blocking. There is an assumption that the church is a high-status institution that can select one from a number of options about how to respond to a given offer. But it is more likely that it can only choose between more or less desirable ways to accept.

A further assumption that violent blocking makes is that if the future is not *made* to come out right, it will certainly come out wrong. A commitment to accept opens a much greater time perspective. For a church operating in Act Four of the great drama, no blocking gains permanent security, and no acceptance incurs decisive damage. One set of alternatives illustrates this longer view. Consider the contrast between the European colonization of North America and the invasion of South America. In the North, the Native Americans chose to block. They took the military option, and began a struggle against impossible odds. They were roundly defeated. The result is the demoralized and degraded state of native North American culture today. The approach of the native South Americans was quite different. They generally accepted the invasion. They were, with few exceptions, unable or unwilling to defend themselves and were rapidly overrun by the Spanish and Portuguese. Yet today their condition is very different from that of their more belligerent neighbors to the north. Their culture and population are a highly significant feature of South American religion and society. Would they have fared better if they had blocked?[6]

The question the church needs to ask itself when confronted with evil is "What is the worst thing that can happen?" If after some consideration it is able to find an answer, it needs to ask itself a second question: "And what would happen then?" The point of the second question is to release the paralysis that tends to surround all thought about the worst thing. The second question is a reminder that the story does not belong to the church, or even to its oppressors—it belongs to God. It becomes possible to think beyond even the worst thing. It becomes possible to imagine accepting it. Then the threatening power of the worst thing over the church is alleviated. Sometimes it even becomes clear that the church's present circumstances, the strenuous efforts it is taking to avoid the worst thing, are actually worse than the worst thing. The worst thing to many medieval Christians was that Muslims had control of the holy places in Jerusalem and the Middle East. But was not much of what happened in the Crusades, that great attempt to block, so much worse than the apparent worst thing?

The key word in learning to accept is the word "and." This small word constitutes a significant statement. It indicates that the sentence is not yet finished. The story is not yet over. There is more to come, even when evil has done its worst. It begins to place the offer one is moved to block into a larger context in which it could be accepted. If one is able to face up to a threat, stare it in the face, and say "And . . . ?" one has gone a long way toward disarming that threat.

The stories of Israel in exile and of the early church under persecution provide many examples of the revolutionary power of a community who can accept the worst thing. These stories tell of the faithfulness of powerless pilgrims and exiles who cannot resist their oppressor but are nonetheless vindicated without using violence. The fact that they accept the fiery furnace and the den of lions disarms the power of those who used such worst things as a threat. They are able to say "And . . . ?" to their oppressors because they know that their own deaths do not mark the end of God's story. When the church is able to face the threats of the world with the same "And . . . ?" it gains extraordinary moral power. This is a power far greater than any physical power it might sometimes have assumed it needed. The courage to accept in this way is derived from its Lord. For the power of Christ lies in the fact that he accepted death, even death on a cross; he was able to do so because he believed in the "And." He believed that his death was not the end of the story: and so it proved. When the church says "And . . . ?" it is faithfully imitating Christ. It is in this faithful imitation that the church finds the power to confront the threats of the world without being intimidated.

The early chapters of Genesis narrate God's attempts to form a sustainable friendship with his creation. That attempt was thwarted in the fall, and the story of Cain and Abel explores the dimensions of fallen society. The flood is God's terrible reaction, his block in response to humanity's woeful failure to accept his offer. But the rainbow that follows the flood is God's commitment never to block so thoroughly again, never to obliterate his creation. The fact that God has to find another way of resolving his creation's many failures creates the Old Testament narrative. The ultimate example of the consequences of this covenant comes in the New Testament passion narratives. Jesus is presented as powerless, in no position to block the impossible and unjust offers of the Jewish authorities and the Romans. He is silent before his accusers. He is betrayed, handed over, waiting. Yet he demonstrates that even this vulnerability, even this condition of being unable to block, can be the ultimate form of faithfulness. This is the greatest test of the words of 1 Timothy 4:4–5: "For everything created by God is good, and nothing is to be rejected, provided it is received with thanksgiving; for it is sanctified by God's word and by prayer."

Subordinate Groups

To give a more nuanced account of blocking and accepting, it is helpful to return to the work of James C. Scott. Scott describes four varieties of political discourse amongst subordinate groups.[7] One takes place wholly within public discourse. It appeals to those principles that the dominant power claims to stand for and lobbies for recognition of legitimate claims within these principles. Thus American slaves in the South were able to appeal for garden plots, better food, and freedom to travel to church. The second, opposite form of discourse is the hidden transcript. "Here, offstage, where subordinates may gather outside the intimidating gaze of power, a sharply dissonant political culture is possible. Slaves in the relative safety of their quarters can speak the words of anger, revenge, self-assertion that they must normally choke back when in the presence of the masters and mistresses." The third realm of discourse lies between these two public and private poles.

> This is a politics of disguise and anonymity that takes place in public view but is designed to have a double meaning or to shield the identity of the actors. Rumour, gossip, folk tales, jokes, songs, rituals, codes, and euphemisms . . . fit this description. As a case in point, consider the Brer Rabbit stories of slaves, and trickster tales more generally. At one level these are nothing but innocent stories about animals; at another level they appear to celebrate the cunning wiles and vengeful spirit of the weak as they triumph over the strong.[8]

> In its most striking form, an entire ersatz façade may be erected in order to shield another reality from detection. Hill villages in colonial Laos, for example, were required by the occasionally visiting French officials to have a village headman and officials with whom they could deal. The Laotians responded, it appears, by creating a set of bogus notables who had no local influence and who were presented to colonial functionaries as *the* local officials. Behind this ruse, the respected local figures continued to direct local affairs, including the performance of the local officials.[9]

The fourth and "most explosive" form of politics is the moment of open challenge and defiance. This is more than a practical failure to comply: it is a "declared refusal." This is a symbolic declaration of war. Scott points out the vital difference between a passive avoidance and an active confrontation: "between failing to sing the national anthem and publicly sitting while others stand during its performance."[10] He points to the public rally called by President Nicolae Ceaucescu on December 21, 1989, in Bucharest, at which public booing and jeering demonstrated the vulnerability and impotence of the Romanian leader. A few days later he was dead.

> In fact, the term insubordination is quite appropriate here because any particular refusal to comply is not merely a tiny breach in a symbolic wall; it necessarily calls into question all the other acts that this form of sub-ordination entails. Why should a serf who refuses to bow before his lord continue to deliver grain and labour services? . . . A single act of successful public insubordination . . . pierces the smooth surface of apparent consent, which itself is a visible reminder of underlying power relations.[11]

Scott's first form of discourse, the campaigning mode, may be experienced as resistance, but since it shares the premise of its opponent, it is not really, in the language of improvisation, a block: instead it is an assertive form of accepting. The second form, the private articulation of the hidden transcript, is more clearly a block, although a largely powerless one. It is a denial of the premise of the dominant power, but one that, unless allied with a series of such acts, makes no practical difference and is thus a truculent form of accepting. The fourth approach is clearly a block. It does not require originality and skill: it requires the courage to make public the hidden transcript. It invites an outright confrontation. Scott argues that the most significant form of discourse is the third kind, that of the disguised meaning. With this assertion I wholeheartedly agree. It is this nether region, between blocking and accepting, that I shall explore more thoroughly in the next two chapters.

Blocking appears to some as faithful resilience. But in that it buries its talent in the hillside it may anticipate the punishment handed out to the third slave; and in that it sets its stall against the inevitable tide of time, it may anticipate the heritage of King Canute, the eleventh-century king of England who notoriously (and legendarily) sat at the seashore and ordered the tide not to come in. I have argued that for the church to block is not desirable, necessary, or possible.

But is accepting the only alternative? It is certainly essential to learn how to accept, and to learn why and how to avoid blocking. But accepting is not the only alternative. I suggest an approach that requires the skills learned through accepting, but does not stop there. Just because the church does not take up arms against evil, that does not mean it simply capitulates to it. The church does not simply accept the story of evil. It has a story of its own. The church's story begins before evil began and ends after evil has ended. As we shall see, this story does not accept evil—it overaccepts it.

8

Questioning Givens

Blocking and Sin

In the previous chapter I invited the reader to imagine what it might be like to be in the habit of accepting all offers—to let go of the impulse to block and to enjoy the freedom of perpetually accepting. This chapter represents a pause in the overall argument. It assesses the instinctive reactions that accepting all offers evokes. These reactions are generally very strong ones, ones that assume that accepting all offers is either impossible, or wrong, or both. Before proceeding in my next chapter to explore *how* all offers may be accepted, I wish here to dwell on the nature of an offer, and some rival approaches to whether offers should be regarded as "givens" or "gifts."

The attitude of accepting all offers may be regarded as an entering into the conditions of life before the fall. In this sense, sin is the refusal to keep the story going, the unwillingness to receive an offer. It is closing one's heart to grace.

John Milbank portrays sin in similar terms, through the narrative of one of Shakespeare's late plays.

In *The Winter's Tale*, Leontes and Polixenes, Kings of Sicily and Bohemia respectively, passed their boyhoods in seeming innocence, as if outside of time. Early in the play, Polixenes interprets their meeting with women, their future wives, or the arrival of "the other" in the course of time, as the

115

moment of the fall. But Hermione (Leontes' wife) to the contrary ascribes marriage still to the reign of innocence, and indeed views the arrival of the women as the event of grace itself (an association that is maintained throughout the play) (Act 1 Scene 2). This is an ironic passage, for in the context of the play the fall is still to come, and involves not a first *misdeed* by Leontes, but rather a first *suspicion* that Hermione has committed the sin of adultery. . . . Leontes misreads the *signs* of Hermione's affection for Polixenes, and therefore offends against necessary trust in the secrecy of the other. Hence "original sin," on this rendering, is the imagination of sin, the reading of the unknown as source of threat or poison rather than potential or gift.[1]

The two young companions, Leontes and Polixenes, had lived a life in which all offers were accepted and seen as benevolent gifts. Sin enters the story when Leontes doubts the offer that presents itself in his wife's innocent affection for his friend. Once he begins to block, the boundless possibilities of accepting all offers are transformed into a prison of fear and suspicion. Milbank continues, "This reading of original sin therefore understands original blessedness by implication, not as deliberately 'doing good,' but as a state of good moral luck or reception of grace."[2] The key emerges again as the ability to receive, to accept the offer, to keep the story going, to resist the temptation to block.

Such a perception of ethics almost invariably evokes a reaction of palpable horror. This is generally accompanied by growing suspicion of culpable naïveté. The reality, it is pointed out, is that the world is not full of generous people offering benevolent gifts; on the contrary it is full of untrustworthy people and intangible forces posing malevolent threats. A commitment to accept all offers means a fast road to manipulation, abuse, loss of identity, perhaps obliteration. Ethics, on this sober estimation, is not about receiving gifts but about negotiating givens. These givens are generally taken to constitute the boundaries of ethical debate. They are like a host of rival superpowers, occupying huge tracts of the globe and threatening the well-being of all who come near their borders. Christian ethics occupies the precarious space between the territories claimed by these competing "givens." Each of these givens places limitations on human and creaturely existence—providing ample reason to block or at least to suspect any offers that might come one's way.

Ethics as the Clash of Givens

There is, for example, the limitation of time and the given of death. There is the limitation of knowledge and the human mind, and thus the given of ignorance. There is the limitation of space and the human body, and thus of freedom. And there is the limitation of goodness and the given of sin and evil. The sum of such givens is sometimes understood as natural law. Tragedy is generally the story of those who have tried hubristically to ignore such givens and have consequently met their fate.

Some see the real givens as lying in the fact that humans are situated in time. The given of time is characteristically explored by existentialists such as Rudolf Bultmann. The self interacts with its human and nonhuman context, and with its own body and mind; how it does so is a question that is always open to renegotiation. Authentic understanding, or freedom, enables the self to be open to each new situation that arises (with its promising and threatening offers, to use the language adopted in the previous chapter). When a person loses himself or herself in the apparent givens of nature or society, that person loses the ability to respond to new situations, becoming wedded to the past—and thus inauthentic. Bultmann identifies this inauthentic form of existence with fallenness: it is experienced by everybody and is a reality that stems from the subject's inability or unwillingness to cope with the passage of time.

Others see the real givens as traceable to the way humans are located in space. The given of embodiment characteristically struggles with the limitations of the self as a part of the natural world. Much of the debate surrounds whether (1) the embodied self is created with an intrinsic propensity to relate to God or (2) God comes to the self as an unpredictable infusion of grace. Either way, the relation of the subject to nature is a constant threat, because the self will always tend to lapse back into amoral behaviour that dishonors its knowledge of values and duties. There is a general tendency to split the natural from the spiritual, and to see the former as standing in greater danger than the latter. But the overall perspective is of the human body as small, weak, and vulnerable.

Others again see the threat to the human subject as lying not outside—in time or space—but within the subject itself. This is the given of sin. The subject has a given and finite heritage, and a given nature, culture, and nurture. The subject must relate itself between the poles of nature and freedom—between the sensuality of overlooking freedom and the pride of ignoring nature. God enables the subject to balance these competing claims of the finite and the finite, and faith can extricate the self from denial of one or another part of its reality. The tendency of this approach is to see sin as the norm, and goodness as an "impossible possibility"—a rare treasure.[3]

The name of Reinhold Niebuhr has come to be identified with the perception of Christian ethics as the clash of competing givens.[4] Niebuhr regrets that the church has talked the language of personal perfection while contrasting that high ideal with a deep pessimism toward the political sphere. By insisting on perfection, Christianity has brought about an unhelpful tension between the ideal and the real. Niebuhr then attempts to save Christian ethics by appending it to a largely Stoic understanding of natural law. Stoicism perceives that there is an absolute spiritual ideal that is constantly trying to bring order to a chaotic, finite world. Niebuhr adopts this pessimistic way of seeing nature and finitude and presumes an original imperfection that humanity sets out gradually to remedy.

John Milbank points out the significant assumptions here made by Niebuhr:

> Niebuhr . . . is surprisingly candid in his opinion that Christianity to be socially effective required to be supplemented by Stoic natural law. But is not this concession, one may ask, precisely an admission of paganism? St Augustine in the *Civitas Dei* would seem to confirm this when he contrasts pagan virtue, which is simply (like Niebuhr's ethic) an exercise in "damage limitation" that takes for granted an *original conflict* which has to be contained, and Christian virtue, which is able to root out the very source of evil because it takes for granted *original created goodness*.[5]

Stanley Hauerwas underlines the way that Niebuhr's stoicism, far from making him the true exponent of Christian realism, jeopardized his whole claim to be a Christian theologian at all. In his hands theology became ethics, and ethics became about sustaining liberal social orders in a Stoic fashion.

> For Niebuhr, God is nothing more than the name of our need to believe that life has an ultimate unity that transcends the world's chaos and makes possible what order we can achieve in this life. . . . Justification by faith is loosed from its Christological context and made a truth to underwrite a generalized version of humility in order to make Christians trusted players in the liberal game of tolerance. . . . [Niebuhr became] the theologian of a domesticated god capable of doing no more than providing comfort to the anxious conscience of the bourgeoisie.[6]

If "Christian realism" scarcely merits the designation "Christian," does it really deserve the name "realism"? Milbank offers examples from Niebuhr's time and ridicules the kind of realism that assumed the absurdities of Cold War logic. He points out that in a situation of enmity so basic that each side had built up a staggering nuclear battery, a promise of "no first use" was meaningless. Deep-laid suspicion or the calculated risk of attaining global advantage could always have undermined any such promise.

In an appeal to drama similar to that which I outlined in chapter 4 above, Milbank perceives that Christianity requires a distinct reading of history. Christians may sometimes see the same historical reality as other people. But they do not take these processes as final, or determined—as "given." Milbank illustrates the way Christianity has exposed features of secular history as anything but natural and given: he cites Augustine's demonstration that Roman justice, which claimed to be restraint of chaos, in fact depended on "the arbitrary coercive power of freemen over slaves, Romans over strangers." The ultimate error of Niebuhrian realism lies in the assumption that there is "some neutral 'reality' to which Christians bring their insights." On the contrary, insists Milbank, "There is no independently available 'real world' against which we must test our Christian convictions, because these convictions are the most final, and at the same time the most basic, *seeing* of what the world is."[7]

Scripture and the Ethics of Givens

The Bible offers a constant stream of challenges to the assumption that the world is the theater of competing givens. To take the presumed given of time, many of Jesus' parables address the listener on precisely this assumption—undermining any confidence that there is one unarguable way of seeing the world, and presenting the listener with a surprising, daunting invitation to live in a very different reality of time.

The parable of the unforgiving servant challenges the boundaries that one might suppose were unalterable and universally accepted.[8] A king wished to settle accounts with his slaves, and had mercy on one who owed him an astronomical sum, releasing the man from his whole debt. But that same slave had no such mercy on a colleague who owed him a comparatively minute sum, and imprisoned the man. When the king heard of his slave's meanness, his mercy turned to harsh punishment. This parable challenges the assumption that the givens of time are birth and death. The boundaries described in the parable are, instead, the moment when the sinner realizes the astonishing offer of forgiveness and the moment when the sinner faces the awesome reality of judgment. God's mercy and justice are much more significant than the apparent givens of birth and death. This suggests a different kind of reality, a different understanding of what is given, from what appeared before.

Likewise the parable of the laborers in the vineyard upsets any correlation between given time and God's time.[9] A landowner goes out early to hire laborers for his vineyard, and agrees to the usual daily wage. Later, several times, even late in the day, he goes out and hires further laborers. When evening comes, each finds they have received the same wage. Those who have worked all day resent this generosity. But the parable has no sympathy for them. They are working with the assumption that God can reward some more than others (the given of the economy). The parable, by contrast, is working with the plenitude of God's sufficient gifts. Why would one wish to be rewarded more than others if one already has more than enough?

Turning to the given of space, the history of Israel abounds in stories of how the human limitations of God's people are no boundary to the potential of his inbreaking reality. One of the most ironic and humorous of these accounts is that of the four lepers of Samaria.[10] The pressure on the northern kingdom from the Aramaeans is such that hunger is driving the people to desperate measures. Elisha promises a plummeting of meal and barley prices within twenty-four hours. His words are heard with skepticism by the king's trusted captain, and Elisha warns that the captain will see this transformation—but not benefit from it. Four leprous men, already excluded from the city, and therefore having nothing to lose, choose to desert to the Aramaeans. They find that the Aramaeans have mistaken them for a great army and have fled. The leprous men, amazed at their good fortune, happily set to loot and plunder. Struck by sudden remorse, they return to Samaria and share the news. On investigation, the king realizes the astonishing turn of events. Food prices fall as Elisha had predicted. The people flood out of the besieged city, trampling the captain to death in the gate, so he does indeed fail to benefit from the miracle. The story unsettles the predictable givens, and the fate of the captain symbolizes the extent to which the boundaries of reality are overthrown. The force of the new reality sweeps away the shortcomings of the people's lack of faith, the isolation and mixed motives of the leprous men, and the overwhelming advantage of the Aramaeans. Nothing is given.

As for the given of sin, no story challenges this constraint more than that of the patriarch Joseph and his brothers. After Joseph has boasted of the destiny disclosed in his dreams, his brothers attempt to do away with him. By a series of twists and turns, Joseph finds himself indeed the master of their destiny. As Pharaoh's chief minister, he can determine whether they live or die, whether they starve at home or settle in Egypt. Finally he reveals himself to them as their brother. The brothers' fear of his vengeance only increases when the restraining influence of Jacob is taken from them. The crucial insight of the story comes in the reconciling words of Joseph himself. Joseph recognizes that God had not been limited by the brothers' sin—and had even used their sin as a means of his grace. He says to his brothers, "God sent me before you to preserve for you a remnant on earth, and to keep alive for you many survivors. So it was not you who sent me here, but God; he has made me a father to Pharaoh, and lord of all his house and ruler over all the land of Egypt." And later he adds, "Even though you intended to do harm to me, God intended it for good, in order to preserve a numerous people."[11] The given of human sin no longer presents the boundary to all possibility, but has instead been transformed by God's providence.

Givens and the Gift

To provide a constructive alternative to what we have seen to be a problematic and questionable notion of the given, I turn again to the work of John Milbank. Must ethics forever be seen as a process of adjustment to competing givens? Milbank launches a full-scale assault on this way of considering the discipline. In a magisterial essay, he takes five of the pillars of a "given" frame of mind and insists that these are the opposite of Christian morality.[12] The pillars are reaction, sacrifice, complicity with death, scarcity, and generality. The five counter theological notes sounded by Milbank are gift, end of sacrifice, resurrection, plenitude, and confidence. His contrast between scarcity and plenitude is particularly telling. Here is his portrayal of the ethics of scarcity:

> Because life is in short supply, because it might run out on us, sooner or later, we must invest, we must insure. Ethics . . . is banks, it is sexual jealousy, it is the sacrifice of self-realisation for the sake of others, it is insurance companies, mortgages and the stock exchange. For in fearing that there may not be world enough or time, we insist on our identity, our truth, our space, denying that of others—thereby rendering their coyness *always* a crime.[13]

Milbank points out that Luther saw the temptation to steal was rooted in a perpetual fear that there will not be enough for oneself. Thus "a man is generous because he trusts God and never doubts but that he will always have enough. In contrast a man is covetous and anxious because he does not trust God."[14] If ethics is characterized by scarcity, it is shaped even more by complicity with death. Milbank sees the two as intimately linked:

> [The moral law] assumes and requires death's existence, since it always views death as an enemy to life rather than as a passage of life to further life; for this reason it seeks to shore up life against death, and to erect an illusory spatial enclave against the ravages of time. Virtue is what holds

death back, inhibits death, protects people from death, even though, from a Christian point of view, death is also remedy and mercy. . . . Thus, . . . given the death-fact, the best we can do is to be virtuous, not kill and not cause to suffer, become doctors and firemen and so forth.[15]

When the time comes for Milbank to display and harmonize the positive notes of the gospel, he identifies as the center of his argument the way the notion of gift addresses the moment of the cross.

Under the dispensation of death indeed, we only see gift via sacrifice, but the genuine sacrifice, supremely that of the cross, is only recognised as such in so far as it is the *sustaining* of joyful, non-reactive giving, by a hastening of death as the only way of continuing to give despite the cancellation of gift by death. We assume that the trained man, the man of uncloistered virtue, the man of Sparta or Gordonstoun who has played at danger, will face danger well. But this man, as Rousseau suggested, will be accustomed to the imagination of danger, which always threatens to outreach any bravery. Moreover, his ever-present danger will have accustomed him to *compromise* with danger, to negotiation with the enemy. By contrast the innocent man, the man who has known nothing but love, will see in even the smallest danger, the slightest hint of death, an absolute harm, a mere nihil, a nonsense, and because he has known something absolutely prior to all fear, he will not now cease from loving, but go on loving fearlessly embracing death. (This is why Tolkein's insertion of "hobbits" into a heroic world is profound, and is profoundly Christian.) Hence only God, who experiences nothing of evil, who does not in any way suffer, acts without fear in the world, does good for the first time in the world.[16]

Thus Milbank has dismantled what he calls morality (and what I am calling the ethics of the given)—the precarious negotiation between the always overbearing and sometimes competing superpowers of brute reality. He concludes with a gesture to the confident man of Luther and the confident worship of Augustine.

The confident man, believing in plenitude, does not steal, and does not need to tell lies to protect himself. The confident man . . . *improvises* exactly good and always non-identical good works all the time, *each* of these good works being of *equal* value—as every good is absolute, and to be good must belong to an entire, an infinite good without exception. The Christian good man is simply for Luther an artist in being, trusting the perfect maker of all things. . . . Only the vision and hope of heaven makes us socially and politically just on earth—and how is it, one wonders, that we have ever come to think otherwise?[17]

What is emerging in my argument is a distinction between the given, on which ethics is often taken to be based, and the gift, on which I am suggesting ethics should be based. Before proceeding further, it is important to recognize the role these terms, gift and given, have played in contemporary debates in Continental philosophy.[18] This discussion will in due course be seen to be a detour, since my understanding of gift and given is subtly different from the notions as used in these debates. But to understand the overall context, such a detour is necessary.

The detour begins with anthropological treatments of gift-exchange in research conducted in the 1920s.[19] Marcel Mauss's celebrated study begins a sequence of anthropological, sociological, and in due course philosophical and theological investigations continuing to the present day. Mauss observes particular cultures and notes how what were in reality obligatory transactions based on economic self-interest are so clothed in pretense and social deception that they are made to appear voluntary, disinterested, and spontaneous. Fascinated by the hold the practice of gift-exchange has on the imagination, Mauss explores the way in which such transactions create and maintain relations between people in these societies. This brings about very positive estimation of the character of gift-based economies. Such societies practice giving within a circle of reciprocation that preserves social cohesion by the redistribution of wealth. A kind of spiritual bond is created in the process. This bond carries with it a sense of surplus that enhances relationship—and thus stands in contrast to barter or cash economies.

This spiritualization of the gift has opened the way to philosophical and theological treatments. Russell Belk seeks to define and describe the "perfect gift." Such a gift is spontaneous, affective, and celebratory. The giver makes a considerable sacrifice and wishes solely to please the recipient; the gift is something uniquely appropriate to the recipient; the recipient is surprised but delighted by it.[20] Robyn Horner sums up the recent notions of gift in two conditions:

> One is that the gift is free. That is expressed in the demand for no motive of return, the requirement of sacrifice, and the need for placing the gift beyond the necessities of the everyday. The other condition is that the gift is present. This relates to the recognizability of the gift as a gift and draws in the corollaries of giving and receiving (or accepting). Freedom and presence are the conditions of the gift as we know it.[21]

The most significant philosophical and theological treatments of the gift have come from Jacques Derrida and Jean-Luc Marion. Marion is captivated by the sense of surplus, of saturation and excess, which we observed above in both Mauss and Milbank. He therefore has a very positive estimation of the role of gift. Derrida, by contrast, sees the gift as almost an impossibility—an aporia, or problem that resists being resolved because it defies any frame of reference. Horner, referring back to her helpful definition of gift, points to why Derrida sees gift as almost impossible. Either a gift is not free, but is instead obligation, payback, sweetener, or peace offering; or it is not present, being misidentified as commodity, value, or status symbol. For Derrida, the gift inevitably gets swept up in a cycle of return—and thus ceases to be a gift.[22]

My treatment of gifts and givens is tangential to the great debate between Marion and Derrida for two reasons. One is that their debate rests on an understanding of phenomenology, that is, the mid-twentieth-century philosophical movement associated with Husserl and Heidegger. This movement seeks to establish a new ground for ontology by considering what is given to consciousness and how it is given—while following Kant in excluding metaphysical speculation from the conversation. Marion is seeking to find a place for revelation within this phenomenological tradition, whereas Derrida is much more skeptical. My concern is neither metaphysical nor ontological, but ethical. I am not asking my reader to pursue such arguments in order to grasp the notion of gift. I am simply questioning the way givenness is so frequently tied in with natural law and Christian realism, and thus taken for granted ("given"!) in Christian ethical reflection. The second reason why my treatment is tangential is that underlying the theological argument in the contemporary Continental debate is the question of whether one can conceive of God as (pure) gift. I am making no such claim, and asking for no such speculation, and so I do not dwell at length here on the work of Marion and Derrida. But I am regarding God as a given. I am arguing that God takes the place in Christian ethics normally reserved for time, death, sin, bodily limitation, and so on—the conventional boundaries. The only boundary, in other words, is the boundary of God. And meanwhile the place that God conventionally takes in Christian ethics—that of a perhaps helpful but largely peripheral and certainly not essential figure—in other words, a gift, a "bonus"—should be taken by those familiar perennial so-called "givens." So what seemed given—the conventional boundaries—becomes gift; and what seemed to be gift—God—becomes the given.

Garrett Green makes a helpful contribution at this point, when he contrasts two forms of living—living "as" and living "as if."[23] Green points out that living "as if" implies living contrary to (given) fact. By contrast, living "as" acknowledges no given, but exposes the presumption of the generally accepted (that is, given) "as," and treats the new "as" as an "is." It is a welcoming of the postmodern rejection of given definitions, and a recognition that each rival "as" must now be argued out—or performed.

Green recognizes that in a postmodern context, there can be no more simply "living." But this does not mean that fantasy is the only option (living "as if"). Instead he offers the notion of living "as" as a way of showing the effect of convictions on practice.

In similar vein, Walter Brueggemann sees the Christian gospel as a "counter-'as.'" He illustrates the revolutionary power of a new "as" by citing André Brink's novel *A Change of Voices*, in which a group of South African slaves hear that the British are about to invade and free them and, anticipating their liberation, rise up and kill their owners. Brueggemann also commends the way David Bryant alters Green's "see 'as'" to "take 'as.'" "Take 'as'" implies a much more active process than simple reception.[24]

I am proposing that the Christian community treat as gifts what may previously have been regarded as givens. This has much in common with Bryant's (and Brueggemann's) notion of "take 'as'"—but the practice I am suggesting is a more far-reaching one. I am also concerned that "take 'as'" implies a choice—to take or to leave. But the Christian community seldom has such a choice. The Christian community needs a way of addressing those forces and issues that threaten to overwhelm it—a way of making part of their destiny what would otherwise become their fate. That is what the next chapter will describe.

There Is Only One Given

It may be helpful to conclude by underlining the distinction between givens and gifts. It is the task of the imagination to change or challenge the presumed necessities of the world, to resist the implication that what the Christian community receives are givens rather than gifts. In this sense, givens are things that are simply there and the community must simply adapt to, if it is to remain in the real world, whereas gifts are largely what one chooses to make of them. For Christian realists, the task of Christian ethics is to adapt to such givens as prevail in the contemporary world—the objective material causes and boundaries of life. Ethics becomes a process of adjudicating between competing givens. Since the emphasis of givenness is on the giver, ethics is primarily seen from the point of view of those who are in the best position to control the majority of the giving—that is, the powerful. It is thus supposed that if Christians put themselves in positions of power they will influence the givens in a positive way.

What I am suggesting, by contrast, is that the only given is God's story, the theo-drama, the church's narrative: all else is potentially gift. It is not therefore a question of putting oneself in a position of power. Ethics is not principally about how to do the giving. God is the only true giver. His story of how he deals with his people is the definitive given. Ethics is done by people who are on the *receiving* end, working out how to accept things that present themselves as givens but cannot be since there is only one given—the narrative of Scripture and the church's tradition. Moreover discernment concerns the reception of God's abundant gifts, rather than the distribution of the world's limited givens. Harry's niece, in the story I related in chapter 6, had only ever seen her uncle as a given. Through Robin's tutorial, she came for the first time to see him, his condition, and his faith as a gift. The process I am describing can therefore be seen as threefold: first, recognizing that much of what seems given is in fact gift; second, realizing that the key to a gift is not its intrinsic nature or purpose but how the receiver responds and accepts it; and third, receiving the gift in such a way that it becomes part of the continuing story of the way God deals with his people. Thus is fate (a given) transformed into destiny (a gift) by placing it within a larger story.

9

Incorporating Gifts

Reconceiving Problems

Christmas Day is experienced by many people as a day of great anxiety, largely because the extensive preparations generate a level of anticipation that the day itself can seldom justify. Nonetheless some people adore Christmas Day—the thought of opening presents and eating food is simply too exciting for words. For other people, Christmas Day is all about the responsibility of preparing gifts and engineering hospitality. There are two distinct kinds of energies required to make the most of Christmas. One is the energy of receiving gifts; the other is the energy of scheming their creation. But a key moment comes when a member of the festive gathering is given something that is far from being what they had always longed for. What feelings does such a gift evoke? Amusement, that the person could have misunderstood them so greatly; anxiety, about how they can feign gratitude; deep misgiving, in pondering what kind of thanks or return gift the giver might be looking for; or anger at such mindless extravagance and misreading of character? Whose fault is the inappropriate gift? Is it the giver's fault if the gift is quickly despatched to the garage or the attic—or is it the receiver's failure to find a use for it, albeit perhaps one quite different from the giver's intention? My argument is that it is the receiver's responsibility to find a use for the gift, rather than the giver's responsibility to ensure the gift is appropriate, and that the church finds itself more often in the role of receiver than of giver.

In an earlier chapter I argued that if the church improvised faithfully it would aim to accept all offers. But clearly not all offers are good. Indeed some are evil. So accepting all offers seems a dubious tactic. The question is, how does one maintain one's integrity without blocking? As I have already suggested, blocking is subtly aggressive and undermines the space of the other. It may also depend on a level of force that may not be available or desirable. But accepting indiscriminately seems naïve to say the least. I want to suggest a third tactic, called overaccepting.

Committed as they may be to accepting all offers, improvisers nonetheless find some offers more difficult to accept than others. The breakthrough in improvisation training comes when actors realize that their performance is not a linear method of getting as efficiently as possible from point A to point B. On the contrary, detours are most of the fun. This changes the whole notion of what constitutes a mistake. As one experienced director puts it, "Mistakes are re-evaluated as possibilities of new directions. . . . Rightness is more a question of *attitude,* not of what you do but of how you do it, whether you are prepared to play with what comes along."[1] The key word here is "play." "Play" describes what happens when the actors are relieved of the responsibility of making the drama "come out right." They no longer have a limited set of possible outcomes at which they must force the story to arrive. They can therefore begin to enjoy the story and not determine the dra   ma.This is what I described in an earlier chapter as the opportunity given to the church by discovering that it lives in Act Four of God's drama. It no longer has to assume that it must make the story "come out right." God will deal with that in Act Five. The church is therefore free to play.

Once the basic skills of accepting have been established, improvisers learn to enjoy such problems as they arise. Problems offer the improviser possibilities for development and exploration. One has to learn to see them as opportunities. A game that teaches this is called "Lantern Lecture."[2]

In this game, A is an explorer showing slides of his exploits to his adoring public. B is the slides. Each accepts and then offers:

A: This is me climbing the Andes, warding off an eagle. . . .
B: [Takes this position, then moves to a new position.]
A: And here I am, being lifted up by the eagle. . . . Now I am being dropped by the eagle. . . .
B: [Responds, then moves to another new position.]
A: And here I am clinging on to a branch further down the cliff. . . .

The game is much more satisfying if the partners cease trying to outwit each other, and simply relish the opportunities for development that arise from the problem. One realizes in this light that simplicity is a subtle form of blocking. The attempt to exclude from the story any material other than that which is relevant for arriving at the goal is a strategy of management and, like all strategies, in the end relies on force. A tactic that has no power to exclude the detours learns to enjoy them, learns to regard them as significant parts of the story—learns to be able to say "Thank you" for them. It learns to regard them as a gift, and in the process, it learns to play.

Presents

This brings us to a simple but immensely significant game, which demonstrates the suggestive power of improvisation for Christian ethics. The game is called "Presents."[3] It is played in pairs. Person A thinks of a present to give to B, and then mimes giving it to her. B has to guess what it is and use it accordingly. The players then swap roles, and B passes a mimed present to person A, and so on.

The trouble with this game is, of course, that it can be difficult to identify what the gift is; the players can get frustrated with each other, as each mimes more and more outlandish gifts, leaving the other more and more bewildered. Each actor seems in competition, and feels it. How can this change? The secret to making the game a success is, as with Lantern Lecture, to concentrate on cooperation rather than competition. The key is not to think of interesting things to give, but to concentrate on making the thing one is *given* as interesting as possible. If A simply holds out two hands, as if proffering something in a box, B may be delighted to receive an array of possible gifts: "Everything you are given delights you. Maybe you wind it up and let it walk about the floor, or you sit it on your arm and let it fly off after a small bird, or maybe you put it on and turn into a gorilla."[4] If the game is played this way, the stifling sense of competition disappears, and great joy and energy are released.

The change to the game might be simple, but the change in thinking is enormous. All offers are now potential gifts. When the burden of the game lies with the giver, the giver requires the kind of imagination that determines the future. Great frustration arises if the gift is misinterpreted. (Remember the feelings engendered by the opening of "inappropriate" gifts on Christmas Day.) When, by contrast, the emphasis lies with the receiver, the imagination cooperates, adapts, and develops.

I want to suggest now that what the gift game pictures is a revolution in thinking about Christian ethics. Ethics as it is generally described is invariably perceived as a matter of choosing when to say "Yes" and when to say "No." But the Presents game shows that there is more to ethics than simply yes or no. In fact person B has three options when offered a present by person A. B can say, first, "No, I am not going to receive this gift." This is a straightforward block. Saying "No" appears, in the short term, to maintain one's own security. This is the approach associated with the Essene sect of first-century Palestine. Throughout Christian history there have always been groups that said "No" to some or all gifts that came their way from wider society. The Amish may appear to outsiders to represent this position today. There are many things to which it is often said the wider church should say "No." The lists sometimes include slavery and murder, often nuclear weapons and embryo research, perhaps abortion and euthanasia, sometimes betting slips, tobacco, and alcohol. Most churches have recognized that one cannot say "No" to one's culture wholesale. To do so is to deny the goodness of God's creation and to declare war on society.

So, what else can B do? B can say, second, "What *is* this gift? What is it *for?* What am I *supposed* to do with it?" This is the way the game is usually played, as I have described above. It is also the way the game is usually played in Christian ethics. B accepts the gift, but does not know what the gift is. The dilemma of B as to the nature of the gift corresponds to the moment of decision that is the focus of quandary ethics. For just as the present is given by A in the game, so are circumstances "given" at moments of decision, and the decision-maker must adjudicate between them. And just as the game is frustrating when played this way, so is decision-making, and ethics that concentrates on decisions is often immensely trying. The assumption is often made that there *is* a right thing to do in each circumstance. Such reasoning is often based on natural law. Natural law arguments tend to assume that everything was created for a purpose, and that when it is employed about its correct purpose all is well. This is the position of B: desperately wondering what this gift is *for.*

There is a third option. Person B can say, third, "How do I want to *receive* this gift?" This is the transition that I have described in the way the gift game is played above. It is not a question of what the gift is *supposed* to be: it is a question of what the gift *can* be. One does not say, "What is this gift *for?*"—and even less, "Is this a good gift?"; one says, "How can this gift be understood or used in a faithful way? What does the way we accept this gift say about the kind of people we are and want to be? What can (or has) this gift become in the kingdom of God?" The ethical issues are less about the gift itself than about where it is perceived to fit into the story of the way God deals with his people and how that fitting-in takes place.

Overaccepting

This is called "overaccepting."[5] Overaccepting is accepting in the light of a larger story. The fear about accepting is that one will be determined by the gift and thus lose one's integrity and identity. The fear about blocking is that one will seal oneself off from the world and thus lose one's relevance and humanity. Overaccepting is an active way of receiving that enables one to retain both identity and relevance. It is a way of accepting without losing the initiative. This often involves a change of status.

Diana, Princess of Wales, was asked in a television interview in 1995 whether she thought she would ever be queen. She famously replied, "I will be queen of people's hearts," thus not blocking the awkwardness of her predicament but overaccepting the sadness of losing her throne, and placing herself in what she saw as a far more significant narrative. Likewise at her funeral, her brother in his address equally famously claimed that "She needed no royal title" to recognize her inherent dignity and grace and the contribution she made to national life—thus not blocking her change of status after her divorce, but again suggesting a more significant context for status than mere royalty. The coal miners of the film *The Full Monty* had been stripped of their dignity by the experience of unemployment. They overaccepted their condition by developing a thriving male-stripper routine. Robin's friend Harry did not block the squalor of his ill health and living conditions, but overaccepted them by converting rubbish into items of usefulness and beauty. Perhaps the best known overaccepting routine is the Monty Python "Four Yorkshiremen" sketch, in which the four men's conversation over a drink descends into a relentless competition of inverted snobbery, as each man's tale of childhood deprivation is overaccepted with the words "You were lucky."

It may be helpful to illustrate the tactic of overaccepting from human experience. The story is told of a concert pianist who was on the point of beginning a performance when there was a scream from the audience. A child had left her seat beside her parent and was running around the auditorium. The concert pianist stepped away from his instrument in order to maintain concentration. The child ran up the steps onto the stage, sat herself down on the stool, and began to play discordant notes at random as she pleased. The hushed audience gasped in horror and embarrassment. The pianist walked toward the child and stood behind her as she played. The pianist leaned over her and, without disturbing her, placed right and left hands outside her two small hands on the keyboard. The pianist then began to play in response to her notes, weaving their discordant sounds into an improvised melody. To have thrown the child out would have been to block: to have let her play on would have been to accept; to weave a wonderful melody around her was to receive her as a gift, to overaccept.[6]

The seventeenth-century spiritual writer Thomas Traherne makes what we are here calling overaccepting a key device in his vision of the world. Because he has such a limitless perception of the dimensions, possibilities, purpose, and eventual harmony of the created universe, he is invariably able to take a challenging starting point and transform it by placing it in a dazzlingly larger context. In this example he begins with the anxiety of a man's deep regard for a woman who is attached to another. He does not block his feelings, nor accept them on their own terms. Instead he places them within a much greater and finer story, thereby turning temptation into renewal, a threat into a point of growth.

> When we dote upon the perfections and beauties of some one creature, we do not love that too much, but other things too little. . . . Suppose a curious and fair woman. Some have seen the beauties of Heaven in such a person. It is a vain thing to say they loved too much. I dare say there are 10,000 beauties in that creature which they have not seen. . . . They love her perhaps, but do not love God more: nor men as much: nor Heaven and earth at all. We should be all life and mettle and vigour to everything. And that would poise us. . . . So that no man can be in danger by loving others too much, that loveth God as he ought.[7]

There is a poem, said to be by R. S. Thomas, in which a priest looks out over the bleakness of his parish, its desolation and despair, and says to God, "Is this what you have given me? All these rocks?" He stares over his unpromising locality and pauses, contemplating the sparsity of the territory and the scarcity of the resources. There is so much reason to block, so little motivation to accept. But he does find the resources to overaccept. Finally he decides, "Well then, I must make a rock garden."

In another overaccepting game, called "It's Tuesday," inconsequential remarks (that is, "dull offers") are overaccepted so as to produce the maximum possible effect on the acceptor. Thus:

A: It's Tuesday.
B: No . . . it can't be. . . . It's the day predicted for my death by the old gypsy! [Dies horribly, saying] Feed the goldfish.
A: That's all he ever thought about, that goldfish. . . . Fifty years' supply of ants' eggs, and what did he leave to me—not a penny. I shall write to mother.
B: [Recovering] Your mother! You mean Milly is still alive? [and so on][8]

The apparently trivial nature of what the actors actually say in this example should not obscure the importance of what is happening. What overaccepting opens up is a whole approach to nonviolent response by a Christian community schooled in the scriptural story. When the Christian community is faced by offers coming to it from the society in which it lives, it overaccepts in the perspective of a story that stretches from creation to eschaton—a far larger story. The method has much in common with what John Milbank describes as Christianity's ability to "outnarrate" all secular narratives. He narrates a "larger story" that stretches from creation to eschaton. The key to the Christian story is "the coding of transcendental difference as peace." This is based on an understanding of the Trinity itself as social, and embodying harmonious difference. Thus creation is peaceable; meanwhile salvation, "the restoration of being," and eschaton together depict the "sociality of harmonious difference." In the light of this larger story, the offer (as an improviser might call it) of violence is always "a secondary willed intrusion upon this possible infinite order (which is actual for God)."[9] In this way Milbank shows how even the most unacceptable offer—violence—can be overaccepted in the light of the larger story.[10]

Many of the offers the church in general or Christians in particular receive are "dull" ones, represented by actor A's first remarks above. But many offers are challenging, threatening, and urgent: the "sectarian passivist" response would be to block, while the "responsible realist" approach might be to accept without reservation. The search for a third way leads us to overaccepting. Overaccepting fits the remarks of the previous actor into a context enormously larger than his or her counterpart could have supposed. This is exactly what the Christian community does with offers that come to it from wider society. It overaccepts in the light of the church's tradition and story seen in eschatological perspective—a perspective much wider than urgent protagonists may have imagined. Conventional ethics, because it is so anxious to establish what is right for everyone, everywhere, at all times, plays down the distinctive claims of the Christian story. It assumes that Christians must accept the givens of the contemporary world, and make decisions based on those givens. What I am suggesting, by contrast, is that Christians use their imaginations to see how the gifts of creation and culture fit into the story of the way God deals with the world, given that the fundamental decision has already been made—God's decision for humanity and creation in Christ. Rowan Williams describes the process of turning from blocking to overaccepting in similar terms, when talking of the Sermon on the Mount:

Christian excellence is in a significant part a matter of how we are to deal with our powerlessness or dispossession. . . . When I am injured, I have the means of possible redress; I have power to restore the balance that has been upset (I can retaliate, I can go to court or whatever). But I also have, as a believer, the freedom to alter the terms of the relation: I can decline to see it as a challenge to equalize the score, and opt to display positively the sovereign liberty of God not to retaliate or defend an interest. In other words, I can either attempt to close off my vulnerability or I can so work with it as to show the character of God. If we come to the Sermon looking either for an ethic of passive obedience to external authority or an ethic of resistance and liberation as conceived in our own age, we shall be disappointed.[11]

Overaccepting imitates the manner of God's reign. For God does not block his creation: he does not toss away his original material. Since Noah, he has refused to destroy what he has made. But neither does he accept creation on its own terms. Instead, he overaccepts his creation. One can see the whole sweep of the scriptural narrative as a long story of overaccepting. The prophet Jeremiah describes how he went down to the potter's house, and saw him working at his wheel. The vessel he was making of clay was spoiled in the potter's hand, yet rather than throwing it away or accepting it as broken, he reworked it into another vessel. The Lord says to Jeremiah that he, the Lord, can do with the house of Israel just as the potter has done.[12] To take another familiar picture, the Lord, the great artist, sees that his painting has been torn and ruined; but rather than throw the painting away, he takes the opportunity to make the painting three-dimensional, the tear in the canvas becoming his broken heart, entered by his redeemed people. The whole narrative shape of the Old Testament, particularly if one accepts that in its historical formation it was profoundly characterized by the experience of exile in Babylon, is a remarkable tour de force of overaccepting. In the face of desperate disappointment, the creation stories and the narrative of Israel place God's people in a far larger context than their distressed circumstances might permit. Here is the Lord who made heaven and earth, who brought Israel out of slavery: of course he can look upon her now in exile, and even use that exile to teach her and others of his character and purpose. Likewise the New Testament describes how God sees what his creation can still be, and how by the way he incorporates it into his kingdom: through election, incarnation, passion, resurrection, and the sending of the Spirit, he demonstrates his character, the kind of God he is. Christians imitate the character of God to the extent that they overaccept the gifts of creation and culture in the same way God does.[13]

Jesus and Overaccepting

The story narrated by the Gospel writers is one long story of overaccepting. In the annunciation and the nativity, God overaccepts human life. He does not reject his people, nor does he simply accept them: instead he comes among them as a Jew. If the gospel story begins with God in Jesus overaccepting life, it ends with God in Jesus overaccepting death. Jesus does not avoid the cross, nor is the cross the end of the story. In the resurrection, God shows that even the worst offer, the execution of the Son of God, can be overaccepted—even death and all its causes can become part of the story.

In between these two key moments lie a whole series of dimensions of overaccepting. Perhaps the definitive episode, because it addresses offers, evil, and issues of identity most specifically, is the temptation narrative. The temptation narratives in Matthew and Luke are a particularly illuminating illustration of overaccepting.[14] Jesus appears to say "No": no to turning stones to bread, no to jumping off the pinnacle of the temple, and no to ruling the kingdoms of the world. As the gospel unfolds, it discloses how each of the temptations is not so much suppressed as fitted into a far greater story, a story of a much larger "Yes," of which the incarnation and resurrection are the most striking elements.

The first temptation, "command these stones to become loaves of bread" (Matt. 4:3), is the desire to be independent of the grace of God, to have food on demand and one's future secure—something Israel had always wanted. Jesus of course says "No" to the gimmick. But he says "Yes" to bread, overaccepting it in the words "This is my body, broken for you," and "I am the bread of life. Whoever comes to me will never be hungry" (John 6:35). The second temptation—to throw himself from the pinnacle of the temple, knowing the angels will bear him up—is the desire, as Hauerwas comments, to be the priest of priests—to force God's hand as the sacrifice God cannot refuse. But throughout the gospel story Jesus fulfills not his own will but the Father's. The resurrection is the Father's thorough endorsement of Jesus' whole life as the manifestation of the kingdom. Jesus says "Yes" to the temple, not as a high diving board, but as the new temple, his body, the church. The last temptation is about power. "All these I will give you, if you will fall down and worship me" (Matt. 4:9). Jesus says "Yes" to power—but the power of God is the power of humility and weakness. Jesus says "Yes" to peace—but peace can only come through the worship of the living God. Jesus overaccepts this temptation in his ascension, ruling at the right hand of the Father, and in his resurrection, as the power of love conquers the tomb. Jesus says "Yes" to the kingdoms because he is the King who reigns from the tree. The kingdom of God is crowned on the cross. Thus each of the devil's temptations is revealed as offering a world far smaller, a story far shorter, than the one the kingdom reveals.

A brief survey of Jesus' ministry displays a series of incidents and encounters that fit the description I have given of overaccepting. They are spread across the genres of miracle, teaching, controversy, and symbolic action. The first miracle in John's Gospel, the transformation of water into wine, is a paradigmatic story of incarnation and thus of overaccepting. Jesus does not block the water by creating wine out of nothing; he does not block his mother by saying that the guests should be happy with water. He accepts the ordinariness of water, the incompleteness of the six (rather than harmonious seven) water jars, and proceeds to overaccept them by transforming them into an abundance of excellent wine.

Likewise the first passage of teaching in Matthew's Gospel, the Sermon on the Mount, demonstrates how Jesus overaccepts the Mosaic law. "You have heard that it was said" (Matt. 5:21, 27, 33, 38, 43), recalls Jesus six times—and each time the disciples and the reader hold their breath to see whether Jesus will abolish (block) the Torah or obediently endorse (accept) it. But on each occasion, with the words "But I say to you," he instead overaccepts the Jewish law, saying it is not murder but anger, not adultery but lust, not unjust divorce but divorce itself, not swearing falsely but swearing at all, not measured retaliation but nonresistance, not loving the neighbor but loving the enemy that constitute the issue. Each of these is a perfect embodiment of overaccepting, none more so than the fifth: "If anyone strikes you on the right cheek, turn the other also; and if anyone wants to sue you and take your coat, give your cloak as well; and if anyone forces you to go one mile, go also the second mile."[15] Going the second mile epitomizes the practice of overaccepting.[16]

Jesus' agrarian parables invite a rather more subtle reading in which overaccepting plays a significant part. James C. Scott uses the term "hidden transcript" to refer to the language of disguise and concealment by which subordinate peoples carry out a performance of deference and consent while subtly undermining those holding power over them. David Toole, following Ched Myers's reading of Mark, sees this pattern at work in the agrarian parables. The context for the parable of the sower is one in which the sower owes the landlord such a large quantity of the grain harvest that he can never hope to achieve economic security. The parable of the sower does not narrate a person either quietly acquiescing or violently overthrowing this oppression. It narrates such an astoundingly abundant harvest that the sower could not only pay his dues to the landowner but pay off his debts and purchase the land, ending his condition of poverty. Thus the parable shows the kingdom overaccepting human oppression. Likewise the parable of the mustard seed, when read in the context of Ezekiel 17, describes the relationship of the tiny people of Israel living in the shade of the great cedar of Rome. Again, there is no armed resistance or passive submission. The parable describes how the kingdom overaccepts the oppressive relationship. As Crossan points out, the mustard plant is after all a weed, growing out of control where it is not wanted. This therefore is the way Jesus commends his revolution—not by accepting or blocking oppression, but by the surprise and abundance of a remarkable crop and by the uncontrollable spread of an infuriating weed.[17]

The Gospels record a number of controversies in which individuals or groups sought to put Jesus on the spot or sought a definitive ruling from him. The issue of Caesar's coin is a typical example. The Pharisees send their disciples, along with the Herodians, to Jesus, saying, "Is it lawful to pay taxes to the emperor, or not?" But Jesus, having elicited from them that Caesar's head and title were on the coin, replies, "Give therefore to the emperor the things that are the emperor's, and to God the things that are God's."[18] He overaccepts the coin, and in the process exposes the true issues of loyalty. In the story generally attributed to John's Gospel, Jesus is confronted with the woman caught in adultery. The Pharisees are all for stoning her—but Jesus says, "Let anyone among you who is without sin be the first to throw a stone at her," and invites a response. Rather than block or accept the Pharisees' demands, he overaccepts the practice of stoning.[19] When his own practice is criticized at the moment of his anointing at Bethany, Jesus commends the nameless woman whose beautiful action anticipated his burial. He does not deny that the money could have been given to the poor, but he overaccepts the poor by saying, "You always have the poor with you, and you can show kindness to them whenever you wish; but you will not always have me."[20] Once again, by neither blocking nor accepting, Jesus identifies the real issue at stake. When his own disciples come to him with an unresolved issue, he responds in similar vein. James and John want to sit at Jesus' right hand and left hand in glory. Jesus does not accept their request, but neither does he deny the notion of glory, nor of greatness—he does not block. Instead he transforms their notion of greatness: "whoever wishes to become great among you must be your servant, and whoever wishes to be first among you must be slave of all. For the Son of Man came not to be served but to serve, and to give his life a ransom for many."[21] By overaccepting the request of the sons of Zebedee, Jesus engages the desire of his followers but puts it to more appropriate ends. The wonderfully ironic story of Jesus' encounter with the Syrophoenician woman completes this series by providing an example of overaccepting being practiced by someone other than Jesus, and of Jesus being greatly impressed. "She begged him to cast the demon out of her daughter. He said to her, 'Let the children be fed first, for it is not fair to take the children's food and throw it to the dogs.' But she answered him, 'Sir, even the dogs under the table eat the children's crumbs.'"[22] By overaccepting the dogs, the woman provokes Jesus into healing her daughter. She has imitated his practice faithfully.

Jesus' ministry, particularly at its outset and conclusion, is characterized by symbolic actions that embody the same pattern of overaccepting. At the outset comes his baptism. The river Jordan was the site of Joshua's entry into the Promised Land, and John's practice of baptizing there was clearly a symbolic statement of preparation for a new kingdom. By going out into the wilderness, the place symbolically between slavery and freedom, to the Jordan, Jesus allows the story of Israel to embrace his own story. By allowing himself to be baptized by John he endorses John's version of Israel's story—that something revolutionary is about to happen. But the events that immediately follow transform those actions of humility. The heavens open, bringing to an end Israel's longing for God to act; the Spirit descends, recalling the end of God's anger at the flood; and the voice speaks, endorsing Jesus as the one on whom the story now focuses. Jesus has not denied the vocation of Israel, nor the ministry of John the Baptist: he has overaccepted them, transforming their reference.

Jesus proceeds to calling his disciples. When he chooses twelve, he echoes the Torah by mirroring the twelve tribes of Israel. In Mark's account Jesus does this by going up a mountain, thus forming a new covenant like the one at Sinai. He chooses a new leadership, rather as God had chosen Moses and Aaron. He is forming a "government in exile"—a fulfillment of Israel in contrast to the authority of priest, scribe, Herodian, and Roman. And he gives new names to his key lieutenants—Peter, and the Sons of Thunder. The disciples are a diverse group, including fishermen, tax collectors, and a future betrayer—a summary of the Israel that Jesus inherited. In all these ways, Jesus overaccepts the tradition of the twelve tribes by placing it in an eschatological context. These are the twelve people through whom the kingdom will come.

The symbolic actions are prominent again during the last week in Jerusalem. The week begins with Jesus entering Jerusalem riding on a donkey. This is perhaps the defining moment of his ministry: he approaches Jerusalem, the heart of Jewish worship and the seat of Roman authority. He comes down the Mount of Olives, the place from which, Zechariah 14 promises, God will fight the nations and restore Jerusalem. Simon Maccabaeus entered Jerusalem this way in the second century B.C., according to 1 Maccabees 13. So did the Sicarius leader Menahem, according to Josephus's account. Where is the horse, the steed that bears the triumphant general, the untamable champion loyal only to the skilled commander, so beloved of great leaders from Alexander to Napoleon?

Not here. In its place, a donkey. Jesus chooses an agricultural tool, not a weapon of war: a tractor, not a tank. He overaccepts the notion of power, of acclaim—of kingship: his kingship rides not on the power of a horse but on the humility of a donkey. He does not block the people's desire to acclaim him, nor does he accept their idea of kingship: he overaccepts and becomes the servant king.

The drama then moves, according to the Synoptic sequence, to the temple. Jesus drives out all who had been buying and selling there and overturns the tables of the money changers and those selling doves. This is one of the most difficult symbolic actions to interpret—the more so because the evangelists appear to have differing understandings of its meaning. It looks like a block—against the temple itself, or at least against the way the temple system was used to oppress those closest to Jesus' heart: the poor, the unclean, the women.[23] But, like the temptation narrative, what seems to be a block may in fact be a form of overaccepting. The key in this case is Jesus' status: he is not in a position *actually* to destroy the temple or end its corrupt practices: this is the only context in which a block would make sense. The underlying significance of the event is a reversal of status, a redefinition of temple: from now on the narrative of what happens to Jesus' body symbolizes or even fulfills the narrative of what will become of the temple. The temple is placed within a larger story—and the two stories are linked, in Mark's Gospel, by the common thread linking them back to Jesus' words about binding the strong man: "No one can enter a strong man's house and plunder his property without first tying up the strong man; then indeed the house can be plundered."[24] These words, originally spoken of Satan, are proved true here of the temple, and later of Jesus' own body.[25] The symbolic action of turning the tables on the moneychangers is a statement that the temple is a part of God's story—with Jesus at the center—rather than God being part of the temple's story. Jesus does not here so much block the temple as outnarrate it.

Perhaps the most self-conscious of all the symbolic actions that embody the practice of overaccepting is the Last Supper. Here overaccepting works throughout the narrative. Jesus overaccepts the Passover tradition. The unleavened bread, of haste and sustenance, becomes his body. The cup becomes the blood of the new covenant. The whole of the exodus tradition—deliverance from slavery and covenant with God—is now embodied in Jesus. And the lamb, the one whose death causes God to pass over Israel? The lamb is, implicitly, Jesus himself—one thinks of Abraham's words, "God himself will provide the lamb for a burnt offering, my son."[26] With deep irony, Jesus overaccepts the purity tradition, not denying that purity must be attained, but nonetheless asserting that purity is attained through blood—his own. And in the process he overaccepts his own death. The ritual last meal becomes an anticipation of the next meal he will eat—in the kingdom. His death is accepted in order that the greater story, that of the transformation of Israel to give life to the world, may be made possible. Just as Jesus in his incarnation overaccepted human life, so here in his anticipation of the cross he overaccepts human death.

Two Stories

I end this chapter with two stories that incorporate all the features of my exposition of improvisation so far—habit, status, questioning givens, and overaccepting. The first is the story of a man named Tom. When he was four years old his parents were told Tom was autistic. The consultant did not mince words. "You must bring him up like a dog," he told Tom's mother, stressing the need for clear instructions and boundaries, and the need to bridle the boy's volatile frustration. The family understood that Tom was going to be a problem. His mother shaped his character carefully. For all the bleak prognostications, Tom found areas of life where he flourished. He played the piano. He sang, growing into a deep bass. He appreciated music so much that he could become ecstatic on hearing a Mozart concerto. He appreciated routine, and before she died, his mother ensured that he would find a regular place volunteering help at a local care home, doing odd jobs and gardening. He died suddenly, aged forty-six.

At his funeral there were the usual seats left for his brothers, their families, and for the extensive wider family. The seats for the wider family were mostly empty. They had always found Tom hard to relate to; they all knew about the dog remark; they could not pretend they really knew him: they stayed away. But behind those rows of empty seats, the rest of the church was overflowing with people. And as the service proceeded, one story after another was told that explained why. One woman recalled how, new to faith, for her first six months she did not sing but simply watched Tom's face as he sang with the choir: he was so enraptured—she wanted to be like him. Few people doubted that, had it been their own funeral, the church would have been much less busy. Tom's life had begun with terrifying and oppressive givens—the given of being thought of as a dog. Through the habits instilled by his mother and father, he learned to take the right things for granted. His low status was unquestioned until his funeral, when it was abundantly clear how God had chosen what is foolish in the world to shame the wise, and what is weak in the world to shame the strong. And his life was revealed as a story of overaccepting—and one that ended with him eating not just the scraps from the master's table but sharing the whole banquet, forevermore.

The second story is told in Ian MacMillan's book *Orbit of Darkness*.[27] One hot afternoon in late July 1941, in the Auschwitz concentration camp, the deputy commandant gathers the whole company of prisoners for a roll call. One of the prisoners has escaped, and so, as a punishment, the deputy commandant selects ten men to starve to death as a warning to the others. The first nine are led away, but the tenth man begins to protest. At that moment a man in the crowd volunteers to replace the tenth man, and his offer is accepted.

The new tenth man turns out to be a Catholic priest. He begins to lead the other nine in songs and prayers in the cell. The incessant sounds inspire other prisoners around the camp, and set some of the guards on edge. Legends circulate around the camp that the priest had habitually given his rations to others, and had not flinched when being heavily flogged by the guards. Days go by, and the guards who come to remove a dead body cannot hold the priest's gaze. The other prisoners realize the guards are scared of the priest. By the tenth day, the guards are beginning to plead with the commandant to be given other duties. Prisoners are beginning to imitate the priest, and share their food with the most needy. By offering himself, the priest has inspired others to gain the upper hand in the primal struggle. On the fourteenth day, one of the guards commits suicide by hurling himself onto the electric fence. The commandant orders that prisoners shall be beaten to death for mentioning the priest's name, for helping each other or giving food away. The following day, the priest is murdered with an injection of carbolic acid. But the unease only grows, and the story ends with a sense that the camp will not be the same again.

This is a story about habit, because it is the habit of prayer, song, and selflessness, the trained ability to take the right things for granted, that enabled the priest to be a witness. His habits were formed in worship and displayed in the camp. "Like Jesus, the priest went to Galilee before he went to Jerusalem."[28] It is a story about status, because the interplay between the powerlessness of the starving men and the growing powerlessness of the guards is the chief dynamic of the narrative. It is importantly a story about questioning givens, because all the givens seem stacked against the prisoners at the beginning of the story, yet gradually each is dismantled, one by one. And it is, of course, fundamentally a narrative of overaccepting, in a particularly Christlike way. The ten men stare death, a slow and agonizing death, in the face. Yet one of them, like Christ, voluntarily submits himself to that from which everyone else strives to escape. He does not accept or block—he overaccepts, actively choosing to die. And once he does so, death is no longer the threat it had always been hitherto. At least, not to the prisoners. To the guards, it is another matter. The priest's death, the death of overacceptance, contrasts with that of the guard who commits suicide—a graphic example of a failed block. This is a story of how a priest fits death into a much larger narrative. At the beginning of the story it is the guards who think about their superior civilization, while the prisoners' minds are on the smoke coming from the gas chambers. By the end of the story, it is the other way round.

10

Reincorporating the Lost

Church History as a Road

I have argued in my treatment of improvisation so far that Christian ethics is about learning to take the right things for granted. It is commonplace to perceive life within the context of a story, and one takes a circumstance or development for granted if it is true to the character of the story. Christianity perceives reality in terms of a particular story, whose broad dimensions I set out in chapter 4 above as a five-act drama, spanning creation—Israel—Jesus—church—eschaton. The key to Christian living is to have a thorough perception and embodiment of what forms of life are appropriate to Act Four. Many, perhaps most, of the church's mistakes derive from a mistaken apprehension of which act it is in. It is not the church's vocation to create (Act One) or to conclude (Act Five) the story. The Messiah has come (Act Three), and it is the church's role to follow in Christ's footsteps (Act Four), not to act as if the fullness of God were yet to be revealed (Act Two). Thus the simple task of the church is to keep the story going, in the face of numerous temptations to block and kill the story when it becomes uncomfortable or threatening. Because the Christian story is larger and greater in depth and scope than the smaller stories that present themselves, Christians can overaccept the offers that come to them from the world in the light of the larger story. Rather than use violence, which bypasses the imagination, kills the story, and sits uneasily in Act Four, the church addresses threats to its integrity by perceiving what such offers could mean in the context of the five-act play.

Two questions persistently present themselves. The first is, on what resources does the church draw in order to overaccept? In other words, how does the sense of being part of a greater story translate into over-accepting in Christian practice? The second question is, how does the church address evil, both in the contemporary world and in the church's own history? In other words, how does the church accept particularly sinister offers, and how does it accept the fact that in the past it has often blocked that which was good and accepted that which was evil?

My answer to these questions begins with the building of a road. I'd like you to imagine church history as a road, stretching from the past into the future. It is in the character of roads to dig and cleave and thrust their way through the countryside, leaving considerable quantities of debris to either side. This is in some ways an ugly process, as environmental campaigners have protested in recent years. To take another, less linear analogy, one may compare church history to a sculpture, at which the sculptor continually chips away, and in so doing creates a great mound of discarded plaster or marble. What has happened in the liberation movement both outside and inside the church in recent generations has been the cry of the discarded marble, the searing pain of the displaced earth. For the church has come to realize that history is written by the winners, whereas the faith of Mary's Magnificat proclaims the God who is on the side of the losers. And the losers in church history have tended to be the same people who have been the losers in society as a whole. The losers have tended to be women, have tended to be races who have experienced domination at the hands of North Atlantic white people, have tended to be people disadvantaged by disability of various kinds. Liberation theology, so prominent in the last thirty years, proclaims that these are the people who are at the heart of God's story—or in the language I have been using, embody the character of Act Four. One can tell the difference between the winners and the losers in the contemporary church by one simple test: the losers long for Act Five, when God will restore the justice of his reign, whereas the winners have too much to lose, and would like a bit of advance notice so as to enjoy their present glory before God brings down the curtain on Act Four.

The revelation brought by the liberation movement in the church in the last thirty years is that the earth cast aside in making the road is at least as much a part of Act Four as the road itself; that the marble discarded by the sculptor is at least as much a part of Act Four as the sculpture. It is now much easier to see, for poor and rich alike, that the losers, whose voice has not been heard, are at least as much a part of Act Four as those winners who have written the history. Charles Péguy, the

French spiritual writer, describes the experience of standing before the throne of God after one's death, and asks the terrible question, "What would God say to us if some of us came to him without the others?"[1] These others are all those we have cast aside in making the road of our own lives—all the marble we have chipped away to carve out the edifice of our own biographies.

The great parable of Matthew 25, telling of the last judgment and the separation of the sheep and the goats, shows the church that its salvation lies exactly in these "others." What the church did or did not offer to the hungry, thirsty, homeless, naked, sick, or prisoner it did or did not offer to Jesus. And why are such people so crucial to judging the practice of the church in Act Four? Because they are the face of Act Five. The church has got to get used to the faces of the poor, because it will see them on thrones in Act Five. Act Five is when the promises of Hannah's song and Mary's Magnificat are realized, when the sorrow of this world is turned to dancing. If the church wants to be a part of Act Five, it has to be shaped and formed by its chief characters as they appear in Act Four. By working with and being with the poor, the excluded, the discarded "earth" and "marble," and in some circumstances being the poor, the church faithfully follows Act Three and anticipates Act Five. The closer the church is to the poor in Act Four, the more prepared it will be to come face to face with God in Act Five.

To imagine what it means for Act Five to be made up of the discarded material from Act Four, it may be helpful to remember the novels of Charles Dickens. The hero of a novel such as *David Copperfield* encounters a gallery of grotesques on his path of life. Some of these have cameo roles, then disappear from the narrative. Toward the end of the book they reappear one by one. If one could not tell where one was in the book by the weight of the pages, one could realize one was nearing the end by the reappearance of characters introduced early on. And so it is with the church. One knows the church is close to the kingdom, that Act Five is breaking in, when it is filled by those who have been written out of the winners' script, when it is close to those who have nothing to lose from the sudden end of Act Four. As a child one of my favorite television programs was called *Mr. Benn*. Each week Mr. Benn would walk into a shop and the shopkeeper would open a door to a new adventure. One knew it was the end of the story when, as if by magic, the shopkeeper reappeared, opening another door to take Mr. Benn back to his everyday world. The poor are to the church as the shopkeeper is to Mr. Benn. They tend to be cast aside by those longing for spiritual adventure; but they are the ones who stand at the door to the next stage of God's story.

The story of the feeding of the five thousand clarifies the respective characters of Acts Two, Three, Four, and Five. The best efforts of Israel, Act Two, can be seen in the loaves and fishes. It is Jesus, in Act Three, who transforms the poverty of our nature by the riches of his grace. The disciples' role, in Act Four, is to see that everyone gets enough and to gather up the leftovers, the discarded elements in the drama of the feeding. In the twelve baskets left over can be seen the new Jerusalem of Act Five, the restored kingdom of God modeled on the twelve tribes of Israel.

Those who have told stories to children will have experienced that vacant, wandering expression that children sometimes have, which masks a razor-sharp allegiance to the conventions of storytelling. Should one try to skip chunks of the plot, or finish before the end of the story, one suffers the accusing wrath of the deeply wronged. This is the case even if one is making up the story as one is going along. How do children know whether one has or has not reached the end of the story? Imagine for one moment that after a long, hard day on the battlefield one was leaving Venus in a spaceship when it experienced a collision with a giant amoeba, whereupon one became part of a cellular development in the amoeba. So far all the narrative has is assorted information—interesting but unsatisfying. Yet if that amoeba subdivides and re-creates the whole universe, so that one finds that one has oneself become a new planet Venus, eating up the spaceship in the process and ending all war, one has a story. The child will recognize it as the end of the story, because the narrative has reintroduced the elements discarded at the beginning. The key to improvising children's stories is not in thinking up clever or original characters or contexts, but in remembering what has been discarded and reintroducing it at the appropriate moment. Likewise the key to improvising on the Christian story is not in being clever or original, but in being so steeped in the discarded elements of the story that one can draw on them when the vital moment comes.

This may be illustrated by the story of St. Laurence. Laurence was a deacon of the church of Rome in the third century, during the persecution of the Christians by the emperor Decius. The Roman magistrate ordered Laurence to bring into the church all its riches. Laurence's response to this highly threatening offer is a perfect embodiment of both overaccepting and reincorporation. He did not refuse: instead he accepted. He asked two days' grace and used the time to set about his pattern of overaccepting. In this case he considered what the riches of the church truly were, and his habit taught him to look back to the neglected parts of the story. On the third day he invited the magistrate back to see the church filled with the poor, the lame, the orphan, and the widow. "These," he said, pointing to the destitute people in front of him, "are the riches of the Church." Laurence had overaccepted the notion of riches, and reincorporated the discarded elements in the story. It was a perfect embodiment of the kingdom. But it was a rival kingdom to the empire, and the magistrate had Laurence roasted on a spit.[2]

Reincorporation

This introduces the final practice within the discipline of theatrical improvisation: the practice known as "reincorporation." A story is not simply a series of events happening one after another. Such sequences have no reason for stopping in any one particular place and not just carrying on. It is not simply a matter of free association: a story requires reincorporation.[3] Reincorporation is what marks the end of the story. When elements found earlier in the story begin to be reincorporated, then some pattern emerges and a sense of completion is possible. Christian ethics seen from an eschatological perspective is always profoundly aware of the end of the story, and of the way this end reincorporates earlier (perhaps all earlier) parts of the narrative. It is reincorporation that distinguishes the end from just another event in the narrative.

The key factor in reincorporation is memory. Memory is much more significant than originality. The improviser does not set out to create the future, but responds to the past, reincorporating it to form a story. This can be illustrated by a game in which actor A provides free-associated disconnected material, while actor B somehow tries to connect it:

A: It was a cold winter's night. The wolves howled in the trees. The concert pianist adjusted his sleeves and began to play. An old lady was shovelling snow from her door . . .

B: . . . When she heard the piano the little old lady began shovelling at a fantastic speed. When she reached the concert hall she cried, "That pianist is my son!" Wolves appeared at all the windows, and the pianist sprang onto the piano, thick fur growing visibly from under his clothes.[4]

The Christian community is in a position much more similar to actor B than to actor A. The community is not able to determine the gifts it is given: it is obliged to use the skill of its convictions to transform the fate (or givenness) of the disconnected gifts into the destiny of a story consonant with the one given story. It does not do this by changing the subject, or by refusing to continue; both of these would do violence to the emerging narrative. This perspective sees all events in creation as offering possibilities for narrative, needing skills nurtured by the gospel to be reincorporated. So the key to successful improvisation is not originality but memory. The more easily forgotten an element is, the more satisfying its reincorporation. Likewise, the deeper the exclusion of a person from the church's story, the more significant that person's reincorporation in the story. As was pointed out to Simon the Pharisee, the repentance of the woman who washed Jesus' feet with her hair was more significant than Simon's own repentance.

In a highly suggestive phrase one author on theatrical improvisation emphasizes that the skills required for improvisation are not primarily those that come in moments of inspiration (or decision). Instead, the future is formed out of the past.

> The improviser has to be *like a man walking backwards*. He sees where he has been, but he pays no attention to the future. His story can take him anywhere, but he must still "balance" it, and give it shape, by remembering incidents that have been shelved and reincorporating them.[5]

This picture of a person walking backwards is an immensely significant and fruitful one. The only given in his life is that at which he is looking—the tradition of which he is a part. St. Laurence was not looking at the risk to the church he was taking by overaccepting the magistrate's demand; he was standing at a moment of crisis and being guided by habits and commitments the church had formed in the past. The only given in the life of the church is the story that is entered at baptism. This contrasts with the model of consequential ethics. An ethic based on the assessment of consequences is likely to have both eyes fixed firmly on the apparent realities of the future. Its solutions to ethical dilemmas need not necessarily have much awareness of the past—indeed, they may well be designed to free the agent from such considerations. The potential for forming the future tends to be dependent on control of the present; by contrast improvisers concentrate their awareness on shelved elements in the past that are ripe for reincorporation. Whereas the improviser looks back when stuck, the consequentialist looks forward. Yet the story told by the consequentialist is far too short: consequentialists live in a one-act play with no awareness of Act Five—their perception of the future seldom accounts for the final resolution of all things.

Lest the story of St. Laurence seem too distant, perhaps too pious, it is worth recalling an instance from contemporary experience. The following story was told to me by a friend called Malcolm. He was a priest in a parish that developed a particular ministry to the rehabilitation of young offenders. This ministry included the development of a furniture resource center, which took in old and damaged furniture, restored it to usable condition, and made it available to those living on low incomes or being rehoused. In the course of this ministry Malcolm came across Paul, who was a fifteen-year-old with a history of misusing drugs. To finance his dependence, Paul had become proficient at breaking and entering homes and pilfering the contents.

Malcolm also came to know a woman called Kristel. Kristel lived with her young daughter in a house in Malcolm's town. She also had a drug habit, and she financed it by bringing men back to her house at night, while her daughter was asleep. When Malcolm came to visit her, he discovered that her house contained no furniture whatsoever, upstairs or down—except the mattress on which she entertained her male customers. Everything else, he realized, was sold to pay her pimp. Malcolm saw that she might benefit from a particularly large delivery of furniture from the furniture resource center.

The day came when Paul and Malcolm filled the delivery truck with tables, chairs, cupboards, chests of drawers, and wardrobes, and in the gaps between them put toys, games, and books for the little girl. They arrived at Kristel's house and knocked on the door. No answer. No Kristel, and no little girl. What had happened? Had she moved, been arrested, died? Was she ill, working, or insulted by the gesture? They had no idea. They couldn't face taking all the furniture back to the center. Then Paul had an idea. "Tell you what," he said, "how about if we just take all the stuff in anyway—she'll get a surprise when she walks in!" Malcolm took a while to realize what Paul was suggesting. "You mean, break into the house?"—but as soon as he said it, he recalled that a mere lock was no obstacle to Paul. In no time they were in the house, and the furniture was all off the truck, the toys all over the floor.

Then Kristel arrived home. She saw the open door and ran into the house, shocked and terrified. She saw Malcolm and burst into tears. "I can explain . . . ," he said—but quickly he perceived that the tears of horror had turned to tears of joy. Her little girl had toys—too many to know what to do with them all. She herself had comfortable chairs and a place to eat and talk and relax. Malcolm was thrilled when he saw her joy. And then he saw Paul. Paul was crying too, but for a different reason. He'd never made someone happy before. He knew how to break into houses—he had been told many times how many hearts he had broken by doing so. Now he had broken into someone's house, into someone's life, and for the first time brought comedy not tragedy, hope not despair. His new life had begun.

This is a story of reincorporation. Paul and Kristel are both people who have been written out of the conventional script of life. The key moment in the story comes when Paul realizes there is a good use for the housebreaking skills he has honed through his adolescence. When these skills are reincorporated into the story, it is the cue for the reincorporation of

Paul himself, then Kristel and her daughter, and finally the formation of a new community. Like an actor walking backwards, Malcolm, and a force greater than Malcolm, found a way of reincorporating lost material—first furniture, finally people—and in the process, stumbled upon the kingdom.

Larger Stories and Smaller Stories

The wonder of a discovery like this inspires the reading of scriptural narrative in a new light. The story of Joseph is most obviously a story about status: the lowly younger brother becomes high and haughty, antagonizing his siblings and being sold into slavery. In lowly prison he becomes high through the gift of discerning the meaning of the dreams of the mighty but needy pharaoh. He is then so high in status that his now lowly brothers do not recognize him. The story is also about the transformation of givens into gifts—of fate into destiny. Rivalry, jealousy, slavery, imprisonment, famine—all these givens are incorporated into the story of redemption and providence, as was discussed in chapter 9. But it is also a story of reincorporation. The solution to Jacob's family's troubles lies in reincorporating the stray element (Joseph) that was cast aside much earlier on. The story is complete when the true victim, Jacob, finally comes to Egypt and sees the extraordinary way God has saved his people. The fact that Jacob has himself been no stranger to the costs and effects of sibling rivalry only adds to the irony and satisfaction of the conclusion.

Reincorporation is a constant theme in the Gospels. If Jesus' calling of the twelve disciples is a rounding-up of the twelve stray tribes of Israel, his ministry to the social outcast is an ingathering of the exiled. Thus Jesus combines the prophecy of Isaiah 2, that the nations will stream back to Zion, and all find a place at the Lord's house, with the injunction of Leviticus 25, that the oppressed will go free, and that if they have fallen into slavery as the years go by, they and their children with them shall go free in the Jubilee year. The most common picture of heaven is of a great banquet, and the most common sphere of conflict in Jesus' ministry is the dinner table. It is in the act of eating that reincorporation is practiced and its significance perceived, by friend and foe. The feeding of the five thousand, as was noted in chapter 4 above, is a paradigmatic story of reincorporation, wherein the disciples take pains to ensure that no morsel of bread is wasted, and they find twelve baskets full. This is a pattern and a promise of reincorporation—a picture of the restoration of Israel through the ministry of Jesus and the mission of his disciples.

Perhaps the most vivid story of reincorporation in the Gospels is the encounter of the two disciples with Jesus on the road to Emmaus. The disciples relate to the stranger the givens of the story, in their tragic finality. Jesus reincorporates every stray aspect of Scripture, so that all the forgotten characters appear on this last page of Luke's story. And after he has reincorporated the Last Supper by his manner of breaking the bread, the disciples then reincorporate the whole experience by realizing they had felt their hearts on fire. Finally they reincorporate the disciples by rushing back to Jerusalem and informing them.

It is time to review the two questions raised at the outset. The first question concerned the resources for improvisation in the church. The answer is that the church has ample resources for every eventuality it faces and it finds those resources among the discarded elements of earlier parts of its story. Church history is theology teaching by examples—good examples like St. Laurence and St. Francis, bad examples like the Inquisition, the Crusades, and the Holocaust. In order to gain access to these resources, the church needs to maintain a lively memory, in which it recalls tales of the good and the bad, and especially of those who have not written their own history—the losers. The greatest improvisers, such as Laurence, did nothing more than reincorporate discarded elements of the story. To do this, one has to be part of a community that knows and lives the story. Remembering the sins of the past is as significant as remembering the saints.

The second question concerned evil. I have argued throughout that for the church to think it can simply block evil is contrary to the example of Christ, has no guarantee of success, bypasses the imagination, and tends to ally the church with powerful forces it may have no place beside. The challenge of evil may be the threat of a rival story, or it may be the denial that there is any story at all. For example Hitler talked of a thousand-year Reich (a rival story), while less exalted Nazis tormented Jews by arguing that if any survivor tried to recall the atrocities of the period, no one would ever believe them (the denial of story).[6] The church's response to both kinds of unpalatable offers should be to tell a much larger story and to stretch its imagination to the full dimensions and cosmic scope of the Christian story.

An example of how awareness of the larger story affects Christian instinct may be seen in reverting to a classic quandary: a violent man pulls out a gun and threatens to kill someone beside you, someone you love. The options available seem to be (1) tragedy—he kills your friend—or (2) martyrdom—he kills you instead. The alternatives (rarely considered) include (3) you emotionally disarm the attacker, or distract his attention, or give something he will settle for instead, such as money, or (4) Providence intervenes in the shape of a banana skin or power outage. But what of (5) attempting to kill the attacker? In a one-act play this is a live option. But recourse to the larger story, the five-act play, offers a warning. One may suppose the loved one is a believer, who is ready to meet his or her maker. One may suppose that the attacker is anything but, and that killing him would close off all possibility of repentance and faith. Thus in the words of John Howard Yoder, "To keep out of heaven temporarily someone who wants to go there ultimately anyway, I would consign to hell immediately someone whom I am in the world to save."[7] The larger story redefines success and failure, victory and defeat. Christian performance is faithful if it follows Act Three and anticipates Act Five; unfaithful if it shoulders all responsibility for resolving all conflicts as if it were in a one-act play. The promise of Act Five is that the person who is shelved will be reincorporated—indeed the story will not be over until the shelved people have been reincorporated; there is no such promise for the one who shelves others.[8]

What the larger story does to the smaller story is to transform givens into gifts and fate into destiny. The tragedy of ethical existence is that one seems to be hemmed in by givens that determine one's range of responses. A commitment to overaccept in the light of the larger story, and an instinct to reincorporate the shelved elements of the story, transforms those givens into gifts. A recognition that the only given is the gospel, the larger story, and that the coming Act Five will resolve all that the church fails to overaccept and restore all that the church fails to reincorporate, transforms blind fate into divine destiny.

To sum up, I have now outlined the dimensions of the analogy between theatrical improvisation and Christian ethics. The analogy arises from the perception that the church exists in Act Four of a five-act play, that the vital event has already happened, and thus that its role is principally to keep the story going, rather than assume it must make the story come out right. It then becomes clearer that the great majority of things that Christians do derive from habit and instinct, and that Christian ethics is more concerned with the development of good habits than with the making of good decisions. Character is formed in a number of ways, but the definitive setting for the embodiment of good habits is worship. The next stage is to recognize the role and significance of status, and to realize that status transactions are simply different tactics and strategies for getting one's way. The interpretation of all human action and gesture in terms of accepting and blocking introduces the practice of overaccepting, in which the church receives the world's offers by placing them in a far larger story than the world ever imagined, and thus comes to see challenges and demands as gifts rather than givens. The last stage is to recognize that the resources for the future lie in the shelved elements of the past, and that the church prepares for Act Five by reincorporating those forms of life and people that were deprived of and excluded from the fruits of Act Four. The church looks back into the history of its situation (the smaller story) and the history of God's providence (the larger story) to see if there are any "lost" elements ripe for reincorporation, and then anticipates Act Five by imitating its pattern—the pattern of reincorporating the gifts of creation in the strength of the givenness of Christ.

A Family Redeemed by Improvisation

My final story happened some years ago and concerns Bill. Bill left school in a town where one went down the mine, constructed aircraft turbines, or learned to build warships. So he did an apprenticeship in the shipyard, and looked forward to a lifetime of employment. He progressed well, moving upstairs to the office, where he ordered parts for future ships. He married, had two children, got a car and a mortgage. All was well. Then one day, along with almost everyone else at the company, he lost his job. His wife worked part-time at the post office and was a highly capable person. She took on a full-time post, and Bill set to cooking and cleaning. It wasn't enough. They realized they would have to sell the house. Bill set about decorating the house to make it attractive to a buyer. His efforts were lamentable. He lived in fear of his highly competent wife and her withering criticism, sharpened by her exhaustion. The two daughters of the house witnessed daily increasing tension. Determined to maintain their Easter observance, the family faithfully shared in the witness of Holy Week, its commemoration of the Passion being borne out in their thinly veiled torture.

Finally, on Holy Saturday, the explosion came. Bill's wife returned after work, desperate to grab some tea and get out to the Easter Vigil, but she was stopped in her tracks by the smell of paint. Bill was on the stairs, his ladder through an involuntary hole in the ceiling, and the contents of an upset paint-pot trickling down the stair carpet. She shrieked: "What's the use of you? You can't get a job, you can't cook, can't keep the house tidy—and put a paintbrush in your hand and you wreck the whole house! You're useless, pointless, hopeless." The silence was louder than the shouting that preceded it, as Bill accepted each word. But his daughter, a precocious eleven-year-old, intervened. She looked up the stairs at her father, and back down to her mother. "He's a good dad," she said, simply.

In five words she had taken the right things for granted, recognized as a child it was not her responsibility to make everything come out right, blocked nothing of what her mother had said, questioned the givens her mother had been assuming, overaccepted her mother's words, and reincorporated the forgotten part of the story—the part that genuinely belonged in the final act of God's drama. All six stages of improvisation in five words. Her simple words brought her mother to humble repentance. The mother tearfully related the story to me later the same day.

PART THREE

Reaping

11

A Threatening Offer
Human Evil

This chapter and the next consider threatening offers. Some threatening offers arise because of what appear to be flaws in the created order, such as disability and illness: these are addressed in the next chapter. In this chapter the flaws in question are those in the human heart and soul. How does a community committed to improvise in the light of the drama of God's story engage with systematic oppression? For many, this may be the most pressing issue of all in Christian ethics: how does a community address sin, particularly when that sin takes a violent, dominant, and potentially obliterating turn?

Much consideration has been given by those writing in Christian ethics to the question of whether and in what circumstances it is appropriate to take up arms to oppose an oppressive regime. In a situation in some ways analogous to warfare, familiar just war arguments such as legitimate authority, last resort, and right intention are frequently aired. But what if there is little or no hope of victory? What if the oppressors have all the cards stacked in their favor, and to block is useless? And what if the oppression is widespread, overwhelming, and yet still officially denied?

This is the situation described by William Cavanaugh in his book *Torture and Eucharist.*[1] Cavanaugh describes the experience of Chile and the Roman Catholic Church there during the dictatorship of General

Augusto Pinochet, 1973–1990. In 1970 the Marxist Salvador Allende was elected president of Chile with 36 percent of the vote. A sweeping program of left-wing reform was implemented, including nationalization of companies and banks, expropriation of land, and controls on prices and wages to favor the workers. Politics was polarized, and the country was close to chaos. On September 11, 1973, a military junta seized power, claiming to put an end to party sectarianism and unite Chile in a depoliticized nationalism. Almost straightaway disappearances, tortures, and killings began. Sympathizers of the ousted government, union organizers, church activists, and people involved in grassroots organizations were systematically targeted; meanwhile many other people, perceived to be in some tenuous way linked to such activists, met the same fate. While its intensity abated somewhat after the new government had become established, this reign of terror continued for the next seventeen years.

Accepting and Blocking

Chile was driven indoors. Those regarded as enemies of the regime had a stark choice: disappear by remaining at home, lying low, and thus risk "being disappeared" when the police came to call; or disappear by fleeing, thereby risking a swift demise. The choice was between passive acceptance and active escape. Even the priests were not immune: in the first four months over a hundred were forced to leave the country.[2]

For senior public figures in the Roman Catholic Church, the choice was slightly different. By September 1973, not a single bishop, not even the most progressive, any longer sympathized with the Allende government.[3] The bishops felt their role was to ensure continuity. It turned out there was a remarkable similarity between their vision for Chile and that of the Pinochet dictatorship. "Both claimed that they intended to subsume societal conflict into a single whole free of essential strife. The church sought a mystical communion of Chileans above the party political fray; the military regime wanted to eliminate party politics altogether."[4] Hence several bishops saw it as their duty to support the new government.

There was in fact remarkably little violent opposition to those who had seized power. As Cavanaugh points out, this was a problem for the Pinochet regime. A month after the coup d'état a general was sent around the country to check on resistance: his visits to military installations led to dozens of executions. The government needed violence and opposition in order to create an atmosphere in which its policies seemed legitimate, in which only the state could be the savior. The senior figures in the church were so concerned to promote the organic unity of Chile that they identified their interests with the regime, seeing church and state as twin guardians of the national heritage. They saw tortures and executions "not as intrinsic to this order but as aberrations, excesses which could be corrected by appeals to the Christian consciences of Chile's rulers."[5] Thus they almost unanimously preferred private conversations to public denunciations—even though those they sought to protect took the opposite view.[6] The bishops never, for example, called for the recognition of conscientious objection to military service.

It was not until 1976 that the bishops began clearly to articulate the hostile nature of a system that "stifles basic liberties, tramples on the most elementary rights, and represses citizens within the framework of a feared and omnipotent Police state."[7] Eventually, in 1977, the bishops began to assert that the church has a social role that had come into conflict with the Pinochet regime. The church, they said, makes salvation visible through soup kitchens, cooperatives, workshops, and aid to the defenseless and oppressed. It "does not let itself be circumscribed only to the 'religious' field, often arbitrarily defined by persons interested in removing the church from other fields. . . . It knows there are those who want to use it: this is a risk inherent in every incarnation. But it knows that absence and silence imply a danger similar to that of word and presence."[8] Finally in May 1980 the bishops, worn out with attacks on themselves in the media, attacks on Christian communities, and having witnessed the effects of torture, issued a document entitled "I Am Jesus, Whom You Are Persecuting," whose title speaks for itself.

Using the language of improvisation, the great majority of citizens in Chile had little or no significant choice between accepting and blocking. Blocking the new regime meant almost certain torture and quite possibly death. The leaders of the church, by contrast, did have a choice, yet in the vital early stages they assumed that accepting was their duty, and that blocking was counter to their role as supporters of the unity of Chile.

Questioning Givens

Why did it take so long? How could it be that even while priests and religious were being brutally killed, their bishops were condoning the regime that was devising a widespread program of torture? Cavanaugh describes in great detail two explanations, one based on the prevalent understanding of the social role of the church and the other based on an inadequate understanding of the true nature of torture.

Cavanaugh summarizes the prevalent understanding of the social role of the church, and the consequences of that understanding, as follows:

> Official Catholic ecclesiology had helped create an autonomous political sphere of arbitrary power by withdrawing to a "religious" terrain in civil society. It was the task of the layperson, acting on general "values" learned in the church, to enter the political realm as an individual and incarnate those values in concrete policies. Unfortunately, this individualization and disappearance of the visible church is also the effect of the military regime's strategy of torture and disappearance. . . . [T]he official church was [ill-prepared] to meet this strategy, since its ecclesiology had already, in effect, disappeared the church as a social body.[9]

The contours of the Chilean bishops' ecclesiology had been set in Europe fifty years before. The period between the two world wars was a highly volatile one in European politics, and the church faced a choice between backing parties that sought to protect its interests against widespread anticlericalism and keeping out of politics altogether. Pius XI, who became pope in 1922, took the latter approach, withdrawing support for political parties and seeking to unite Catholics on a religious and moral level. His great initiative was Catholic Action, a largely lay movement under clerical supervision, that aspired to address contemporary social problems particularly through infusing the institutions of civil society with Catholic values and personnel. "Pius envisioned a brigade of committed laypeople, under the direction of the hierarchy, who would take the Gospel into the everyday world and rewin society for Christ."[10]

Pius XI assumed that the spiritual and the temporal were different spheres. The clergy's task is above nature; they form the laity in a Christian conscience, and through the labors of the laity the gospel finds an indirect route to the world. Every true Catholic thus becomes a model of a patriotic obedient subject and an excellent and loyal citizen. This ideology shaped the generation of Roman Catholic leaders that served Chile in the 1960s–1980s. Its theoretical basis was derived from the New Christendom ecclesiology of the French Catholic philosopher Jacques Maritain. For Maritain the key New Testament text is Jesus' instruction to render to Caesar that which is Caesar's and to God that which is God's. Thus Jesus affirmed the autonomy of the temporal and the superiority of the spiritual. What this means in political terms is that the church holds sway over an interior, mystical realm while leaving the body to the state. Maritain aspires to a "New Christendom," a new and truer Christian culture independent from the church, yet imbued with the Christian spirit.

Cavanaugh explains how Maritain's ecclesiology made available the space for Chilean oppression. "Maritain may declare that only God, and not the state, is truly sovereign, but once the church has been individualized and eliminated as Christ's body in the world, only the state is left to impersonate God. As the state itself becomes the guarantor of rights, human rights become tied, in bitter irony, to the security of the state."[11] The emphasis on the mystical quality of the body renders the church invisible. The key to the problem is the distinction of planes, the separation of the temporal from the spiritual—which rests on a still more fundamental mistake, the distinction of body and soul. Cavanaugh has no doubt that this is from beginning to an end a matter of the definition of the political, which rests not on Constantinian nostalgia but on the theological understanding of the body.

> If we understand the unity of body and soul, we must understand that what is really at stake is not body-power versus soul-power, but competing types of body-soul disciplines, some violent and some peaceful. Christians must understand that the state's control of the body is a control of the soul as well. The church must see that its own disciplinary resources—Eucharist, penance, virtue, works of mercy, martyrdom—are not matters of the soul which must somehow "animate" the "real world" of bodies, but are rather body/soul disciplines meant to produce actions, practices, habits that are visible in the world. For the church to be a true social body it must reclaim not only its body but its soul from the state, and institute a discipline which is truly Christlike—a power based in compassion and martyrdom, suffering and reconciliation, and not in a revived Christendom.[12]

And it is likewise the body that is in question in a proper understanding of torture. In November 1973, the Dirección de Inteligencia Nacional, or DINA (later the Centro Nacional de Informaciones, or CNI), began its implementation of the bureaucracy of terror. The following account from a peasant union official is typical. "They put four of us inside a container no bigger than a table. In the dark, we could hear screams all day and sobbing all night. It was how I imagined hell would be. . . . The guards would splash in the pool and pass by the cells, saying they were going to kill this one or castrate that one.[13] The motive seems to be interrogation, and the search for answers apparently justifies the brutality. But the reality is invariably that the torturers already knew the answers. Torture is not the seeking of truth through the imposition of pain, but conformity to the voice of the state.[14]

As Cavanaugh acknowledges, ethical judgments about torture have tended simply to denounce it as evil and demand that it stop. They can be summarized as "Torture is very bad."[15] The claim is generally based on an understanding of individual rights. Torture is regarded as a violation of personal integrity. For Cavanaugh, this is based on a misunderstanding of the nature and purpose of torture. For torture is *not* primarily an attack on individual bodies. Individual bodies suffer great pain and distress; but the purpose of torture is the disintegration of *social* bodies. "Torture is not merely an attack on, but the creation of, individual bodies."[16] Torture is an extreme version of the process common to modernity, of the state dismantling intermediate social bonds in the name of giving individuals equality under the law, with the result that none of the ties and bonds by which medieval persons identified themselves any longer hold sway.

It is not that rights are in any sense equivalent to torture. It is that rights contribute to the atomization of civil society, transferring power from intermediate social bodies to the state as a whole, in the name of protecting the individual. But this protection counts for nothing when a more sinister power atomizes society and leaves the individual naked before the merciless power of the state, as was the case in Chile under the Pinochet regime. There is no one to whom to report and denounce incidents of torture, other than the very state that is carrying out the torture.

Cavanaugh's argument makes it painfully clear that the disappearance of the church (following Pius XI and Jacques Maritain's ecclesiology) was related to the disappearance of bodies in torture. Once the corporate body becomes invisible, there is no body that can safeguard the citizen against the predation of the state. What is required of the church therefore is to reassert itself as a body in its own right. The church's response to torture is not to campaign for individual rights, because the notion of individual rights colludes with the assumption that the individual is at the mercy of the state. Instead, the church needs nothing less than to remember and demonstrate that it is the true body, a body more significant than either individual or state, a body entered in baptism and shaped by the Eucharist. It is the body of Christ.

Reincorporating the Lost

The beginnings of a renewal in the Catholic Church's perception of its role in Chile came first of all through its commitment to the poor. The Committee of Cooperation for Peace in Chile, or COPACHI, was created to address the immediate social fallout from the coup d'état in 1973. Gradually it developed a wide network of parish-based social program. The COPACHI was forced to close by General Pinochet in 1975, but the following day the cardinal created the Vicariate of Solidarity, which expanded the work to a range of legal, informational, and social organizations.

It responded to the neoliberal economic policies of the new government with assistance to unions, with the establishment of cottage industries, and with the fostering of cooperatives in which unemployed people could work together at finding alternative sources of income, train in new skills, and share the burden of daily necessities. Self-employment workshops included shoe-repair and pipe-fitting enterprises. It responded to the dismemberment of the state health system by setting up health clinics to meet primary health care needs. These clinics employed doctors excluded from conventional work by finding themselves on a political blacklist, and trained local people to become nursing assistants. It served children and young people by creating soup kitchens to provide nutritional lunches and by running youth clubs. Gradually the emphasis of the nutritional work moved more toward helping people grow their own vegetables and creating cooperatives to bulk-buy wholesale goods cheaply. Most of the work had an educational dimension, and some explicitly set out to train labor leaders and build capacity among neighborhood organizers. Through these educational programs people learned to name the regime's abuses and discovered that "the only way the regime's social control could be resisted was through cooperation and membership in one another."[17] The Vicariate logged thousands of the regime's abuses, and provided almost the only source of information to rival the government's propaganda. Perhaps most symbolically (and in a way reminiscent of the story of Harry and Robin in chapter 7 above), sewing and handicraft workshops began to use scraps of old material to produce scenes of everyday life known as *arpilleras*, and these tapestries became some of the most significant forms of social protest in Chile.

The focal image of reincorporation portrayed by these programs is that of knitting. Knitting is a perfect image of reincorporation because the strands of wool could represent diverse stories, rejected material, or oppressed and atomized people. Knitting is about the reintegration of diverse strands, and thereby the creation of something beautiful and useful. It is an appropriate image of how reincorporation represents the church's response to torture. Torture and disappearance undermine and attempt to obliterate all social bodies between state and individual. The church, through its program of social solidarity, set about knitting them back together. By constituting a new body, by knitting together a renewed social fabric, the church responded to torture and disappearance. The programs of the Vicariate "refused to recognize and legitimise the omnicompetence of the state over matters bodily."[18]

Another aspect of reincorporation represented by the social programs of the Vicariate was that they were not limited to Catholics alone. Non-

Catholics and non-Christians benefited, especially in relation to work with victims of torture and families of the disappeared. As Cavanaugh notes, this hospitality is an eschatological sign of the final ingathering of God's people in the reconciliation of the world. "The church therefore remembers not only its own martyrs but also the many other victims of the antievangelical powers of the world. As Matthew 25:31–46 startlingly reveals, victims are members or potential members of Christ's body, but this is revealed only on the Last Day."[19] This is particularly true of the soup kitchens, which echo Jesus' prediction that "people will come from east and west, from north and south, will eat in the kingdom of God" (Luke 13:29). These meals are not merely humble gestures made to alleviate basic needs; they are, like the Eucharist, prayers that Christ might come in judgment and institute the kingdom of justice that the heavenly banquet represents.[20] The eschatological perspective sees this heavenly banquet as epistemologically prior to the contingencies of the earthly soup kitchen. The injustices of the regime in Chile are thus judged by the fulfillment of Christ's promises.

Forming Habits

The central argument of *Torture and Eucharist* is that it is the regular practice of the Eucharist that forms and constitutes the body of Christ as a body that is capable of addressing torture. In chapter 6 above I argued for the significance of the imagination in ethics and suggested that the habits and practices of the church formed the moral imagination of Christians. This is how Cavanaugh understands the Eucharist and its importance in Chile. "The Eucharist is much more than a ritual repetition of the past. It is rather a literal re-membering of Christ's body, a knitting together of the body of Christ by the participation of many in his sacrifice. . . . If torture is the imagination of the state, the Eucharist is the imagination of the church."[21] The Eucharist is the principal way in which the church resists torture, because the problem is the invisibility of the church, and the Eucharist more than anything else makes the church visible. "If anyone is to 'discern the body,' then it must become visible in present time. . . . The Eucharist, as the gift which effects the visibility of the true body of Christ, is therefore the church's counter-imagination to that of the state."[22]

Cavanaugh derives his notion of eucharistic imagination from Augustine's understanding of the Eucharist. Augustine argues that human beings can become a sacrifice to God, not because God needs appeasing, but because they belong with him. They are united with him by dying to the world and rising with Christ, being not conformed to the world, but transformed into fellowship with God.

> Christ adopted the form of a servant. His self-gift to humanity, his complete *kenosis*, is such that he gives over his very identity to the community of his followers, who thereby become in history his true Body, which in turn takes the form of a servant. The Christian sacrifice unites both to each other and to God in the body of Christ, so that we become what is offered on the altar. This, says Augustine, is the import of the Eucharist.[23]

Cavanaugh notes, again in the same spirit as chapter 6 above, that the Eucharist is about actions more than words. While contemporary Christians talk about hearing or attending or (in the case of the priest) saying Mass, the early church spoke of doing or making or performing the mysteries. Doing the Eucharist corresponds with other kinds of doing. "The church's performance of self-sacrifice is in fact the 'proof' of the presence of Christ in the bread and wine. In order for the church at the Eucharistic table to offer what Christ offered, the church must offer its own self in sacrifice."[24]

In order to create and maintain a visible body capable of standing apart from the world, the church requires considerable discipline. Discipline is that pattern of practices which strengthens the body so that it can withstand the power of those forces that refuse the sovereignty of Christ. The Eucharist is central to that discipline, because it makes the body visible and because it is the sacrament that anticipates the parousia now. Cavanaugh refers to Cyprian's understanding of discipline in the third century. The body of the believer is the battleground between God and the forces that refuse his sovereignty. This is especially the case in martyrdom; but every day the Christian faces a kind of martyrdom in controlling the body's desires and resisting the world. "The body of the Christian is a microcosm of the church body which is under constant threat from the *saeculum*. Christian discipline is the antidote to the world's attempts to discipline the body."[25]

Hippolytus, the Greek theologian of the early third century, and author of the account of early church practices known as the *Apostolic Tradition*, states how right conduct is required for participation in the Eucharist. The community inquires into the professions of those seeking membership. Brothel-keepers, idol-makers, gladiators, soldiers, magistrates, and prostitutes are among those who are expected to change profession in order to be accepted for baptism. Baptism only goes ahead if the candidate is shown to have performed works of mercy during the three-year preparation: right doctrine is secondary. Likewise in the Eucharist, reconciliation is not just a fruit of participation in the sacrament, but a requirement. Those who are at odds with one another are not to take part. The instructions of Matthew 5:23–26 are crucial: coming to the altar is coming to God's judgment seat; and to come unreconciled is to come unprepared. Paul's warnings in 1 Corinthians 11:27–32 about the fate of those who do not discern the body (and Cavanaugh insists that the body means the church, not just the eucharistic bread) mean that withholding the sacrament from the dire sinner is done for the sinner's sake, and is not simply exercised as a punishment. Referring to the reincorporation of those who had apostasized during the Decian persecution, Cyprian insists on a long penance to retrain as a disciple, to reorient the body and soul of the believer from the discipline of the Roman state to the discipline of the Christian body.[26]

The existence of this understanding of discipline, focused on the Eucharist, makes possible the use in notorious circumstances of excommunication. The Eucharist, with the bishop as president, is the eschatological gathering of the whole body of Christ: exclusion of one unreconciled member is therefore a very serious affair—but one that concentrates the minds of those gathered on the disciplines of being part of the body.

After seven years of the junta, finally in December 1980 seven bishops issued a decree of excommunication for those responsible for conducting or commissioning torture, and for those who could prevent it but do not. No torturers or torture centers were actually named. Nonetheless a threshold had been crossed. At last the language of unity and order that had previously been used to support the regime started to be used to emphasize ecclesial discipline against the marauding state. Torture is recognized as attacking the body of Christ. "Excommunication is an exercise of church discipline which makes, however temporarily and faintly, the true church visible as an alternative society of peace and justice where torture has no place."[27] The specific excommunication of General Pinochet himself never came. A variety of explanations for this have been advanced, largely based on the flawed ecclesiology that hindered the bishops from perceiving the significance of what Pinochet was doing. But despite its only partial implementation in Chile, Cavanaugh demonstrates how integral this practice is to the church's response to oppression—in his own words, "excommunication is one of the clearest examples of how the Eucharist is a resource for the social practice of the church."[28]

Incorporating Gifts

Perhaps the central insight of Cavanaugh's remarkable treatment of Chile under Pinochet is the portrayal of torture as a perverted liturgy. In other words, torture and Eucharist emerge as rival practices that compete to define the social nature of the body. The task of the church in the face of torture is not so much to block it, since it does not have the power do so, but rather to interpret it as a liturgy and to renew its own liturgy in the face of it.

Cavanaugh argues that "torture is a kind of perverted liturgy, a ritual act which organizes bodies in the society into a collective performance, not of true community, but of an atomized aggregate of mutually suspicious individuals."[29] There is a kind of drama going on, in which the victims are made to speak the words of the regime, to "double the voice of the state." The questions and answers do not seek or provide new information but seek to conform the individual to the torturers' reality.

> Torture may be considered a kind of perverse *liturgy*, for in torture the body of the victim is the ritual site where the state's power is manifested in its most awesome form. Torture is liturgy—or, perhaps better said, "anti-liturgy"—because it involves bodies and bodily movements in an enacted drama which both makes real the power of the state and constitutes an act of worship of that mysterious power.[30]

By contrast "the Eucharist is the true 'politics,' as Augustine saw, because it is the public performance of the true eschatological City of God in the midst of another City which is passing away."[31] It is important to understand the relation of the church to the world in this sense. "The point is not to politicise the Eucharist, but to 'Eucharistize' the world."[32]

Cavanaugh narrates the church's liturgical overacceptance of torture by describing the practices of the Sebastian Acevedo Movement against Torture. Sebastian Acevedo was a construction worker whose two children were abducted in November 1983. After three days spent fruitlessly searching for them, he doused himself with gasoline and set himself alight outside the Concepción cathedral. Taking his name, members of the movement began to perform public ritual acts of solidarity and denunciation with their bodies at key locations such as torture houses, courts, government buildings, and media centers. As many as 150 figures would emerge from the crowd, unfurl banners, distribute literature, sing songs, and recite a liturgy detailing the atrocities of the executive and the silence of the judiciary. Usually the police would envelop the protests, but sometimes a ten-minute liturgy would be completed.

These subversive street liturgies not only reclaimed time, in that they anticipated, as the eucharistic liturgy does, the irruption of the kingdom; they also created space, short-term public spaces in which the dominance of the state and its police was subverted. The grip of fear is overcome when a group can defy and satirize. "The future Kingdom of God is brought into the present to bring the world's time under the rule of Divine Providence, and thus create spaces of resistance where bodies belong to God, not the state."[33] Meanwhile the places of torture, which have been hidden, are exposed and made visible through the street liturgies, as if the veil covering them were rent in two. Names of torturers themselves are sometimes made known, and techniques identified. Victims become martyrs.

It is from beginning to end a battle over the body. The bodies of the protestors are gassed, beaten, hosed, and dragged away. Defenseless bodies use their weakness to expose the oppression of the state. "The ritual is designed to make the tortured body, which has been disappeared by the state, miraculously reappear in the bodies of the protestors."[34] Pain is overaccepted by being transcended. "Torture plays on the incommunicability of pain to isolate the victim. Here, however, this isolation is overcome by the sharing of pain."[35] The protestors see themselves as holding chained hands and embracing broken bodies. And, most of all, they identify their sufferings with the tortured Christ. "The bodies of those disappeared reappear in the reappearance of the visible body of Christ."[36] This unity in Christ is, more than anything, the tactic that subverts the isolation of torture. Torture can separate victims from one another, but nothing can separate them from the solidarity of Christ's flogging and nailing, and in that suffering they become martyrs not victims. That sense of being united with one another by participating in Christ's sufferings corresponds to the eucharistic understanding of participation. "Christ's body reappears precisely as a suffering body offered in sacrifice; Christ's body is made visible in its wounds. But this body is also marked with future glory. . . . We witness a liturgical anticipation of the end of history and the resurrection of the body."[37]

Cavanaugh's summary is worth quoting in full. In it he uses language that combines the notions of status, habit, reincorporation, and overaccepting.

> If torture is essentially an anti-liturgy, a drama in which the state realizes omnipotence on the bodies of others, then the Eucharist provides a direct and startling contrast, for in the Eucharist Christ sacrifices no other body but His own. Power is realized in self-sacrifice; Christians join in this sacrifice by uniting their own bodies to the sacrifice of Christ. Christians become a gift to be given away to others, as illustrated in the practices of the Vicaria and the Sebastian Acevedo Movement. In giving their bodies to Christ in the Eucharist, a confession is made, but it is not the voice of the state that is heard. The torturer extracts a confession of the unlimited power of the state. The Eucharist requires the confession that Jesus is Lord of all, and that the body belongs to Him.[38]

12

A Threatening Offer
Flawed Creation

The previous chapter looked at a threatening offer, where the flaw lay in the evil within the human soul. In this chapter I examine a very different kind of flaw—that of chronic disability and illness, a natural evil to balance the human evil of the last chapter. I shall look at two testimonies. One speaks of parenting a child with a profound mental disability. The second tells of personal physical pain compounded by the experience of parenting a child with a chronic debilitating illness. Like the previous chapter, the stories explored here do not crystallize into an ethical "issue": but like the previous chapter, the expectation from the argument of the rest of this book is that this is exactly the kind of context in which "God's works might be revealed."[1]

Forming Habits

The Methodist theologian Frances Young is a professor at Birmingham University. In her book *Face to Face*,[2] she tells the story of her life with her son Arthur, from the joint perspective of theologian and parent. She begins to write in 1984 on the day after her sixteen-year-old son Arthur stood unsupported for a few seconds for the first time. Arthur was born brain-damaged due to a small placenta. Frances Young describes in detail a life that "lacks event . . . a kind of slow motion in which all track of time gets lost."[3] The details concern sleeping in leg splints, withstanding fits, getting dressed, feeding, school, games, bathing, and so on. She goes on to raise questions of grief, frustration, and theodicy, as well as tracing her own vocation to the ministry and discussing the role of the church and wider society with respect to a child like Arthur.

Let us first look at what Frances and Arthur's story tells us about forming skills. Frances Young opens her book with what could be called a detailed, uncritical, dispassionate description of her life with Arthur. It is a description of common behavior in an uncommon situation. The considerable detail demonstrates the depth and complexities of the story: its ethics are not to be decided by detached observers making timely decisions at crisis moments. The heart of the story, as told in Young's first chapter, is of the mundanities of standing, walking, sleeping, dressing, feeding, being a family—mundanities that struggle to become habits. In her detailed account, she recaptures the social significance of common behavior, just as I set out to do in chapter 6.

Alongside Frances Young's story of her life with Arthur I shall set a rather different story. Margaret Spufford is a historian specializing in the seventeenth century who stands in the middle of three generations of profound physical suffering. In her book *Celebration* she tells of the trauma of being ten years old and seeing her mother collapse amid grotesque noises upon having a massive stroke.[4] In her late teens Margaret started to develop serious bone problems that fifteen years later were diagnosed as osteoporosis. She could not sit for more than two hours at a time and she had experiences of agony. She had a looming fear that life after the menopause could be much worse. And into this situation came a daughter, Bridget, and only gradually did it become apparent how ill she was. Bridget was diagnosed with cystinosis, a genetically caused metabolic disease that slowly kills by damaging the kidneys, and her life became a constant cycle of routine (and sometimes horrifying) pain and doctor's interventions. Meanwhile her parents strove to offer emotional normality while instinctively seeking to protect their child. In time the increase in cystine, an ancillary symptom or side effects of treatment, affected her pancreas, thyroid, ligaments, hip, feet, and sight, and the threat of dementia loomed. Bridget's parents faced this stark daily reality:

> Nursing a child who would have died without constant and continuous medical interference, knowing with accurate foreknowledge that she was going to die in a few years, and transforming this situation to a "normal," good, loving, family life that felt as ordinary as possible, given the nursing restrictions. It is an almost impossibly taxing situation.[5]

Frances Young's and Margaret Spufford's accounts have three things in common, all of which relate to the formation of habits. One is that both writers see their stories in the context of their academic studies. Both at different times considered setting aside their vocations and careers, but both were advised that laying down their own lives would be a sacrifice that would not take away their children's suffering, and might well remove a vital source of rhythm and purpose in the family's life. So instead their accounts each tell of their wrestling with pain and frustration through their chosen fields of patristic theology and seventeenth-century social history, and through the patterns of life imposed by the discipline of research and the practices of academic interaction. Both are aware how much the cerebral virtues of research and teaching are a part of their own notion of human flourishing.

Both writers also take for granted, second, that the struggles of their lives must find a place within the central reality of worship. Margaret Spufford credits the regular habit of participating in worship as the reason why she has not followed Ivan Karamazov in "returning her ticket" to heaven:

> Sometimes the complete and total accuracy with which the Eucharist embodies the totality of experience as I know it is in itself nearly unendurable. Like all total accuracy, it also brings relief. Then the Offertory is taken onwards, the action moves from Crucifixion to Transformation and Resurrection. . . .
>
> [I]t is because the celebration of the Eucharist and Christ's offering of himself in it seems to comprehend all the realities of acute pain and death that I have not handed in my ticket.[6]

For Frances Young it is the social dimension of worship that speaks most clearly. She found a particular welcome and a special sense of identity through joining with Christians living in an area of social deprivation, a deprivation that mirrored or refracted a different kind of deprivation in her own life with her son. She describes an experience of community in her worship in an inner-city church, an experience of shared vulnerability. "The sense that every single member of that very assorted congregation mattered and had a gift to contribute and that there was something about even the least to be respected . . . created an atmosphere and a level of relationship which I have scarcely encountered anywhere else."[7]

Having seen diversity accepted in the inner-city church, she was able to take on chaplaincy work at a mentally handicapped hospital with a renewed vision.

One of Origen's arguments for the truth of Christianity was that while philosophy had only made the elite good, Christianity had lifted people of

all levels of society and of every different type and race to a "philosophical"
way of life. . . . Just as male needs female, rich needs poor, white needs
black, so intellectuals need the simple. . . . The church is itself when it
bridges all these gaps and tensions between people of different kinds.[8]

What she has described here is the way worship forms character, and
how a community that worships faithfully together learns to take the
right things for granted.

And, third, this confluence of suffering and worship led in the case
of both writers to a specific vocation. Frances Young was called to the
ordained ministry in the Methodist Church, and Margaret Spufford was
called to be an oblate amongst Anglican Benedictine sisters. As Spufford
puts it, "all I have is the hardly prayable prayer of the Annunciation."[9] In
the habits and practices and disciplines of their religious traditions, the
two writers find a rhythm of life that affirms and challenges the otherwise
dominant narrative of need they experience as parents.

Accepting and Blocking

Both writers give over considerable space in their accounts to the
heartfelt soul searchings and mental bargainings that followed the di-
agnosis of chronic problems, and both acknowledge that these times of
bewilderment have never been fully resolved.

A number of ways of what this book has called "blocking" present
themselves. Both writers acknowledge the sense of death as a way out.
Margaret Spufford describes the troubled conscience shared by a fellow
parent in Great Ormond Street Hospital. "After eighteen months, one
night she could not stand the screaming and the endless prospect of
her son's pain, and had put a pillow over his face, intending to suffocate
him. She had taken it away in time, but the guilt and the memory would
not leave her alone."[10]

This is a form of blocking that arises from stress, but there is another
form of blocking that arises from intolerance of difference—particularly
in relation to people with a severe mental disability. In a success- and
independence-oriented culture, it is easy for retardation to be seen as an
evil that needs to be eliminated. "Our society is really only interested in
achievers; it admires the handicapped who achieve, like the blind student
at university, or the wheelchair-bound marathon-runner."[11] Sometimes
the severely mentally disabled are kept out of public sight—in institutions, often geographically secluded. Another approach is to dispose
of those whose difference is intolerable. A third approach is to assume
that there is no difference between the mentally disabled and the rest of

society—to obscure any suggestion to the contrary by means of euphemisms such as "differently abled." Each of these approaches represents a failure to cope with difference.

More subtle is the realization that this child will not grow away from its parents in what the parents might regard as a natural or at least conventional way. Frances Young acknowledges the sense of despair, facing up to the difficulty in perceiving what kind of a life Arthur might have, and "voicing my protest at the success of antibiotics which kept children like Arthur alive into adulthood for no reason at all; was there not a moral difference between killing and letting nature take its course? Next time Arthur had a chest infection, why could I not refuse treatment?"[12]

The reverse of this is what Frances Young calls the "I will do anything" syndrome. This is an obsessive need to make things better that she regards as probably inevitable for parents in such a situation. For example, "armies of friends and relatives are needed who will devote their whole lives to getting the maximum development out of the handicapped child . . . twelve hours a day," resulting not infrequently in family breakdown.[13] Margaret Spufford similarly acknowledges her debt to those who persuaded her to continue her own life and maintain that of the rest of the family in spite of the intense demands of caring for Bridget.

Another kind of blocking emerges as both authors recognize the ambivalence of the notion of healing. For Frances Young, seeking healing in a case like Arthur's is a masked form of blocking.

> Suppose . . . all his damaged brain cells were miraculously healed, what then? Brains gradually develop over the years through learning. There are twenty-two years of learning process that he has missed out on. . . . I find it impossible to envisage what it would mean for him to be "healed" because what personality there is is so much part of him *as he is*, with all his limitations. "Healed" he would be a different person.
>
> . . . I have no doubt it is possible to maximise potential, to stimulate other cells to take over lost functions, and so on. But . . . to arouse hopes of miraculous healing seemed to me to be dangerous and cruel, delaying the effective acceptance of the situation in a positive way.[14]

Margaret Spufford's reflections on healing are more sanguine, being concerned for example with the emotional deprivation of her adolescence. "A very large proportion of the healing process, it seems to me, is to come to accept, with some kind of loving tolerance, that it is so, that the deficiencies which frighten you remain, . . . but that you are still usable, and can still be used."[15]

More subtle still is the blocking that is disguised as piety. Frances Young was told that one could see the soul peeping out through Arthur's eyes. She finds meaningless the notion of a soul that thrives in contra-diction to the damaged brain and resultant incapacity to make sense of or communicate with the world, and unsustainable the notion that the soul is separable from the body. "To justify [Arthur's] condition in terms of the soul peeping out through the eyes which will be refined by the afflictions of this world and suddenly come to some sort of flowering in the life to come, is entirely implausible. . . . There is no 'ideal' Arthur somehow trapped in this damaged physical casing. He is a psychoso-matic whole."[16] Frances Young points out that the scriptural view of the resurrection of the body gives no justification to this common notion of the escape of the soul.

Two further kinds of blocking are observed. One is the inclination humbly to recognize that others are worse off than oneself. Margaret Spufford discovered that this was avoidance, not engagement.

> I must somewhere have acquired some muddled thinking about "count-ing one's blessings" and "looking on the bright side of things." . . . It took me a while to discover that I was actually stopping myself from getting on with living by trying to persuade myself that there was no problem. . . . [A] failure to face one's own problem, because one feels guilty in the face of someone else's difficulties—which can, by definition, only be imagined, probably wrongly—assists no one. . . . One can only live where one is, now.[17]

The final form of blocking, and perhaps most subtle of all, is laughter. What can be an insight into and glimpse of heaven can also be a barrier to truthfulness.

> I think laughter at your own utter absurdity brings home your own total inadequacy and dependence on grace, which is very necessary. . . . A strong sense of the absurd is a very useful ally.
> But laughter can also accidentally turn into armour-plating, and im-prison the wearer. Sometimes grief does need expression. We had so much grief to carry that we were desperately afraid of boring anyone with it. . . . The people we came to value most highly were those with whom we could be honest, and those from whom we did not feel we had to shield our grief or anxiety.[18]

How does a community begin to "accept" a severely mentally disabled child? The communal virtue mentioned most often by Frances Young is the acceptance of difference. The way disabled people are perceived is itself an ethic. To begin reflection by saying "How should the church treat mentally disabled people?" is already too late. Disability is already a moral notion—one that asserts that there is a norm and that those who fulfill this norm get to name and describe those who differ in significant ways, putting the latter at a disadvantage. The disadvantages that result from most conditions derive more from society's prejudices than from the disability itself. The question should be more like this: "What kind of community is required that can welcome and care for the other in its midst without that 'otherness' being used to justify discrimination?" What is required is to become "that kind of people who are capable of recognising the other without fear and/or resentment."[19]

Truthful stories such as Frances Young's remind Christians of both the necessity and the cost of rearing severely mentally disabled children in the family. But the recognition of difference is implicit in the delegation to the family of the rearing of *all* children. For those who are different know that being treated equally is not sufficient for being treated justly. If being treated equally means having to forget who one is, then the price is not worth paying, as the experience of black Americans bears out. It goes beyond equality. "The commitment of parents to their retarded children . . . implies a more profound and richer sense of community than the language of equality can provide. . . . The retarded are a concrete test of the moral implications of a society's willingness to let the differences occasioned by our familial heritages flourish."[20]

Thus the church starts with what it already takes for granted—that parents should bring up their own children, even if the parents are strange (or sick, like Margaret Spufford) or the children different (or sick, like Bridget)—and see that this assumption makes diversity inevitable. The challenge is not to make new decisions, but to face the consequences of assumptions already made.

Assessing Status

Status is a very significant issue in all parent-child relationships, and throughout the language of "disability" and sickness, particularly in all questions of mental well-being. I shall suggest four dimensions in which status has an important bearing on these issues.

The first dimension is the question of whose story this is. Both Margaret Spufford's and Frances Young's accounts beg the question of whose story is being told. It is notoriously difficult to tell a story from the point of view of all the parties involved. Is it a story of need: the parents' (or families') need for community support, the child's need for parents, the parents' need to be needed, or the community's need for parents of character, who will not shy away from the discomforts of such parenting and the lack of hope? Or is it a story of learning: the child learning from the parents to live, the parents learning from the child what being a parent means, the community learning from both what the issues at stake are and whether "experts" are the best placed to settle them? Or is it a story in which all the parties discover on their "journey" that their own self-understanding needs reassessment: parents reassess why people have children, communities reassess what they mean by "achievement," "normal," "suffering," and indeed "community" itself (which community, for example, do we have in mind?), while the child grows and gains some self-understanding for the first time? Or is it merely a story of the marginalization of the weak and different by the strong and normal, in which the child (if mentally disabled) cannot share the parents' or community's benefits, the parents cannot share the child's inner life, and the community (including the experts) can never understand the grief, struggle, joy, or insight of the parents? In a significant way, Margaret Spufford's account is the more complex of the two because it tells the story of a sufferer who is at the same time a caregiver.[21]

Margaret Spufford speaks of the shock of facing a decision about whether Bridget should go ahead with a kidney transplant and realizing that, now that Bridget was nineteen, the decision had nothing to do with her parents. This presented the parents with an extreme status paradox: "if the decision and the power were nothing to do with us, the responsibility of the background care was still entirely ours. And to be utterly powerless, and almost completely responsible, is a bad combination."[22] Frances Young describes a related process of renouncing the need to exert power over people's lives. Realizing that her need to control Arthur's life derived from her own needs and not from his, she became more detached and allowed him to be more free from his parents' instinct for possessiveness. The status issues become similar to those expressed in chapter 6 above. Christian community is not about those in the center succoring those on the margins: this would be another "strategy" of the powerful. The Christian tactic is to find itself on the periphery and make friends with those others it finds there. But this leads to some profound paradoxes.

The second dimension of status is the subtle critique that needy children make of society in general. Frances Young appeals to the medieval understanding of the holy fool. For William Langland, in *Piers Plowman*,

> The "lunatics" who take no thought for the morrow, and do not kow-tow to anyone are "God's apostles," the only incorruptible members of society. They are to be valued and given hospitality. They perform a very special kind of service to society, in being a comment on the attitudes of everyone else. It reminds me of the long-standing, but very odd, Christian tradition that some are called to be "fools for Christ": there were those who quite deliberately concealed themselves in the guise of witless and irresponsible beggars, living on trust, as a way of ascetic discipleship.[23]

Young goes on to point out that people like Arthur are not failed versions of somebody else: they can be something that no one else can be. "The basic truthfulness, lack of inhibitions, and that indefinable virtue—simplicity—often seen in the mentally handicapped, may be the very qualities that it would be criminal to educate out of them. This could be their potential—and an area where the rest of us fail desperately."[24]

The third dimension of status is the way that deeply needy children become a microscope through which the rest of society is explicitly judged. Frances Young is unapologetic about this.

> Handicap is a kind of judgment. Clearly it is not some kind of punishment for sin. . . . Handicap discriminates between those who rise to the occasion, and those who fail to do so. It discriminates between the good marriage and the shaky marriage, the stable family and the unstable family. . . . In this life it has to be borne, with all its accompanying distress and pain. There is a sense in which we can "do" nothing about it. . . . But the way we handle it is crucial for the creation of true human values and true human community. It provides a constant living parable of frailty, but also of its potential transcendence through the grace of God.[25]

The times in which the church has faced judgment most acutely—particularly in the persecution of the early centuries—have tended to be the times when the church has been the strongest and most true to itself. The church needs, she says, to "discover how to follow Christ in taking the judgment upon ourselves on behalf of our society and our world. . . . [T]hat purging and testing is the process whereby the miracle of grace is brought about. In a sense this is what I have lived through and what this book has been about."[26]

The fourth dimension of status is the realization that the story could not be told without these most needy of people. Frances Young recalls a tramp who often calls on her, and often says as he leaves her door, "I always say a prayer for you, lady." This "reflects a view that goes right back to the time of the early church, namely that the rich are dependent on the poor for their salvation."[27] She points out that "there is a sense in which we are all handicapped"; and likewise "it's not the handicapped who need community care—it's US. To learn from the handicapped requires a new heart and a new spirit within us, but . . . it will be our salvation."[28] She adds, later, "in a sense we normal people are the rich: our judgement comes in the way we respond to the challenge of the handicapped, they provide us with an opportunity for repentance, and so we depend on them for our redemption."[29]

Thus the most needy have come from the fringes of the story to the center, and from the center of the story to a Christlike place, the stone that the builders rejected that becomes the cornerstone of salvation.

Questioning Givens

Among the many givens that appear to present themselves in Margaret Spufford's and Frances Young's accounts, three stand out.

The first is that this is an enlightened and humane modern world in which suffering and evil have in large part been eradicated. Margaret Spufford recalls, with deep and conscious irony, the observation of a social anthropologist that "we are very handicapped in two ways, you know: we cannot understand the meaning of chronic pain, and we do not any longer understand the meaning of ritual." She thought of explaining to him that these were in fact the two central realities of her life—but decided not to bother. Instead she reflects,

> Am I, I wonder, profoundly privileged, or profoundly handicapped, by being, as it were, an insider in the tradition of the lives of the people I study? . . . What may be different is that I do not regard the evils which torment me as punishment from the hand of God, or signs of his wrath. I do, though, share their belief that these evils may be turned to his purposes.[30]

The second apparent given is that the therapeutic optimism of contemporary medicine is the principal lens through which issues of profound need should be perceived. Frances Young neatly summarizes this culture.

> Because science has apparently been so successful—particularly medical science so successful in ridding us of so many of the common ills of human life, so that infant mortality has dropped drastically and length of life expanded beyond belief compared with even a century ago—the delusion of our society is that humanity can resolve all its problems, and *something* can be done about *everything*. Even if we cannot yet cure a given condition, research presses on in the confidence that one day we will, and meanwhile effective therapies are devised to ameliorate its effects. At the very least this keeps up morale. So programmes are clothed in ambitious quasi-scientific language, what is done is given sanction by the appeal to the enhancement of human dignity, and an effective diversion from facing up to the reality of the situation is created.[31]

However, Margaret Spufford relates in vivid detail the other side of this coin. She describes the human cost in family life of an apparently limitless series of medical interventions, designed to ameliorate conditions, correct side effects, introduce new organs, test out new equipment and treatments, and so on endlessly.

> I do think it has taxed my husband and me almost to the limit, and there are times when I wonder frankly how much longer I can endure the pain and uncertainty of it. The situation itself is almost unendurable. Essentially, modern medicine sticks a family down on one of the "frontiers of medical knowledge," and says "Make your home here, and make it a good one; make your children secure, and safe, and loved." We try, but could anyone succeed?[32]

The third apparent given, related to the second, is that the goal of care for the most needy is "normality." The term "disability" implies a "fall" away from the norm. In a context where it is felt "something should be done about everything" it becomes difficult to recognize a condition like Arthur's as in any sense natural. The dominant language is that of "potential." This is helpful in that it affirms that the most needy children are "different" not "sub-." But the tendency is to equate normalization with realizing potential. Frances Young questions this assumption.

> Does self-help, if it has been mechanically drilled into behaviour and is merely the response of an automaton, actually increase dignity? . . . Isn't behaviour modification . . . a way of manipulation and a denial of true humanity? . . . Might not the real triumph be the ability to receive from one another, to discover interdependence, to find values which make success and death equally irrelevant? Should we not allow the handicapped to stimulate questioning about the value of autonomy and conformity, and look for other forms of transformation?[33]

This brings us to the beginnings of overaccepting.

Incorporating Gifts

As Frances Young notes, in words that could have come from chapter 9 above, "the desire to exclude may be an inevitable reaction, but it is not the effective answer. The desire to deny that any anomaly exists may be the other way out, but that is a delusion. Somehow the reality of difference must be accepted so that something new and creative may emerge."[34] There are three kinds of overaccepting in the two accounts that fulfill this longing for something new and creative.

One kind of overaccepting is to see the parent's struggle as part of the larger struggle of humanity with life and with God. Frances Young identifies with the story of Jacob wrestling with a man at the Jabbok ford. Jacob was wounded, but would not let the man go until he had received a blessing. He realized that it was God with whom he had wrestled, and who gave him a new name, Israel. "I had to go on wrestling. I will always be marked by the struggle. But it is through it that I have seen God. . . . I too have demanded a blessing before I would let go, and I have received it."[35] A slightly different version of overaccepting in the same vein is to see the role of those caring for a child like Arthur as aspiring to be "very special parents" who will experience "stronger faith and richer love" through the vocation they have been chosen to perform.[36] Margaret Spufford's insight, derived from Pierre Teilhard de Chardin, is similar in relation to the sufferer of pain: "it is exactly those who bear in their enfeebled bodies the weight of the moving world who find themselves, by the just dispensation of providence, the most active factors in that very progress which seems to sacrifice and to shatter them."[37]

A second kind of overaccepting realizes that the experience is one that cannot be determined but must be actively received. Margaret Spufford cites W. H. Vanstone's understanding of God as the great creator-artist, subject to the discipline of all art. Vanstone's words closely resemble the argument set out in chapter 10 above.

> We see, at the moment of lost control, the most intense endeavour of the artist: and his greatness lies in his ability to discover ever-new reserves of power to meet each challenge of precarious adventure. . . . The problem arises not because the artist has chosen the "wrong" form but because he has chosen *some kind* of form. . . . One must "find the way" in which, through risk and failure and the redemption of failure, the other may be able to receive.
>
> . . . The demand on the artist is to overcome the unforeseeable problem, to handle it in such a way that it becomes a new and unforeseen richness in his work. The artist fails not when he confronts a problem but when he abandons it: and he proves his greatness when he leaves no problem abandoned. Our faith in the Creator is that he leaves no problem abandoned and no evil unredeemed.[38]

Margaret Spufford adds that she now defines "almighty" as "there is no evil out of which good cannot be brought."[39] As Frances Young makes clear, the way God "overcomes the unforeseeable problem" is to take it into himself. "Jesus did not waft away the darkness of this world, all its sin and suffering and hurt and evil, with a magic wand. He entered right into it, took it upon himself, bore it, and in the process turned it into glory, transformed it."[40] Margaret Spufford adopts a similar pattern in her response to the pain of her own condition:

I have found it to be somehow *absorbing darkness*—a physical or mental suffering of my own, or worse, of someone else's—into my own person, my own body, or my own emotions. We have to allow ourselves to be open to pain. Yet all the while we must resist any temptation to assent to it being other than evil. If we are able to do this, to act, as it were, as a blotting paper for pain, without handing it on in the form of bitterness or resentment or of hurt to others—then somehow in some incomprehensible miracle of grace, some at least of the darkness may be turned to light.[41]

Frances Young also recognizes the key role of active receiving, although her notion is on a more human level. Nonetheless her notion of receiving complements that of Vanstone. "Those of us who are privileged in society think we ought to give to the less privileged, but so easily that becomes charity at arm's length, or a sense of debilitating good because we don't do enough, or patronage. What we need to do is receive. . . . To receive from someone is to accord them a deeper respect, and to do them far more good than to give them our charity."[42] She explains what this means in relation to Arthur, again in words that echo the description of overaccepting in chapter 9 above.

The key, it seems to me, is in establishing a reciprocal relationship with the handicapped. The most fundamental aspect of this is the recognition, not that we are doing them good, but that they are doing something for us. The thing that finally resolved my distress was the discovery that I had to give thanks for Arthur. It was no longer a case of accepting him, but rejoicing in him and receiving from him. . . . It is with him that I find the fruits of the Spirit: love, joy, peace, patience, kindness, goodness, faithfulness, humility and self-control.[43]

A third kind of overaccepting sees the most needy people as redefining the whole understanding of God. Frances Young hints at this when she sees Christ as "marginalised, vulnerable, exposed to the sins of the human race," in short, like many disabled people, the scapegoat. She is also alive to redefining humanity in terms of weaknesses as well as potential. But a full understanding of how God is revealed in such stories, and how the church may learn to overaccept, requires a revision of the kind of story that is being told. Earlier I listed four possible themes that could each be regarded as central in the telling of the same story: need, learning, the journey of discovery, and marginalization. Each is attractive as a unifying theme. Marginalization appeals to the Christian concern for the weak and downtrodden—though it is important to remember that the most needy are integral members of Christian community, not simply recipients of charity. The journey of discovery appeals to a positive approach to the most needy, but may not do justice to the suffering involved. Learning clearly has an important place, so long as learning that life is under God's direction is not limited to the tragic climax of Creon (in Sophocles' *Antigone*), who through suffering has become wise.

The theological issue here is that of need. The issue in question is the same as between Athanasius and Arius in the fourth century: is the dependent, derived Son a blot upon God's divinity or, from the perspective of self-communicating love, a mode of its perfection? There must be a receptive, dependent, needy pole within the being of God.

Like God therefore, severely mentally disabled people show the church the character of human neediness; they are "a prophetic sign of our true nature as creatures destined to need God and, thus, one another." Centrally,

> The challenge of learning to know, be with, and care for the retarded is nothing less than learning to know, be with, and love God. God's face is the face of the retarded; God's body is the body of the retarded; God's being is that of the retarded. For the God we Christians must learn to worship is not a God of self-sufficient power, a God who in self-possession needs no one; rather ours is a God who needs a people, who needs a Son. Absoluteness of being or power is not a work of the God we have come to know through the cross of Christ.[44]

Frances Young confesses that her experience with Arthur has placed her face to face with God—hence the title of the book. And Margaret Spufford's book is remarkably, miraculously, called *Celebration*.

Reincorporating the Lost

Reincorporation is a backward-looking exercise: it seeks out the lost or neglected parts of the tradition and restores them to a place in the fulfillment of the story. Frances Young describes an evening at a fellowship group in which reincorporation on a personal level took place at the instigation of one member's remark: the result is a vivid portrayal of the transformation of fate into destiny.

> I began by confessing that every now and again things happened which revealed that I still had not resolved my deepest questioning. . . . When I had finished my long confession, one member of the group commented that it sounded like a tragedy, and yet what a rich life I had had. It still felt like a tragedy, living with meaninglessness. . . . The tragedy was not so much Arthur as my sense of abandonment, my inability to accept the existence and love of God at those deeper levels where it makes a real dif-

ference to one's life. . . . I had no hope for the future. Despair was lodged deep down inside. . . . It felt like tragedy. Yet my friend's comment on the richness of my life came across as a healthy rebuke. It is since that evening that I have been enabled to climb out of my black hole and find complete release from the doubts and fears and self-concern that had imprisoned me.[45]

Frances Young considers fate and destiny in her prelude—and, with hindsight, decisively favors the latter.

I can only look back on all that has happened with a sense of gratitude and awareness of the grace of providence. Somehow now God seems behind and before everything. . . . [I]t is there in the Bible; whether you look at Jeremiah, or the Psalms, or Paul, you find that sense that God had known, consecrated and appointed even before birth, a sense of destiny.[46]

In her personal narrative, Frances Young is especially aware of this in relation to her call to ordination. She talks of feeling overwhelmed by the sense that God had loved her all along, "and somehow everything in my life fell into place." She found herself fulfilling the vocation of her dead brother Richard, while her other brother had fulfilled Richard's other vocation to be a cellist. "Somehow between us we had fulfilled what the lost member of the family should have been."[47]

Reincorporation on a community level takes place most visibly in worship. Frances Young describes a sense of profound identification with adults in a residential hospital for people with mental disabilities. She was particularly struck by the sense of grace at the receiving of communion.

Before God we were all equally vulnerable human beings in need of his grace. . . . The rush to the rail, the grateful "thank you," the simple receptivity, seemed to bring a new depth to what we shared together. . . . To receive with that simple desire and genuine gratitude, trusting that here is the bread of life . . . would that we were all like that every time we communicated.[48]

In sum, "in sharing the confession and absolution, the communion and celebration of the handicapped, and of people very different from myself, I have experienced a foretaste of the heavenly banquet."[49]

Having explored the significance of reincorporation on the level of personal narrative and corporate experience, Frances Young, third, touches on the way a whole people may be able to reintegrate its lost elements.

There is this intractable "crookedness" in humanity, and you cannot make it straight simply by re-definition. . . .

Once we have defined it, how can we "sacralise" it? "The special kind of treatment which some religions accord to anomalies and abominations to make them powerful for good," said Mary Douglas, "is like turning weeds and lawn cuttings into compost." What you throw away becomes manure, contributing to new life.[50]

In conclusion the final unity of the severely mentally disabled and the "able-bodied" is an eschatological one, portrayed perhaps in the relation of the *gerim* to the Israelites in the Old Testament. The *gerim* were sojourners or resident aliens who could not be integrated into society. In other words the analogy for the mentally disabled is not the poor or marginalized, for there is no question of full integration. The analogy is of the sojourner, who always reminds the Israelite that once the Israelites were sojourners in Egypt. Part of the experience of the able-bodied is that, in the land of the mentally disabled, they too feel like resident aliens. And in the language of the New Testament, the whole people of God are *gerim*, longing for their homecoming in heaven.[51]

13

A Promising Offer
Perfectible Bodies

Accepting and Blocking

Cloning means the production of an identical copy of an organism by manipulating the genetic material of another organism without a sexual interaction of any kind. It is the DNA equivalent of a photocopy. It occurs naturally in the case of identical twins. It is important to note at the outset that the general term cloning refers to three separate practices, which are advocated on different grounds by different people. These are reasons to "accept" cloning. I propose now to go through each of these three practices, explaining why each has its advocates.

Babies for Life

Perhaps the most common notion of cloning is the one closest to science fiction—to clone, gestate, and bring to birth a human being, in much the same way as Dolly the sheep came to be born on the 277th attempt in 1997. Scientists are a long way from being able to do this for humans, but a few well-publicized geneticists are actively researching in this area. Besides the scientific thrill, why should anyone want to do such a thing? I suggest four possible scenarios.[1]

185

1. Childlessness. Imagine Sam and Kerry were several years into what they saw as a lifelong union, still in love but sadly childless. They had tried everything that technology offered but with no fruit. Given the widespread desire in contemporary society to have children (and parents) of one's own genetic inheritance (I refer to misgivings over adoption), it would seem logical to try this new method of having children of one's own.

2. Bone marrow. Imagine a second scenario. Suppose Sam became very ill and required a bone marrow transplant. No compatible bone marrow could be found. The possibility of cloning Sam in order that his child might provide the required bone marrow becomes irresistible, especially from Kerry's point of view. Can you imagine, if the technology were available and Kerry had the money, explaining to her that she couldn't do it?

3. Child death. Imagine a third scenario. Imagine that Sam and Kerry did succeed in having a child by conventional means and that they loved her dearly but that, in accordance with every parent's nightmare, at six months old she had a terrible accident that over the next two weeks led to her death. Surely one could understand Sam and Kerry's desire to clone the child in order to come to terms with the situation.

4. Lesbianism. Imagine a fourth scenario. Imagine that Sam and Kerry were both women. Imagine that they lived in a society that had passed laws preventing discrimination against lesbian and gay people. But this society continued to prize genetic continuity between parent and child. Would not cloning seem an attractive option for Sam and Kerry then?

Organs for Medical Use

Despite the appeal of some of these claims, many advocates of cloning would not go so far as to desire the cloning of a fully fledged human being. A more modest form of cloning would be to reproduce individual organs—a liver, for example, or an ear—for transplantation. In fact, even more modest forms of cloning—using cloned bacteria or human cells to produce human proteins, such as insulin for diabetes—are already routine. Cloning techniques applied to mice to generate new organs and even whole animals are used in biomedical research for a wide range of purposes, such as the search for a cure for multiple sclerosis, cystic fibrosis, and hemophilia. A blanket ban on cloning would include work that is already commonplace. Though it is not unusual for people to react to cloning by saying that it is not "natural," one should be aware that there are already a host of practices surrounding human reproduction and biomedical research that would be hard to describe as "natural" in any conventional sense.

Embryos for Research

Perhaps the most significant area in the short term is a third practice, that of cloning embryos who will never become anything more than embryos, and using those embryos not to generate new citizens but for experimental research. This research would help to treat degenerative diseases and spinal cord injuries, as well as opening the way to discoveries in early embryo development and cell differentiation. Some of this research is already being carried out on "spare" eggs fertilized during assisted-conception processes such as in vitro fertilization. It is this third area, embryo cloning, that is up for discussion at the present time, since the technology is nearly available and the benefits of research are easy to understand.

The issue focuses on stem cells. Stem cells maintain and repair tissues; without them, the brain, liver, skin, gut, and blood systems could not function. It used to be thought that these adult stem cells only made cells of one type, so that liver stem cells only made liver, and so on. It has recently become clear that adult stem cells can be reprogrammed, so that cells from the bone marrow, for example, can form liver, brain, and other organs. This opens up the possibility of repairing a sick tissue by injecting manipulated adult stem cells from another tissue, for example by using bone marrow stem cells to repair a badly damaged liver. But there is another possible source of stem cells: human embryos. If manipulated correctly, these stem cells can generate cells from all the different organs in the body. In cell culture in the laboratory and in animal experiments, embryonic stem cells have been shown to be able to repair damaged tissues, for example in models of Parkinson's disease. The drawback is that generating each batch of embryonic stem cells requires an average of six human embryos to be destroyed.[2]

In reality many years of research are needed to validate either form of stem cell as a viable treatment. Nonetheless the messianic promises of certain stem-cell researchers dominate the debate. The paraplegic is set to walk and those imprisoned by brain disease are on the brink of being freed. Who could block this remarkable offer?

I would like now to move on to the areas in which there have been criticisms of cloning from a variety of sources. These are reasons to "block" cloning. I shall distinguish two broad lines of argument, the first maintaining that cloning is wrong in itself, the second concentrating on the undesirable consequences likely to arise from cloning.

Deontological Objections to Cloning

One line of objection is along deontological lines, concerned with the process in itself.

1. Dignity. Perhaps the most common criticism is that cloning is an affront to human dignity. This way of arguing goes back to the late-eighteenth-century German philosopher Immanuel Kant, whose widely respected categorical imperative maintained that one should always treat others as ends, rather than means. Cloning is therefore wrong because it treats people as objects, rather than subjects. The child or embryo becomes an object of manipulation. A person who results from the process could hardly be seen as a gift—but rather more as a product. What would happen to "mistakes" that come into being? Would they not inevitably be thrown away? This is a situation that already arises in relation to certain kinds of assisted fertilization. It is also argued that cloning violates the dignity of the parent, not just the child. Reproduction is taken out of the province of human relationship and placed in the lap of impersonal technology.

2. Choice. Underlying this sense of violation is an implication that cloning is an abuse of power. It appears that an embryo has no choice, no future prospect of life, and is a mere toy in the hands of researchers. This seems to be a straightforward case of the weak being at the mercy of the strong. In a society that prizes individual choice very highly, this is an argument that earns close attention. It is particularly pertinent in the case of the six embryos that are required to generate each batch of stem cells. In the case of full-fledged cloning, the problem is even greater: for every live healthy "Dolly" born, hundreds of malformed animals are created, most of whom die in utero.

3. Resources. The abuse-of-power argument can be extended beyond the one-to-one relationship. One can see the whole project of developing extensive technologies to allow parents to have children "of their own" as being highly questionable. Even if the technology became generally available, in the aged populations of the West, demand would far outstrip supply. There are so many children in the world dying of malnutrition, so many whose growth is inhibited by chronic hunger, that it would seem more worthy to attend to their needs than to find ever more complex ways of augmenting the privileges of the few. How can one seek to generate and nurture new children when there are so many already deprived of minimal welfare?

Consequential Objections to Cloning

The second set of arguments against cloning dwell less on the act itself than on the likely consequences. These are of two kinds: one concentrates on the cloning and birth of children, the other on the misuse of technology.

1. Psychology. Some of these consequences affect the children themselves. What would be the psychological effects on a person who discovered he or she was genetically the same as someone else? How would he or she be treated by others? In a world where so many problems can be traced to the difficulty found in coping with difference—of class, race, religion, color, nationality—there would be an even more profound difference, ironically one based on sameness. It is not difficult to imagine a new apartheid developing by which clones are not treated as true human beings.

2. Physiology. Dolly showed signs of premature aging. All adults have damaged DNA, containing mutations that can give rise to diseases like cancer; these mutations would be transmitted to the clone and might contribute to an accelerated aging process. It seems that not only would the clone be different, but he or she would begin life with a profound physiological disadvantage.

3. The family. Some of the fears address the likely effect on society as a whole. There seems to be at work in cloning a dangerous desire to control the future. This is a deeply conservative impulse, one that assumes that all that could be wished for is already here, and that there are no grounds for faith or hope. What would happen to the family if its place in reproduction could simply be bypassed? Would it be possible to develop clones who lived much longer than the rest of the population, and, if so, would the population increase unsustainably? Questions of this kind can be deeply unsettling and point out the irony involved in trying to manage the future. Unforeseen side effects are the curse of new technologies.

4. Master race. Thus far I have assumed the good faith of those advocating cloning, but it is not difficult to imagine more sinister motives. Perhaps the most widespread concern about the misuse of technology is the fear of power falling into the wrong hands. The genetic experimentation by the Nazis in their concentration camps during the 1940s is well known. It evokes an apocalyptic picture of the attempt to produce a master race by cold-blooded genetic means.

Questioning Givens

The debate about human cloning is a complex one, particularly so because the three dimensions of cloning outlined at the beginning of this chapter appeal to different constituencies. Many who, for example, long for embryo research to relieve the condition of a child with a currently untreatable genetic disorder would nonetheless recoil from the prospect of the full-scale cloning of babies. Another reason why the debate is complex is that in many cases the advocates and opponents of the new technology share a host of largely unquestioned assumptions that are common in contemporary North Atlantic cultures.

The way the debate is conventionally set up, it is a battle between those who are clinging to outdated religious and cultural comfort blankets (false givens) and those who are bravely opening up a realm of new possibilities, with exciting prospects for the quality and quantity of human life. But this configuration of the arguments misses the fact that advocates for human cloning have their own givens. These givens are ones that are shared with a great deal of the culture of health care in the contemporary West.

Two recent cases in the United Kingdom made these assumptions transparent. In the children's hospital in Liverpool known as Alder Hey it came to light that one particular consultant had been undertaking the sequestration of a quite extraordinary number of organs, to the bewilderment of bereaved parents. The organs were apparently taken for the benefit of research, and thus for the wider benefit of society. However the parents appeared to have no idea of what the consultant seemed to regard as this quite reasonable practice. Now the collection of specimens from dead bodies is hardly new; it would be impossible to tell the history of medicine without the taboos broken by medieval anatomists. But anatomy and autonomy belong to different mind-sets.

Attention immediately focused on the professor at the center of the story. Why so many organs might be required remains a mystery. More significant seems to be the attitude toward the dying children. The central good, in the eyes of the professor and his colleagues, seems to have been life itself. Nothing wrong with that, we might say, but look at the practices entailed by this assumption. If life is the central good, and a child has, sadly, given up the struggle for life, there are two ways that child can still serve the central good: their organs can either directly save another life by transplant, or indirectly save many lives by being used for research. In a kind of Platonic move, the individual dying child is secondary or instrumental to the greater good of the "form" of Life itself. This way of putting the matter sounds much less agreeable, and perhaps this discomfort accounts for the reticence of the hospital in thoroughly explaining the situation to the parents. After all, it takes a lot of courage to face grieving parents with the truth. It transpired that appropriate parental consent had not been gained. The anguished response of many of the unfortunate parents was to focus on the particular organs of their own precious child, thus restoring the dignity that had been lost in the professor's instrumental view. Funeral services took place in relation to various anatomical parts—some great, some much smaller. The irony of this is that both the professor and these parents displayed rival but complementary philosophies. Both had faith in the preservation of life—the former in the future life of other children, the latter in the respect and care for the organs of the individual child.

Another painful recent case, that of the Siamese twins from the island of Gozo in Malta, Jodie and Mary, reveals a great deal about contemporary nostrums. Just as the Alder Hey case demonstrated the assumption that life is the central good in the National Health Service, so the case of Jodie and Mary reveals assumptions about what form that life should take. In the modern world people are valued by their ability to be independent, to live what many like to call a "normal" life. If anyone was never going to live a normal life, it was Jodie and Mary. Jodie and Mary were born as twins who had separate heads and upper bodies, but who were united around their middle bodies and formed a single body with a head at either end. Their parents came to Britain because they believed their children were a gift and that that gift could be treasured in Britain more than anywhere else. They entered a culture in which the assumption of central good of independence and autonomy has attained such prized status that few people notice it. It is in the air and the water, and it has become the guiding principle of health care. Mary, the so-called "weaker twin," could be deeply loved and treasured—but she could never be independent, autonomous: she could never lead a "normal" life. Jodie, meanwhile, the so-called "stronger twin," though equally loved, could perhaps also live an independent life. Extensive surgery in the early months and years of life could lead to an autonomous life for Jodie. Without it, both would die.

What seemed intolerable about Jodie and Mary was that they could never live an autonomous life because, by definition, Siamese twins could never be autonomous. Autonomy is about the moral activity of a freely choosing individual—and Jodie and Mary could never be an individual. In the moral world of autonomy it is very difficult to conceive of the value of those whose lives are dependent, inarticulate, and brief. In the case of young children, the principle of autonomy is generally negotiated by transferring its benefits onto the parents. But in this case the parents seemed to favor caring for the twins as they were and not separating them. In the logic of autonomy, they had chosen the "wrong" option. The news media explained that this was for "religious" reasons. In the relentless logic of this debate, "religious" could only mean obscurantist, irrational, and muddleheaded. Against this lay all the benefits of modern technology and skill—benefits that meant that the twins could be separated and Jodie could become autonomous. The courts decided that a decisive intervention on Jodie's behalf was preferable to watching both twins die. There was no meaning in the short dependent life of the twins to compare with the meaning to be found in the long independent life of Jodie. So Mary died—less, perhaps, so that her sister might live, than that the assumptions of contemporary culture and medicine be kept intact.

This narrative of two distressing cases, though not concerning human cloning directly, nonetheless highlights the givens in the arguments used in favor of cloning. The assumption is that suffering is the great enemy. There is one way to avoid suffering, and that is to cure it. In order to find a cure, some quite extraordinary practices may be performed, practices that may do extraordinary things either to the patient, as in the case of Jodie and Mary, or to those who have not been cured, as in the case of the children at Alder Hey. It is remarkable what practices are described as cures. The truth is that there are very few maladies that medicine can actually cure. Most of the practice of medicine is instead about reducing, delaying, dispersing, sometimes cutting out. But the language of cure resonates so much with the culture of autonomy and fulfillment that ever more drastic forms of intervention are spoken of as cures. The quest for a cure killed Mary and led to remarkable goings-on at Alder Hey. The National Health Service is better funded than ever but still desperately short of money. The answer is partly because it costs so much to fund ever more extraordinary cures that there is little left to care for those for whom "cure" does not adequately name the need.

Which brings us back to the assumption that cure is not just the best, but the only approach to suffering. The second reason why the National Health Service is in such straits is that caring is out of fashion. The vocation of nursing is under threat: is the central place of the nurse secure in an organization that is not sure it is still primarily concerned with caring for those one cannot cure? If caring is still central, why do so few resources go toward, for example, psychiatric services in inner cities, where people who are sometimes incurable and may well be less articulate frequently seem to be left comfortless? The reality is that today it is more difficult to care than to cure. It is more difficult to be with a child when she dies, more difficult to offer respect and dignity to each tragic case, than it is to search frantically for a solution, a remedy, an escape. However many cures researchers find, each person needs to face up to the time when all the curing has to stop. When all the emphasis is on curing, on happy endings, there will inevitably be a tendency to ignore, neglect, or even destroy realities that tell a different story. But it is these realities, the weak and the dying, that should be closest to the heart of medicine, just as they are closest to the heart of God.[3]

In common with almost all whose arguments are tied to technology, the advocates of human cloning assume that the human story is one of progress. Just as "Christianity, Commerce, Civilization" was the threefold clarion that motivated the European scramble for Africa in the nineteenth century, so a similarly uncritical view of progress governs the scramble for bio-utopia today. "Nature" is an uncharted, uncivilized, trackless waste, and biotechnology offers an invading force that promises to bring huge benefits to human life in every aspect. Galileo was opposed by blinkered reactionaries, so the story goes, and the "martyrdom" faced by contemporary advocates of cloning only proves their membership of Galileo's great tradition. But is it civilization or commerce that is really driving the clamor for biotechnological "cures"?

Perhaps the deepest assumptions lie in reasons for having children in the first place. Human cloning in its fullest sense offers a different way of having children. But why have children anyway? The most common response to this question is "Because it's natural"—and the most common objection to cloning is that it is correspondingly "unnatural." But the word "natural" is very slippery. Use of this kind of language can be highly manipulative and disingenuous. There are a host of natural things such as the common cold that most people do their best to avoid, and a host of nonnatural things such as the motor car that many people employ every day. The debate about human cloning tends to resolve into a split between those who see human nature as expressed most fully when it subdues the limitations of existence and those who see the fulfillment of human nature in the acceptance of those limitations.

Assessing Status

Having explored the respective arguments for accepting human cloning and for blocking it, and having questioned the apparent givens largely assumed by both sides, it is time to assess where the church lies in the debate.

In the case of full-scale cloning of "babies for life," the question is relatively clear. There is a simple division in the theological designation of human identity. On the one hand there is the definition of the human as that which chooses—and therefore a perception of cloning as a perfectly human fulfillment of the capacity to choose.[4] On the other hand there is the definition of the human as one who is chosen, one who is assumed by God in becoming flesh in Christ, one who is created for a purpose and earmarked for destiny, whose salvation is won by Christ's cross and depicted in his resurrection. This latter perception of the human as God's creature, adopted through the sonship of Christ, sees cloning as comparable to the fall, in other words as a rejection of creatureliness and an arrogation of a role that belongs to God. Fundamentally humanity is a creature not the Creator.

In the case of the development of organs for transplant, where the fundamental identity of humanity as creature is not in question, the use of cloning techniques need not be so troublesome. The question here is not so much about whether to accept human limitations, but about whether the manner of engaging them leads humanity into an even greater prison. A reexamination of Michel de Certeau's work, cited in chapter 6 above, helps us grasp the subtlety of the issue at stake here.

Cloning offers itself as a way of overcoming the limitations of the human body and, rather like the Liverpool professor mentioned earlier, places instead the value of Life as the higher good—backed up with pictures of happy children and older people facing aging without fear. The contrast is between Life (as a kind of spirit) and the body (as a kind of doomed given). This contrast evokes two reasons for concern, one economic, the other theological.

The theological cause for concern relates to de Certeau's distinction between a strategy and a tactic. De Certeau describes a strategy as a triumph of place over time, and a tactic as its opposite. This helps us see why cloning is so threatening to the church. This quest for Life is in many respects like the church: it talks of a transformation of the body in the name of an ideal higher and grander than mere mundane existence. It aspires to a future that transcends that which is possible in the present. Although it operates from the power base of the laboratory, and is thus, in de Certeau's terms, a strategy, its ideology is of a minority holding out for liberation in the face of the heavy hand of oppressive conservatism, and is thus more like a tactic. Its ideology places its faith in the triumph of time over place—in the triumph of life over the limitations of the body. It has its own notion of sin, its own perception of nature (as opposed to creation), its own sense of choice (as opposed to vocation), its own means of salvation (as opposed to Christ), and its own utopia (as opposed to the kingdom). It is, in other words, a rival church—or, to use the church's jargon, a heresy.

The economic cause for concern is whether this "Life" force is in fact no more than a product of a capitalist economy. Biotechnology is a burgeoning industry. Like any industry, it has to find a market for its products. The conventional way for an industry to do this is through a variety of methods that bring a sufficient proportion of the population to feel their life is considerably the poorer without this new product, and to enter the imaginary world of the utopia that might be accessible with the help of this new product. The money accrued through sales is then plowed back into research and development, with a little profit for the shareholders. It does not require too much cynicism to suppose that the drive for "Life" is in many respects rather like the drive for most other things, and deeply shaped by the market.

Reincorporating the Lost

The improvisatory tactic of reincorporation picks up where the theological analysis of rival stories and the economic analysis of bio-utopia leave off. For both the church and the biotechnology industry claim to be concerned for the needy child. The difference partly lies in the rival eschatologies of the two forms of salvation.

The logic of the practice of full-scale human cloning is the logic of refinement. The ability to eradicate all impediments to human perfection involves a subtle redefinition of what it means to be human. That definition comes to resemble the same qualities as I have previously alluded to in identifying the spirit of Life to which many involved in contemporary health-care innovation aspire. Life, in this understanding, involves rationality, self-consciousness, and autonomy. It does not involve a particular notion of the body—on the contrary, the possibilities of the body are an ever-receding boundary of experimentation. It is not a definition of Life that offers much good news or consolation to those who currently experience disability, disease, or decay. Children with special physical needs or older people with Alzheimer's disease are not the priority in this perspective—and, when the definitions are pushed to their extreme, they may not even find themselves to be regarded as "persons" at all.

Yet these are exactly the kinds of people that the Christian story perceives as being reintegrated in Act Five. The question of whether a novel practice promises to reintegrate such people in the story is a test of whether it belongs to the ethics of the kingdom. For a practice that offers to bring salvation to humanity, human cloning has a daunting list of casualties. The list does not just include those whose disadvantages threaten to exclude them from any prospect of sharing the bio-utopia: there is also the rather large matter of the fate of the embryos upon which the vital research and experimentation is performed. These embryos have given their life so that others might enter the promised land. Yet they have no say in making this sacrifice. And there is no guarantee that the promised land is worthy of any sacrifice, let alone one on such a colossal scale. A sacrifice that does not take away sin is a characteristic emblem of a heresy—that was the heretical gesture of the suicide pilots on September 11. But in this case the sacrifice is not a suicide.

It is the elimination and use of the weak in order to fortify the strong. This is not the kingdom.

Incorporating Gifts

If the church is to overaccept human cloning it must first identify what this gift or heresy could really be used for, could really become. The answer lies in identifying the potential of the gift. The gift, in the case of human cloning, is all about the human body. What does the church understand about the body?

Cloning is a matter that concerns the body. St. Paul promises the church the fruits of salvation:

> We know that the whole creation has been groaning in labor pains until now; and not only the creation, but we ourselves, who have the first fruits of the Spirit, groan inwardly while we wait for adoption, the redemption of our bodies. (Rom. 8:22–23)

Salvation involves "the redemption of our bodies." This phrase, the redemption of our bodies, incorporates two of the greatest frustrations of the Christian life. The first frustration is a present anxiety: namely, the limitations of the human body, the fact that it cannot do everything our hearts and minds want it to do, cannot be everywhere we want it to be, is far from the beauty we desire for it, and is prone to disease and decay. The second frustration is a future anxiety: there is a growing anxiety that the promised redemption of our bodies is so slow in coming.

Given these two frustrations, it is easy to see how, over the history of the church, a host of heresies has grown up that strive to bypass or overcome the limitations of the human body. These heresies are of two general kinds. One is the bypass approach: frustrated by the limitations of the body, it escapes into a secret knowledge, the possession of which guarantees salvation without the need to trouble with the ponderous details of ordinary life. The alternative heresy is the overcoming approach: circumventing the delay in the redemption of our bodies, it seeks to perfect individual human bodies and thus attempts to evade the ravages of death. Cloning represents this latter quest. Recognizing, rightly, that one cannot live without the body, human cloning attempts to live without God—or, at least, impatiently refuses to wait for God's good time.

When Christians consider that human cloning is largely about the limitations and the delay in the redemption of the body, they may quickly realize that their tradition has always been about addressing these two anxieties. They already have a practice that is all about the nonsexual (and, for that matter, nongenetic) regeneration of the body. It is none other than baptism. In baptism Christians are made a part of the body of Christ. The body that matters for Christians, the body they seek to "clone," is not their own individual body but the body of Christ. In baptism Christians die and are buried, and thus begins a transformation and a reproduction by which their body is made new in the image of Christ. This transformation is witnessed in discipleship and perfected in sanctification. This is what Christians mean by progress—indeed, it is the only form of progress in which the church has any real stake. The transformation is developed through worship, most especially in the Eucharist, wherein Christians eat and are renewed as the body of Christ. The purpose of the whole process is that Christians should be ready for the destiny long prepared for them: and that destiny is friendship with God.[5]

The issue becomes one of sovereignty. The challenge to the Christian imagination is not whether it can condone cloning, but whether Christians genuinely uphold the belief embodied in baptism, namely, that the body of Christ is their true body. Do Christians really believe in the sovereignty and wisdom of the God who rules through the broken and risen body of Christ, or do they secretly think that the information in their genes is master after all?

Forming Habits

The conventional way for the church to respond to heresy is to take the claims and practices of the rival ideology and dismantle them piece by piece. It can take the ideology of human cloning and point out that its notion of sin is insufficient, its understanding of salvation is inadequate, its heaven is a hell. If the church is to overaccept human cloning, however, it must attend to the practices that embody its convictions. The church can only have something to say on an issue such as this if it places it within the context of its entire perception of God's plan for human salvation and the practices that accord with the character of God revealed in that plan. To put it another way, Christian ethics is about learning to imitate God, not about keeping one's nose clean; about being transformed, not trouble-free.

When the church addresses an issue such as cloning, it should not be saying, "How can we ensure this troublesome question makes as little difference to our lives as possible?" but rather, "How can our response to this issue stimulate a renewal of the faith and practice of the church?" The vast majority of the things Christians do in their lives they do from habit and instinct—they take them for granted. A response to cloning will only be meaningful if it arises from what Christians already take for granted, but have perhaps neglected—hence the apparent complexity of the questions. Christianity is not primarily a set of beliefs, but a transformed pattern and perception of being in the world. Christians are formed into communities—called the church—which have specific practices—such as baptism, Eucharist, the reading of Scripture, penitence and reconciliation after sin, and so on—which shape and order their common life according to the character of God revealed in Jesus Christ. The notion that Christians are individuals who freely choose from a supermarket shelf of beliefs and go along with a new development such as cloning after going down a checklist of such beliefs and finding no just impediment—such a notion is the creation of capitalism, not of Christianity. The church's witness in the face of an issue like human cloning lies not so much in its arguments as in its practices. The two practices that address the issues raised by human cloning are the way the church welcomes the stranger and the way the church engages suffering.

The principal way in which the church welcomes the stranger is through catechesis, baptism, and discipleship. These are the ways a person becomes part of the body of Christ. If the body of Christ is God's answer to the human limitations and the delay in the redemption of our bodies, how then are Christians to become disciples, how are they to be conformed to Christ, how does this process of transformation take place? What is this nongenetic, nonsexual regeneration? By imitation, says St. Paul.

> For I think that God has exhibited us apostles as last of all, as though sentenced to death, because we have become a spectacle to the world, to angels and to mortals. We are fools for the sake of Christ, but you are wise in Christ. We are weak, but you are strong. You are held in honor, but we in disrepute. To the present hour we are hungry and thirsty, we are poorly clothed and beaten and homeless, and we grow weary from the work of our own hands. When reviled, we bless; when persecuted, we endure; when slandered, we speak kindly. We have become like the rubbish of the world, the dregs of all things, to this very day.
>
> I am not writing this to make you ashamed, but to admonish you as my beloved children. For though you might have ten thousand guardians in Christ, you do not have many fathers. Indeed, in Christ Jesus I became your father through the gospel. I appeal to you, then, be imitators of me. For this reason I sent you Timothy, who is my beloved and faithful child in the Lord, to remind you of my ways in Christ Jesus, as I teach them everywhere in every church. (1 Cor. 4:9–17)

He states quite simply, be imitators of me. Paul regards this imitation as so intense that it is like the relation of father and child. In other words this is the kind of cloning to which Christians are invited—imitating the apostles as they imitate Christ. Paul insists that salvation takes place in and through the body, not despite or outside the body.

> But someone will ask, "How are the dead raised? With what kind of body do they come?" . . . There are both heavenly bodies and earthly bodies, but the glory of the heavenly is one thing, and that of the earthly is another. . . . It is sown a physical body, it is raised a spiritual body. If there is a physical body, there is also a spiritual body. . . . Just as we have borne the image of the man of dust, we will also bear the image of the man of heaven. . . . For this perishable body must put on imperishability, and this mortal body must put on immortality. (1 Cor. 15:35–53)

Any pursuit of salvation without the body is condemned. Accordingly Christians believe the church is the body of Christ, since salvation in Christ comes through the embodied practices of the common life of Christians. Thus Christians believe in nonsexual reproduction, but of the body of Christ; and they believe in the copying of lives, but in the imitation of discipleship.

This brings us to the question of suffering. Some years ago I spent some time in northern India. The thing that struck me most was that in Delhi, people trusted their relationships, but distrusted their technology. If the computer systems were down, everyone laughed—but if one left a social or business engagement without sharing a cup of tea, everyone frowned. It made me realize that in the West our investment in technology reflects our distrust of relationships. Technology is designed to overcome the shortcomings of relationships. In fact, of course, technology often exacerbates the fragility of relationships. The technology of cloning is an illustration of this. When Christians share the peace at the Eucharist, they experience the body of Christ as an interlocking network of supportive relationships. They are promised that Christ's peace passes all understanding. But do they really believe in it?

The great test of the Christian belief in the church as their true body, the body of Christ, is whether it helps them in their suffering. What of the suffering that could be alleviated through cloning? Is it not inhumane to oppose it? Just think for a moment about how cloning alleviates suffering. Cloning attempts to perfect individual bodies and make them sufficient in themselves. It thus bypasses the need for human care by substituting technological intervention. By contrast, the church, the body of Christ, offers a tapestry of relationships. Contemporary society has come to believe that suffering and death must be, if not abolished, at least delayed as long as possible. The pursuit of this unattainable goal has coincided with a decline in the pattern of care and relationships that make life sustainable in the face of suffering and death. Cloning is an intense example of what has become of medicine in modernity. What was once fostered by the churches as an embodiment of the Christian commitment to care when it could not cure has now become a demand to cure even if that means ceasing to care. But the truth is that suffering and death cannot be legislated or researched away. What is needed is a company of friends who will care even when they cannot cure, a communion of saints whose membership is stronger than death, and a savior whose presence and promises of redemption abide despite the eventide. Cloning offers none of these: indeed it undermines each of them by treating the body as an isolated organism. But each of these is available in humble faith through the grace of Christ and the ministry of the church, and they come through baptism.

Summary

In cloning, as in so many other issues, secular arguments pose an irresolvable conflict between a promise to alleviate suffering and a fear of undermining human identity. Christians have tended to enter such debates with little or no sense of their own identity as a church, and consequently their arguments have carried little authority. But the body is at the very heart of Christian theology and practice, and the issue of cloning offers a stimulus for renewal. While the practice of developing organs for transplant seems little more than an extension of current medical practice, research on embryos emerges as the sacrifice of the weak to fortify the strong. It is time to remember what the church has always believed: that it is the true body, the body of Christ, whose reproduction and transformation in baptism and Eucharist is a foretaste of its ultimate regeneration. This is a promise far more profound than the promise of cloning.[6]

14

A Promising Offer
Unlimited Food

For thousands of years people have relied on the manipulation of living organisms to make bread, cheese, and beer. In the last thirty years it has become possible to identify the genetic code of an organism and to modify that code by introducing particular genes from another organism. There are three such types of gene transfer:

1. Wide transfer—where a gene from one organism, such as a fish, is transferred into a very different organism, such as a tomato. Plants can be engineered with genes taken from bacteria, viruses, insects, animals, or even humans.
2. Close transfer—where genes are moved between similar organisms, such as wild plants and commercial crops.
3. The alteration of activity levels of genes within the one organism affecting, for example, the conditions in which a crop can flourish.

Although it is possible to modify the genes of animals in this way, I shall confine the following remarks to the implications of this technology on plants grown for food.[1]

Accepting and Blocking

Let us begin with reasons that are presented why the "offer" of genetically modified (GM) foods should be readily "accepted." There are three applications of GM foods that commend themselves. They can be divided broadly between the kinds of people who respectively stand to benefit from them.

1. We may start with the applications that directly benefit the food producers themselves. The introduction of a gene from a soil bacterium can make soya insusceptible to herbicide. This means that a field can be sprayed to prevent weeds growing without fear that the spray will also damage the crop. In other words, the food won't be killed by the weed killer. Similar technology can make the plant more resistant to viruses and insect predators. This not only enables far more food to be produced but also reduces the use of environmentally damaging insecticide sprays. Recent research has suggested that bananas may become extinct in the next ten years unless such developments are introduced.

2. The second group that stands to benefit from GM foods is consumers. Few consumers in the West are going to complain if they find their supermarkets stocked with rosier, tastier tomatoes that keep fresh longer than before and sell for half the price, or cheaper chickens fed with modified maize. Few people will be against foods with a greater iron content, to combat anemia. The promise of GM foods is a consumer's paradise, with an ever-expanding range of foods available year-round for decreasing relative cost. Gone will be the awkward pips in the grape or the tiresome skin on the orange, which takes so much effort to peel. It will be difficult to remember the days when the range of goods was arbitrarily limited by weather and season.

3. The third group of beneficiaries may be producers in the two-thirds world. Many crops in the developing world are grown in hostile environments, with little water or too much salt. If rice or wheat could grow in such domains, using atmospheric nitrogen, or if they could grow tall enough to overcome flooding in the paddy fields, or if barley could grow shorter so it did not blow down in the wind, much more food could be produced. With world population set to rise by a quarter in the next twenty years, someone needs to find some more food from somewhere.

So GM foods have a wide range of appeal. They offer increased crop yield, improved resistance to pests, disease, and adversity, novel plant products, more efficient processing with less waste, and products that could be beneficial to medicine. This constitutes a remarkable step forward on the path of human progress. They promise to end world hunger, increase quality, and bring down costs. Who could ask for anything more?

Nonetheless there are a variety of arguments put forward suggesting vigorously that the offer of GM foods should be "blocked." Conventional ethics considers issues under two broad headings: things that are right or wrong in themselves and things that are considered good or bad depending on their consequences. It is common for the first, deontological, kind of objection to be an immediate, reflex response, while the second, consequential, reaction tends to emerge with considered reflection and dwells on both what can be predicted and what cannot.

1. The most frequent deontological reaction to genetic modification is that humanity should not "play God" by "interfering with nature." A coalition of opposition to GM foods has grown up around a general sense of human arrogance and hubris. Nonetheless, the majority of arguments concern the foreseen or unforeseen consequences.

2. The unforeseen consequences largely concern the safety of the GM foods themselves.

a. Novelty. The novelty of GM foods leads to the inevitable concern that some of these foods may prove to be toxic in themselves or, at least, likely to provoke allergic reactions among consumers, in either the short or long term. Although there is a statutory authority advising on novel foods and processes, confidence in such bodies has been undermined by recent food scares such as salmonella, E. coli, and the bovine spongiform encephalopathy infection that caused British beef to be banned in Europe for a considerable period. There is particular concern over one kind of gene with a resistance to antibiotics, which could cause problems in the human body's immune system. The so-called "precautionary principle" asserts that where harm to human health or the environment is possible, the burden of proof should rest on the innovator, rather than the opponent, of the new technology.

b. Irreversibility. If GM foods become widespread, and then are considered to be undesirable, it may prove very difficult to turn back the clock. Pollen from GM fields can be carried by wind or insects. There could be such a thing as a "superweed," resistant to almost every herbicide. Some kinds of pollution never go away, and genetic pollution may be one of those kinds. Apocalyptic speculation, of the kind indulged by science fiction, quickly derives from this kind of specter.

3. The foreseen consequences largely concern the imbalance and misuse of the power over human food.

a. Labeling. In the West the concern has focused on labeling. Many people feel that the consumer should have the right to know whether the food they are buying is genetically modified. Although this is reasonably straightforward in the case of simple foods, such as the tomato, it has proved more problematic for processed foods.

b. Power. The more general fear is that such a basic source of life as food has passed into the power of a handful of multinational corporations who stand to hold the world at their mercy. The world is voluntarily handing over power to people unaccountable to the democratic process. A particular example of the way power has come to be used is in the way that, in the last twenty years, it has become possible to hold a patent on a living organism. Besides those who see this as being wrong in principle, there are many others who see it as a first step toward being able to own a patent on another person, and thus to return to slavery.

c. In the two-thirds world there is the positive prospect of increasing yield by growing crops on marginal land: but this must be set against fears that the process will continue to be dominated by multinational companies and thus reinforce the local producers' dependence and indebtedness. The so-called "green revolution" of the 1970s forced millions of small farmers off their lands in countries like Brazil and India by making them dependent on expensive seed technology. It will continue to be possible for the multinational seed suppliers to devise methods of keeping their small clients dependent and powerless. The voices for GM foods come not largely from the two-thirds world, but from the West, and this tells its own story. The nutritional potential of GM crops in the two-thirds world is enormous, but the reality is that the research resources are largely going instead toward convenience for Western appetites. Instead of providing more food, many Africans expect genetic modification to undermine their countries' capacity to feed themselves by destroying the diversity, local knowledge, and sustainable agricultural systems they have acquired over centuries.

Questioning Givens

Thus far I have attempted simply to outline the principal arguments employed by those involved in the debate about GM foods. I have said little that might indicate how God or the Christian tradition might speak or act amid this contemporary confusion. I want now to identify some of the deeper issues that underlie the debate, in order to explain why I believe the Christian response lies in practices already dear to its heart.

The heart of the argument in favor of GM foods is that they offer to end two–thirds-world hunger and at the same time increase the choice and quality of foods for the Western consumer while decreasing the price. Each of these arguments raises a deeper question for Christians.

1. The promise to end two–thirds-world hunger through creating more food presupposes that two–thirds-world hunger is due to lack of food. But it is highly questionable whether the two-thirds world really has a food problem in that sense. Rather, it has a war problem and a wealth-, land-, and food-distribution problem. Several countries currently export food while their own people go hungry. Malawi has recently been expected to do this by the strictures imposed upon it by the International Monetary Fund. There is an assumption that producing more food will bypass these problems. But there seems no evidence for this. If people cannot share the food they currently have, what reason is there to suppose they would be better at sharing if they had more? This is a problem of the cruelty and selfishness of the human heart, not one that can be addressed by scientific progress. The advocates of the new technology are offering a way to solve a major problem without changing the human heart. To Christian ears, this must be nonsense. The heart needs converting, not ignoring.

2. The promise to give the Western consumer more choice and quality while decreasing the price buys into an assumption that progress means getting more and more for less and less. This represents a failure to come to terms with human limitations. It is an understandable outworking of the perception that this life is all there is. If there is nothing to be hoped for, the barriers of this life—of length of days, depth of experience, degree of health, acuteness of mental awareness—must be pushed back to the ultimate, to keep oblivion at bay. In this sense, GM foods find a parallel in the moves toward human cloning: each is offering a salvation of the human body in this earthly life. For a Christian, such an assumption about progress is a denial of faith in the church, that body whose members support one another in this life and look forward to ultimate fulfillment in the next.

The heart of the argument against GM foods is that it epitomizes human hubris, that the technology releases potentially dangerous and polluting organisms into the food chain, and that it further concentrates power in the hands of the rich. Again these arguments each raise deeper questions for Christians.

1. In the case of humans "playing God" by "interfering with nature," both of the key elements are more problematic than they at first appear. "Interfering with nature" is taken for granted by a great deal of current technology and almost the whole practice of medicine. It is very

difficult to agree on the threshold beyond which interacting becomes interfering. An objection to the apparent novelty of GM foods quickly becomes a wholesale renunciation of most of what takes place in a modern hospital. There is in fact nothing new about biotechnology: the novelty lies only in its extent. Meanwhile the frequently repeated expression "playing God" carries a host of generally underexamined theological and philosophical presuppositions. One notable assumption is a latent Deist notion that God set "nature" up as a self-sustaining mechanism, and then withdrew to let the "clock" tick away unimpaired. This understanding of the "God" in "playing God" is alien to the Christian understanding that God himself "interfered in nature" by becoming flesh in Christ. Not only does this transform any understanding of God, surely it also subverts any static reading of "nature."

2. The fear of poisoning the food chain, while genuine, rests on an assumption that what really damages the body comes to it from the outside. There abides a humanist, and, in Christian eyes, a somewhat naïve perception that if legislation can keep the human body pure, most significant ills will be kept at bay. Now legislation and regulation has an undeniably important role, but the Christian cannot look principally to the government to solve problems largely beyond its jurisdiction. The contemporary cult of the body and concern about the purity of what enters it ignores the deeper impurity—of sloth and jealousy and greed and pride—that comes from within. It rests on an understanding of ethics that is largely individualist and broadly concerns the desire and right to keep one's soul and body unsullied by the world. It is not to be mistaken for a concern for the world per se.

3. The concern about the concentration of power in the hands of the multinational companies, though commendably true to the Christian bias to the poor, represents a similar naïveté. The problem is not just the fact that a few people have all the power—it is that power tends to corrupt all kinds of people.

Assessing Status

The irony is that the proponents and opponents of GM foods agree on more than they disagree. One side claims to give more power to the consumer and to the two-thirds world; the other side claims that power is going to the business moguls and that consumer order is being threatened with chemical chaos, and thus that the government should use its power to legislate and its executive authority to police that legislation to ensure that its orders are not subverted by the clever or the devious. Both sides thus believe the issue is really about power.

They also believe it is about technology. One side thinks technology is the answer, the other side thinks technology is the problem. The proponents of GM foods think of it as a significant symbol of human progress, and they line up a series of benefits that show what technology can do. The opponents of GM foods see the technology as an alien imposition on an otherwise harmonious order, like an invader from another planet or a virus that threatens the delicate equilibrium on which the earth balances.

For Christians, technology is not the problem, but it is not the answer either. Technology is attractive because it offers to make a better world without us needing to become better people. Those who oppose technology tend to assume the problem lies in technology, not in ourselves. By going along with the way the argument is generally set up, Christians underwrite the presumption that power and technology rule the world. In so doing, Christians fail to proclaim the heart of their faith: that it is God the Holy Trinity, the creating Father, the crucified Son, the outpouring Spirit, who rules the world. He has given the church resources that, if properly employed, make GM foods a secondary issue.

So from the Christian perspective the issue is not principally about power or technology, but about who is at the center of the world's story. The treatment in chapter 3 portrayed the church as standing in the fourth act of a five-act play. In this sense neither the business moguls, nor the scientists, nor the government stand in the center of the story; neither does the church. It is Jesus who stands, in Act Three, in the center of the story. In the strength of this belief, Christians are released from the relentless urgency of putting "Christian figures" in what are taken to be the most influential positions, in boardrooms, laboratories, or councils.

The Christian claim that Christ is at the center of history, at the center of the world's story, is indeed a claim about power. It is a claim about providence, a statement of faith that God, in ways corresponding to those he has already disclosed, will sustain his people throughout Act Four, even when their future seems most uncertain and insecure. It is certainly not a claim that Christians, because their Lord is Lord of heaven and earth, will always be in control of politics, technology, and food.

The issue of GM foods turns out to be only secondarily about power and technology, and primarily about food. In realizing that the issue is about trusting God to give them enough food, Christians learn about the form of God's power and the method of his technology, for his power lies in transformation and his technology lies in the social relations created and shaped by the Eucharist.

Forming Habits

The Eucharist is the technology God uses for constructing a new society. God gives his church not more food, but a way of distributing food that shapes the way it henceforth thinks about power. This is manifested in a number of ways.

One way is that when Jesus talked about power he did so in terms of food. He said that anyone who wished to be powerful should be a *diakonos*, a table-waiter.

> You know that among the Gentiles those whom they recognize as their rulers lord it over them, and their great ones are tyrants over them. But it is not so among you; but whoever wishes to become great among you must be your *servant*, and whoever wishes to be first among you must be slave of all. For the Son of Man came not to be *served* but to *serve*, and to give his life a ransom for many. (Mark 10:42–45—italicized words are derivations of *diakonos*)

Thus from the very beginning, food distribution shaped the church's understanding of power. (It is notable that Luke places this interchange between Jesus and the disciples in the context of the Last Supper.) The way to learn how to be great is to distribute food.

A second dimension linking food and power is that one of the first acts the early church took upon itself was to ensure justice in the distribution of food. Conflict was already arising because of the alleged neglect of the weak and marginalized. A particular ministry was created and seven people were set apart for the administration of food. They were known as deacons.

> Now during those days, when the disciples were increasing in number, the Hellenists complained against the Hebrews because their widows were being neglected in the daily distribution of food. And the twelve called together the whole community of the disciples and said, "It is not right that we should neglect the word of God in order to wait on tables. Therefore, friends, select from among yourselves seven men of good standing, full of the Spirit and of wisdom, whom we may appoint to this task, while we, for our part, will devote ourselves to prayer and to serving the word." What they said pleased the whole community, and they chose Stephen, a man full of faith and the Holy Spirit, together with Philip, Prochorus, Nicanor, Timon, Parmenas, and Nicolaus, a proselyte of Antioch. They had these men stand before the apostles, who prayed and laid their hands on them. (Acts 6:1–6)

Thus not only is food distribution about power, but it also shapes the whole ordering of the church as the body of Christ.

The third dimension of this intimate relationship between food and power in the early church comes through the admonition delivered by St. Paul. Finding that food distribution at the Eucharist was not such as to glorify God, but instead mirrored the unjust ordering of resources in the "world" beyond the Lord's table, he gave the Corinthians the full force of his grief.

> When you come together, it is not really to eat the Lord's supper. For when the time comes to eat, each of you goes ahead with your own supper, and one goes hungry and another becomes drunk. What! Do you not have homes to eat and drink in? Or do you show contempt for the church of God and humiliate those who have nothing? What should I say to you? Should I commend you? In this matter I do not commend you! (1 Cor. 11:20–22)

And this is his introduction to the narrative of the Lord's Supper.

These three passages demonstrate the "technology" of the Eucharist. The Eucharist is a practice that shapes the church, transforms social relationships, and defines power. Repeated practice of this pattern of action should form Christians in the habits that identify the real issues in the GM foods debate. In chapter 5 above I portrayed Christian ethics as being about learning to take the right things for granted. These three passages show how the church learns to think about food. But they are not yet the whole of the church's understanding of GM foods.

Incorporating Gifts

The church overaccepts offers that it receives from the wider world by placing the narrative of the offer within the larger narrative of God's ways with the world. The most significant way this is done in relation to GM foods is to dismantle the abiding notion that the transformation of food is an unthinkable, ungodly thing. On the contrary, it is at the heart of the gospel. The gospel narrative is interwoven with godly modified foods.

At the very beginning of his ministry, as recorded in Matthew and Luke, Jesus was faced with the temptation to turn stones into bread. The ultimate genetic modification. The solution to all the world's food shortages. He resisted the temptation. Why? This becomes a more pressing question as the Gospel accounts proceed. The first miracle (or "sign") in John's Gospel is the transformation of water into wine. The ordinary stuff of life is converted into the exuberant symbol of joy. Clearly John does not see food transformation as outside Jesus' power or purpose. The one miracle recorded in all four Gospels is the occasion when he turned five loaves and two fish into a feast for five thousand followers. If ever there was a statement that the Eucharist is God's answer to issues of mass hunger, this is it. A child brings a token gift, the sum of the resources available, and Jesus transforms it into a superabundant supply of nourishing food for all. A sublime act of overacceptance. It is hard to sustain an argument that Jesus was against "unnatural" food transformation.

Jesus' anxiety about turning stones into bread remains a mystery, but there is a clue, albeit in a different Gospel, in the discussion that follows the feeding in the fourth Gospel. Here Jesus connects what has taken place with what Christians experience in the Eucharist, and in the process identifies himself.

> Jesus answered them, "Very truly, I tell you, you are looking for me, not because you saw signs, but because you ate your fill of the loaves. Do not work for the food that perishes, but for the food that endures for eternal life, which the Son of Man will give you." . . . So they said to him, "What sign are you going to give us then . . . ? Our ancestors ate the manna in the wilderness; as it is written, 'He gave them bread from heaven to eat.'" Then Jesus said to them, ". . . [T]he bread of God is that which comes down from heaven and gives life to the world." They said to him, "Sir, give us this bread always."
>
> Jesus said to them, "I am the bread of life. Whoever comes to me will never be hungry, and whoever believes in me will never be thirsty." (John 6:26–35)

What is beginning to emerge is that Jesus is not against food, or the transformation of food, but is eager to draw attention to that which truly nourishes and to reveal that he himself is God's sustaining food for his people. At the Last Supper all becomes clear. The Passover that commemorated God's deliverance of his people from slavery becomes a renewed act of liberating and sustaining food-sharing. Jesus takes the ordinariness of bread and transforms it into the bread of life. He takes the cup of suffering and joy and transforms it into the cup of salvation, his own blood, the embodiment of the forgiveness of sins. And this breaking, this sharing—this is what constitutes his body. What Christians can miss by getting into the wrong kind of debate about genetically modified foods is that they already have the Eucharist. They already have God's modification of food. The key to a Christian understanding of GM foods is not the transformation of food but the social relations created and presupposed by that transformation. For the Eucharist is not just about transforming food. It is about transforming the people that share the food, and the society those people share.

Reincorporating the Lost

The real question about GM foods is what kind of a society people want to live in. Do people want to live in a society where they are obsessed with the quality and purity of what goes into their bodies, where they have to produce vastly more food because they take it for granted that real sharing is impossible, where they assume that the control of technology is all they mean by power? Or do they want to live in a society where food comes alive when it is broken and shared, where they only discover who they are when they gather to receive the fruits of God's sacrifice for them, where people of all shapes and flavors and aptitudes and stories bring their different gifts to the table and find that each of their gifts is accepted but they nonetheless each receive back the same?

As the extraordinary social ethic of the New Testament comes together, food emerges as the key to unraveling every relationship, both personal and "public."

> When you give a luncheon or a dinner, do not invite your friends or your brothers or your relatives or rich neighbors, in case they may invite you in return, and you would be repaid. But when you give a banquet, invite the poor, the crippled, the lame, and the blind. And you will be blessed, because they cannot repay you, for you will be repaid at the resurrection of the righteous. (Luke 14:12–14)

Here is a plea for the formation of habits that embody the new society made possible by the Eucharist. It is also an indication that the Eucharist prefigures an eschatological meal at which the poor, the crippled, the lame, and the blind have a special place, and at which Christians look forward to shared food, transformed bodies, and new hearts. The test of GM foods becomes a eucharistic test: does this technology resemble the technology of the Eucharist—in other words, does it prefigure the kingdom by enabling a greater sharing of food and power among all God's people? If not, are GM foods a heresy—a rival to the Eucharist, a rival transformation of food that rather than creating more just relations in fact perpetuates and enhances injustice and dismantles the social relations made possible by the Eucharist?

Summary

GM foods offer the world everlasting food, but God has given his people everlasting food through the Eucharist—the bread of life, spiritually modified food. The Eucharist is God's word to the advocates of GM foods because its fellowship challenges the cynicism of their selfish world. The Eucharist is God's word to the opponents of GM foods because its sacrifice challenges the naïveté of a world based on humanist assumptions. Most of all the Eucharist proclaims to all people that there is only one way to save the world—not through more food, not through pure food, but through shared food, the broken bread received from Christ's body broken on the cross.

Analysis of the arguments for and against GM foods shows the debate to be principally one about power and who should hold it. Close regulation is clearly required to protect the interests of the poorer countries and future generations. Christians need have no problem with the transformation of food because it is a repeated theme in the gospel, but they need to renew their understanding of the Eucharist as a practice that transforms power relations as well as food if they are to understand how the church can embody God's word on this issue.

Epilogue

The Extent of Improvisation

I hope I have said enough to establish that improvisation in the theater offers very helpful resources for clarifying and enriching the practices of Christian ethics. The claims I have made cover a wide range of theological disciplines.

Most evidently, there are claims about the conduct of Christian ethics. I argue that Christian ethics must always be grounded in the practices of the church. I suggest that the central role of Christian ethics is the formation of habits and disciplines—that it is those habits and disciplines that largely shape what the church regards as crises and dilemmas—and that it is those same habits and disciplines that largely govern the church's response to such crises and dilemmas. I propose that status questions are invariably the key to understanding ethical "issues" as they are conventionally posed, particularly as such questions are so often overlooked. And I describe two central practices, overaccepting and reincorporation, that epitomize how communities should seek to reflect the pattern of God's activity and embody the Christian story in their common life.

The claims about Christian ethics involve subsidiary arguments about four other aspects of theology. By arguing that the practices of the church should ground the deliberations of ethics, I am not just making a claim about ethics—I am making a claim about the church. Hence there is an ecclesiological dimension to this argument. The practices I have discussed are largely those embodied in local congregations. I have not engaged in proposals for national and international institutions. In this I seek to reflect the emphasis of the New Testament, whose injunctions for the life of the church largely assume the common life of small communities. Seeing such communities as the heart of the church by no means excludes discussion of issues of global scope—such as cloning and genetically modified foods. It simply offers a context in which the church may best understand such complex issues.

The early chapters make explicit that my argument concerns the way the Bible is treated in Christian ethics and thus involves a hermeneutical dimension. I question the assumption that the Bible is a script that the church performs and suggest instead that it is more like a training manual that forms what Christians take for granted. In my proposal of the five-act play I illustrate the relationship of the church to the Bible, showing how the church is located between the key events in the story, which have already taken place, and the ultimate fulfillment of the last act. This attention to hermeneutics is also related to the dimension of the argument that involves church history. The first chapter suggested that church history is theology teaching by examples, and the practice of reincorporation amply demonstrates how the contemporary church engages with church history as a resource in ethics.

There is a fourth aspect of theology on which this study touches, in addition to ecclesiology, hermeneutics, and church history—that aspect is doctrine. In arguing that overaccepting is central to the way God makes himself known in history, particularly in the incarnation and the resurrection, I am making a significant claim about Christology and soteriology. In describing reincorporation as the practice of the reign of God, I am making a claim about eschatology. In both ways I am seeking to explore continuities between the way God is recorded as working in the scriptural narrative and the way he works today. Meanwhile improvisation may prove helpful in understanding the development of doctrine. I have not elaborated this proposal at all in this present study, but there may well be possibilities in perceiving the formulation of, for example, the doctrine of the Trinity in the second to fourth centuries through the lens of improvisation.

The Potential of Improvisation

Given that the practices of theatrical improvisation have implications for ethics, ecclesiology, hermeneutics, church history, and doctrine, where might their potential be further explored? I have given only four worked examples of how the practices of improvisation might enrich an understanding of pressing questions in Christian ethics. Are there other questions on which improvisation might offer similar resources?

The categories under which I treated the four examples are by no means accidental ones. Each offers potential for development in the same vein.

The discussion about the church in Chile under the Pinochet dictatorship concerned the role of improvisation in relation to human evil. In many ways the church defines itself by how it responds to human evil, from inside as well as out. On a personal scale, any thorough treatment of the church and human evil today must engage with the question of the sexual abuse of children. As with most questions of human evil, this would quite possibly begin with a consideration of issues of status, and the horrifying reality that the church has been implicated in countless numbers of such crimes. On a global scale it might have been possible to discuss the role of the church in relation to war in general and perhaps terrorism in particular. For example, there is much to reflect on once one begins to perceive the war between al-Qaeda and the United States in status terms. Al-Qaeda shows all the advantages of a tactic over a strategy. Strategies seem to have no way of dealing with those who are unafraid to die. The al-Qaeda story in significant ways overaccepts the Pentagon story, to such an extent that its fighters are prepared to die for the cause in suicide bombings. However, the fact that al-Qaeda's fighters are murderers prevents them from being regarded as martyrs. While they appeal to a greater story than the one-act play of liberal-democratic, consumer-capitalist fulfillment, the fact that they are prepared to kill in such a brutal and random way exposes that this is by no means the fourth act of God's story. The habits of discipline formed in their training camps are a lesson that the issues of terrorism are largely fought in the moral imagination. But an appropriate response has to be one that offers a more compelling story, not just a more terrifying military power. And that is why the horror of terrorism is a challenge to the United States to identify what really is the story that characterizes its nationhood, and whether that is a story that presupposes violence or not.

The treatment of accounts of disability and physical suffering moved the discussion to questions of disordered creation, or what is sometimes called natural evil. There is no doubt that the pastoral potential of reflection on practices of improvisation is considerable. Recently I buried a faithful member of my congregation. In May she told me about all the things that meant most to her—family, music, work, garden, faith. In early July we spoke again. If she had just a few weeks, what were the key things she wanted to do, to say, to complete? She pondered, and planned, and later carried out her remaining projects. In early August she asked me to spend some time with her as she let go of the one or two things that still lay uneasy on her heart, and together we allowed God to release her from the burden of them. Later that month, three days before she died we prayed together, and I commended each part of her life, body, mind, and spirit, to the God who had made and so much cherished her. And finally, shortly after her death, I had the opportunity to sit with others beside her body and recognize before God everything that had happened. And afterward there was only one word spoken: that word was "beautiful." She instinctively knew that ministry is about the power one is given when one is given mundane ways of encountering the unfathomable. What this account demonstrates is the significance of ordinary practices of the church in overaccepting even death. This person's death showed that the one who has been given ways of fitting her death into a much larger story becomes extraordinarily powerful: such a person's witness can affect and shape a whole community in ways that technological remedies never could.

The discussion about cloning quickly became a discussion about the body more generally. Many issues cluster around the notion of "body." There can be no doubt that the issue of homosexuality is demanding from the church a response that requires a renewal of understanding concerning the Christian body. It is evident that the conventional responses of blocking or accepting are inadequate. If the church is to overaccept homosexuality as an issue, it needs to review its relevant practices. For example, there needs to be consideration of whether marriage is primarily about a quality of relationship, or rather whether it centers more on the protection of the most vulnerable, initially children and, increasingly, aging parents. There needs to be consideration of friendship and what constitute the key practices of friendship—for it could be the case that the companionship involved in homosexuality is more pertinent to friendship than to marriage. But no consideration of overaccepting could ignore that Jesus talks much more about the inclusive kingdom than he does about the exclusive relationship of marriage, and the church may need to face a far more sweeping redescription of a whole pattern of relationships, placing the needs of the most vulnerable—the hungry, the stranger, the prisoner—and the relationships that they require and make possible as more normative in Christian ethics than the paradigm of marriage.

The discussion about genetically modified foods developed into an exploration of the significance of the Eucharist in modeling a series of social relations and practices. If the previous examples offered potential for further reflection in the areas of the body and of society, this example encourages consideration of issues of global concern, such as the deterioration of the created environment and the changes in climate and biodiversity. Arguments in these areas could adopt a similar structure to that used about GM foods. Status issues are again important here, since the absurdity of the destruction that has followed human mastery of the planet is increasingly evident. Reincorporation must have a large part to play, because salvation needs to be found in such obscure parts of the created environment as have yet to be harnessed by acquisitive consumerism. And overaccepting is central to the argument, if it is to be affirmed that the Eucharist is the epitome of humanity in harmony with creation, food and drink at last taking their ordered place in a social practice that meets need but exposes greed.

The Limits of Improvisation

Before closing, a few words of caution seem in order. I have frequently used terms such as "play," have often highlighted the humorous dimensions of my subject, and have, in the last two chapters especially, taken quite bold steps in asserting the validity of the practices of the church in relation to apparently "worldly" issues. It has been understood throughout, but should be underlined in conclusion, that this is not an exercise in the disembodied play of ideas, in any negative sense of that term. Improvisation depends on and assumes an active community conducting regularly the practices of the church and discerning an appropriate (or "obvious") engagement in the light of the habits formed from those practices. It is not a secret game, a kind of Gnosticism as described in chapter 2 above, in which an individual can get an answer to a vexed ethical question by toying with a few spiritual motifs.

I have been cautious throughout about using the word "new." This study is rather more interested in description than prescription: it is an effort to reincorporate neglected traditions in the church through reinvigorating their memory by redescribing them with a new vocabulary. But it is not trying to invent practices or create new traditions. This study is new in the sense that there seems never before to have been a sustained treatment of the similarities between the discipline of Christian ethics and the practices of improvisers in the theater. But if the treatment is new, I have tried throughout to suggest that the practices I commend have always been there. It is not necessary for a community seeking to be faithful in trying circumstances to learn how actors improvise in the theater. But if such communities, formed by Christian habits and practices, are to be regarded, as I hope they will come to be, as the principal focus of Christian ethics, then it is helpful to highlight the significance of their moral formation and discernment by describing their witness using terms such as status, overaccepting, and reincorporation. If these terms are new, they are directed not so much at novelty as at renewal. Part of that renewal may indeed be a greater understanding of the significance of play, seen not as childish irresponsibility (a term that itself wilts under theological scrutiny) but as the imagining that, in the reign of God, last might be first and the mighty might lose their seat by a method other than by force.

Thus this is not designed to be another disembodied theory. And it does not set out to be another bright new idea. It aims to inspire the community of readers to rediscover the significance of the ordinary practices of the church, and perhaps to their surprise to realize that in these practices may be found ample resources to engage the most intractable issues and questions in the contemporary world. Although I am wary of developing my argument into a theory or a technique, I still assert that improvisation is a set of practices that a community can foster over time, and in that sense can become better at. Like all habits, they cannot be picked off the shelf or learned overnight. They must be formed doggedly, persistently, undemonstratively, before being employed playfully, subversively, faithfully.

The Challenge of Improvisation

This epilogue has briefly summarized the theological significance of improvisation, the kinds of specific further areas where it could prove particularly fruitful, and the pitfalls that need to be avoided in embracing its potential. Given this measured style of drawing the study together, it is appropriate to end on a more challenging note.

This has been a study in how to enhance the practices and the self-understanding of the church in order to resource its practical service and witness to contemporary society in a spirit of generous orthodoxy. It offers encouragement and proposals that address some of the most controversial and inhibiting concerns of conventional Christian ethics. It offers a way of treating the Bible in ethics that respects the authority of the text but receives that authority as empowering rather than constraining. It aims to inspire those seeking to practice the Christian faith in the humble disciplines of community, not by becoming sentimental about the virtues of community but by offering suggestions as to how to go about the process of communal discernment. It thus sets out to help Christians engage with their environment without losing their identity.

This study offers ways of overcoming a number of dichotomies familiar in ethical discussion. It points to grounding a theology that affirms the centrality of the poor in the purposes of God without assuming that that centrality rests on secular assumptions of either inherent class conflict or integral individual rights. It emphasizes the key role of an eschatological perspective in Christian ethics, without that automatically casting

creation into a theological backwater. The balance between reincorporation on the one hand and overaccepting on the other permits a holding
together of created (and incarnate) goodness and teleological purpose.
Likewise the treatment of nonviolence points to a perception of active
engagement that breaks through the assumption of the "passivity" of
peace set against the "responsibility" of war. The discussion of worship
and play dispels any suggestion that ethics that is concerned with the
"real" world must divorce itself from the imagination. And part of the
overcoming of those other dichotomies is an assumption that the split
between church and academy is not an inevitable one.

I am asking the church to open up its practices so their social significance becomes more widely apparent. I am asking the Christians to take
seriously the place of the imagination in ethics and the need to train that
imagination through corporate practices. I am inviting communities of
faith to discover the power and vocation they can find when they enjoy
the play of tactics and cease to assume their significance is determined
by whether they can make the story come out right. Meanwhile I am
asking the academy to take the church seriously in ethics. I am asking
scholars to attend to the embodiment of practices in liturgy and life
that the church usually takes for granted. And I am asking theologians
not to justify their work to the world as responsible but to offer it to the
church as constructive play, play that perhaps comes closer to the reign
of God than the earnest striving for ethical solutions ever can. Thus this
study is a request, and an invitation; a challenge, and a gift. And that is
how it seeks to imitate the gospel that is its inspiration.

Notes

Introduction

1. No one epitomizes this generation more than Stanley Hauerwas. See especially *The Peaceable Kingdom: A Primer in Christian Ethics* (Notre Dame, IN: University of Notre Dame Press, 1983; London: SCM, 1984) and John Berkman and Michael Cartwright, eds., *The Hauerwas Reader* (Durham, NC: Duke University Press, 2001). I have sought to cover the arguments of Hauerwas and others in Samuel Wells, *Transforming Fate into Destiny: The Theological Ethics of Stanley Hauerwas* (Carlisle, UK: Paternoster, 1998).

2. A more comprehensive attempt to pursue this constructive agenda may be found in Stanley Hauerwas and Samuel Wells, eds., *The Blackwell Companion to Christian Ethics* (Oxford, UK: Blackwell, 2003).

3. For the best account of imagination in theology, see Garrett Green, *Imagining God: Theology and the Religious Imagination* (Grand Rapids: Eerdmans, 1998). A stimulating account of the role of the imagination in shaping history may be found in John Lukacs, *At the End of an Age* (New Haven, CT: Yale University Press, 2002).

4. Lurking behind the contrary assumption that ethics is about jostling between competing givens is the long shadow of Reinhold Niebuhr. For a quite remarkable analysis of the sources and assumptions of Niebuhr's approach, see Stanley Hauerwas, *With the Grain of the Universe: The Church's Witness and Natural Theology: Being the Gifford Lectures Delivered at the University of St. Andrews in 2001* (Grand Rapids: Brazos, 2001).

5. For treatments of my experience of bringing the proposals made in this book into engagement with the process of social and economic regeneration, see for example my "No Abiding Inner City: A New Deal for the Church," in Mark Thiessen Nation and Samuel Wells, eds., *Faithfulness and Fortitude: In Conversation with Stanley Hauerwas* (Edinburgh: T & T Clark, 2000); "Generation, Degeneration, Regeneration: The Theological Architecture and Horticul-

ture of a Deprived Housing Estate," *Political Theology* 3/2 (2002): 238–44; and *Community-Led Estate Regeneration and the Local Church* (Cambridge, UK: Grove Booklets, 2003).

6. See Hans Frei, *The Eclipse of Biblical Narrative: A Study in Eighteenth- and Nineteenth-Century Hermeneutics* (New Haven, CT: Yale University Press, 1974) and *The Identity of Jesus Christ* (Philadelphia: Fortress, 1975); David Kelsey, *Uses of Scripture in Recent Theology* (Philadelphia: Fortress, 1975); George Lindbeck, *The Nature of Doctrine: Religion and Theology in a Postliberal Age* (London: SPCK, 1984).

7. The benchmark for treatments of musical improvisation and theology is Jeremy Begbie, *Theology, Music, and Time* (Cambridge: Cambridge University Press, 2000), esp. 179–270. A contribution that has direct relevance to the present study is Sharon Welch, "Communitarian Ethics after Hauerwas," *Studies in Christian Ethics* 10/1 (1997): 82–95, where she draws on jazz to illustrate the importance of listening to foster community. See also Albert R. Jonsen, "The Ethicist as Improvisationist," in Lisa Sowle Cahill and James F. Childress, eds., *Christian Ethics: Problems and Prospects* (Cleveland: Pilgrim, 1996).

8. My understanding of Mark's Gospel has been especially influenced by Mary Ann Tolbert, *Sowing the Gospel: Mark's World in Literary-Historical Perspective* (Minneapolis: Fortress, 1989) and Ched Myers, *Binding the Strong Man: A Political Reading of Mark's Story of Jesus* (Maryknoll, NY: Orbis, 1988).

Chapter 1: Ethics as Theology

1. See Aristotle, *The Nicomachean Ethics*, trans. David Ross, rev. J. L. Ackrill and J. O. Urmson (Oxford, UK: Oxford University Press, 1980) and *The Politics*, trans. T. A. Sinclair, rev. Trevor J. Saunders (Harmondsworth, UK: Penguin, 1981).

2. For the contrast between Aristotle's assumption of violence and the Christian (that is, Augustinian) assumption of peace, see John Milbank, *Theology and Social Theory: Beyond Secular Reason* (Oxford, UK: Blackwell, 1990; Cambridge, Mass.: Blackwell, 1991).

3. For a stark, if perhaps a little overdrawn, portrayal of this transformation, see John Howard Yoder, "The Constantinian Sources of Western Social Ethics," in *The Priestly Kingdom: Social Ethics as Gospel* (Notre Dame, IN: University of Notre Dame Press, 1984).

4. A marvelous narrative account of this worldview is given in Sigrid Undset's remarkable trilogy, *Kristin Lavransdatter*, trans. Tiina Nunnally (3 vols.; Harmondsworth, UK: Penguin, 1997, 1999, 2001).

5. For a significant challenge to the way this story is generally told, see William Cavanaugh, *Theopolitical Imagination: Discovering the Liturgy as a Political Act in an Age of Global Consumerism* (Edinburgh: T & T Clark, 2002), esp. 9–52. Cavanaugh argues that "to call these conflicts 'Wars of Religion' is an anachronism, for what was at issue in these wars was the very creation of religion as a set of privately held beliefs without direct political relevance" (22).

Chapter 2: Theology as Narrative

1. An author who might be taken to epitomize the universal strand in contemporary Christian ethics would be Hans Küng. See, for example, his *A Global Ethic for Global Politics and Economics*, trans. John Bowden (London: SCM, 1997).

2. Among a wide range of titles, see for example Susan Frank Parsons, ed., *The Cambridge Companion to Feminist Theology* (Cambridge: Cambridge University Press, 2002); Gustavo Gutierrez, *A Theology of Liberation: History, Politics, Salvation*, rev. ed. (London: SCM, 1988); and Michael Northcott, *The Environment and Christian Ethics* (Cambridge: Cambridge University Press, 1996).

3. See for example Rosemary Radford Ruether, *Sexism and God-Talk: Towards a Feminist Theology* (London: SCM, 1983).

4. Adrian Hastings, *The Church in Africa, 1450–1950* (Oxford, UK: Oxford University Press, 1996).

5. Gustavo Gutierrez, *We Drink from Our Own Wells: The Spiritual Journey of a People*, trans. Matthew J. O'Connell (Maryknoll, NY: Orbis, 1990).

6. Richard L. Fern, *Nature, God, and Humanity: Envisioning an Ethics of Nature* (Cambridge: Cambridge University Press, 2002).

7. I owe this understanding of Saint Antony to Brian S. Hook and R. R. Reno, *Heroism and the Christian Life: Reclaiming Excellence* (Louisville, KY: Westminster John Knox, 2000).

8. See John Howard Yoder *The Christian Witness to the State* (Newton, KS: Faith & Life, 1964).

9. I discuss sectarianism at greater length in my *Transforming Fate into Destiny: The Theological Ethics of Stanley Hauerwas* (Carlisle, UK: Paternoster, 1998), 90–125, and 141–50, where I see the issue as one of the triumph of time over space. See also chap. 6 below.

10. A painful example of this is described vividly by Duncan Forrester in his treatment of the church at Dachau. See his "The Church and the Concentration Camp: Some Reflections on Moral Community," in Mark Thiessen Nation and Samuel Wells, eds., *Faithfulness and Fortitude: In Conversation with Stanley Hauerwas* (Edinburgh: T & T Clark, 2000), 189–207.

11. It is significant that James Wm. McClendon begins his three-volume systematic theology with *Ethics*, in the place where philosophical theology might conventionally go, and ends with a volume on *Witness*, in place of a volume on philosophical theology and in the location in the series usually reserved for ethics. See his *Systematic Theology*, vol. 1, *Ethics*, 2nd ed. (Nashville: Abingdon, 2002) and James Wm. McClendon with Nancey Murphy, *Systematic Theology*, vol. 3, *Witness* (Nashville: Abingdon, 2000).

12. For further exploration of heroes and saints, the violence of the nation-state, and the contrast between Aristotle's city-state and Augustine's church, see Samuel Wells, "The Disarming Virtue of Stanley Hauerwas," *Scottish Journal of Theology* 52/1 (1999): 82–88; Jean Bethke Elshtain, "Citizenship and Armed Civic Virtue: Some Questions on the Commitment to Public Life," in Charles H. Reynolds and Ralph Norman, eds., *Community in America: The Challenge of Habits of the Heart* (Berkeley: University of California Press, 1988); and John

Milbank, *Theology and Social Theory: Beyond Secular Reason* (Oxford, UK: Blackwell, 1990). There are also significant issues raised by Stanley Hauerwas and Charles Pinches in *Christians among the Virtues: Theological Conversations with Ancient and Modern Ethics* (London: University of Notre Dame Press, 1997) and by Brian S. Hook and R. R. Reno in *Heroism and the Christian Life*.

Chapter 3: Narrative as Drama

1. Among those who have considered the Christian narrative as a drama are the following: Dorothy L. Sayers, *The Man Born to Be King* (New York: Harper and Brothers, 1943); Alasdair MacIntyre, *After Virtue: A Study in Moral Theory*, 2nd ed. (London: Duckworth, 1984); Susan Schreiner, *The Theater of His Glory: Nature and the Natural Order in the Thought of John Calvin* (Grand Rapids: Baker, 1995); Walter Brueggemann, "Preaching as Reimagination," *Theology Today* 52/3 (October 1995): 313–29; Raymund Schwager, *Jesus in the Drama of Salvation*, trans. James G. Williams and Paul Haddon (New York: Crossroad, 1999); Kevin Vanhoozer, "The Voice of the Actor: A Dramatic Proposal about the Ministry and Minstrelsy of Theology," in John G. Stackhouse, Jr., ed., *Evangelical Futures* (Grand Rapids: Baker, 2000); and Michael Horton, *Covenant and Eschatology: The Divine Drama* (Louisville: Westminster John Knox, 2002).

2. Hans Urs von Balthasar, *Theo-Drama: Theological Dramatic Theory*, vol. 1, *Prolegomena*, trans. Graham Harrison (San Francisco: Ignatius, 1988); *Theo-Drama: Theological Dramatic Theory*, vol. 2, *Man in God* (San Francisco: Ignatius, 1990); *Theo-Drama: Theological Dramatic Theory*, vol. 3, *Dramatis Personae: Persons in Christ* (San Francisco: Ignatius, 1992); *Theo-Drama: Theological Dramatic Theory*, vol. 4, *The Action* (San Francisco: Ignatius, 1994); *Theo-Drama: Theological Dramatic Theory*, vol. 5, *The Last Act* (San Francisco: Ignatius, 1998).

3. Translated by T. M. Knox (Oxford, UK: Clarendon, 1988).

4. I have been greatly helped in my understanding of von Balthasar's project by conversations with Ben Quash and Ivan Khovacs. See J. B. Quash, "'Between the Brutely Given, and the Brutally, Banally Free': Von Balthasar's Theology of Drama in Dialogue with Hegel," *Modern Theology* 13/3 (July 1997): 293–318; and Ben Quash, "Drama and the Ends of Modernity," in Lucy Gardner, David Moss, Ben Quash, and Graham Ward, *Balthasar at the End of Modernity* (Edinburgh: T & T Clark, 1999), 139–171; also Ivan Khovacs, "Robbing Peter to Pay Paul: Theology's Indebtedness to the Theater with Reference to the *Theo-Drama* of Hans Urs von Balthasar," unpublished paper delivered at the Performance and Responsibility Research Colloquium convened by the Institute for Theology, Imagination and the Arts at St. Mary's College, University of St. Andrews, March 2002. Ivan Khovacs provides an illustration from the Munich Olympic Games that inspired my story from Tunisia that follows.

5. Catherine Pickstock, "Necrophilia: The Middle of Modernity," *Modern Theology* 12/4 (1996): 407–8, quoted in Ben Quash, "Drama and the Ends of Modernity," 148.

6. TD 3:514 (hereafter, "TD" refers to von Balthasar, *Theo-Drama;* see n. 2 above), quoted in Aidan Nichols, *No Bloodless Myth: A Guide through Balthasar's Dramatics* (Edinburgh: T & T Clark, 2000), 132–33.

7. Nichols, *No Bloodless Myth,* 164; Rene Girard, *Violence and the Sacred* (Baltimore: Johns Hopkins University Press, 1977).

8. TD 5:518, quoted in Nichols, *No Bloodless Myth,* 247.

9. Nichols, *No Bloodless Myth,* 248.

10. See Ben Quash, "Drama and the Ends of Modernity," 164–67.

11. N. T. Wright, "How Can the Bible Be Authoritative?" *Vox Evangelica* 21 (1991): 7–32 at 18–19, italics original. For other comparable treatments, see Gabriel Fackre, *The Christian Story: A Narrative Interpretation of Basic Christian Doctrine* (Grand Rapids: Eerdmans, 1984); Paul D. Hanson, *The People Called: The Growth of Community in the Bible* (San Francisco: Harper & Row, 1986), 519–46; Bernhard W. Anderson, *The Unfolding Drama of the Bible,* 3rd ed. (Philadelphia: Fortress, 1988); Frank Anthony Spina, "Revelation, Reformation, Re-creation: Canon and the Theological Foundation of University," *Christian Scholars' Review* 17/4 (1989): 326; and J. Richard Middleton and Brian J. Walsh, *Truth Is Stranger Than It Used to Be: Biblical Faith in a Postmodern Age* (Downers Grove, IL: InterVarsity; London: SPCK, 1995), 240.

12. See Walter Wink, *The Human Being: Jesus and the Enigma of the Son of the Man* (Minneapolis: Fortress, 2002).

13. The placing of the church in Act Four and Israel in Act Two should not be taken as an endorsement of supersessionism—the claim that the church has replaced Israel in God's purposes. The abiding place of the Jews in God's providence must always be an open one for Christians, and to use this schema to resolve that question would be to expect too much from it. For a helpful perspective, see John Howard Yoder, *The Jewish-Christian Schism Revisited,* ed. Michael G. Cartwright and Peter Ochs (London: SCM, 2003).

Chapter 4: Drama as Improvisation

1. Nicholas Lash, *Theology on the Way to Emmaus* (London: SCM, 1986), 37–46.

2. Lash, *Theology on the Way,* 42.

3. Lash, *Theology on the Way,* 46; italics original.

4. Frances Young, *The Art of Performance: Towards a Theology of Holy Scripture* (London: Darton, Longman & Todd, 1990). See also Stephen Barton, "New Testament Interpretation as Performance," *Scottish Journal of Theology* 52/2 (1997): 179–208.

5. Walter Brueggemann, *The Bible and the Postmodern Imagination: Texts under Negotiation* (London: SCM, 1993), esp. 64–70.

6. This observation has much in common with Hans Frei's notion of the way Mark's Gospel "renders" the identity of Jesus. See Hans Frei, *The Identity of Jesus Christ* (Philadelphia: Fortress, 1975).

7. Brueggemann, *The Bible and the Postmodern Imagination,* 67.

8. Brueggemann, *The Bible and the Postmodern Imagination,* 68. Brueggemann's most suggestive words are these: "Barth has made clear that the God of the Bible

is 'Wholly Other.' In conventional interpretation, the accent has been on 'wholly,' stressing the contrast and discontinuity. When, however, accent is placed on 'other,' dramatic interpretation can pay attention to the dialectical, dialogical interaction in which each 'other' impinges upon its partner in transformative ways. That is, 'otherness' need not mean distance and severity, but can also mean dialectical, transformative engagement with" (106 n. 19). One senses that Brueggemann is thinking here of the early Barth of the commentary on *Romans*, rather than the later Barth of the *Church Dogmatics*.

9. "The minister enacts the drama and invites members of the listening, participating congregation to come be in the drama as he or she chooses or is able" (Brueggemann, *The Bible and the Postmodern Imagination*, 68).

10. Kevin Vanhoozer, "The Voice and the Actor: A Dramatic Proposal about the Ministry and Minstrelsy of Theology," in John G. Stackhouse, ed., *Evangelical Futures: A Conversation on Theological Method* (Grand Rapids: Baker, 2000), 90. I am grateful to Ivan Khovacs for bringing this essay to my attention, and for his comments on it.

11. Vanhoozer, "The Voice and the Actor," 69.

12. Vanhoozer, "The Voice and the Actor," 82.

13. Ivan Khovacs, "Robbing Peter to Pay Paul: Theology's Indebtedness to the Theater with Reference to the *Theo-Drama* of Hans Urs von Balthasar," unpublished paper delivered at the Performance and Responsibility Research Colloquium convened by the Institute for Theology, Imagination and the Arts at St. Mary's College, University of St. Andrews, March 2002.

14. Shannon Craigo-Snell, "Command Performance: Rethinking Performance Interpretation in the Context of *Divine Discourse*," *Modern Theology* 16/4 (October 2000): 475–94, at 482.

15. Craigo-Snell, "Command Performance," 479.

16. Craigo-Snell, "Command Performance," 480.

17. Craigo-Snell, "Command Performance," 481–82.

18. Gerard Loughlin, *Telling God's Story: Bible, Church, and Narrative Theology* (Cambridge: Cambridge University Press, 1996), 20, quoting Rowan Williams, "Postmodern Theology and the Judgement of the World," in Frederic B. Burnham, ed., *Postmodern Theology: Christian Faith in a Pluralist World* (New York: Harper Collins, 1989), 97.

19. Jeremy Begbie, *Theology, Music, and Time* (Cambridge: Cambridge University Press, 2000), 222–23.

20. The following have been my chief texts in clarifying my understanding of theatrical improvisation: Keith Johnstone, *Impro: Improvisation in the Theatre* (London: Methuen, 1981) and *Impro for Storytellers* (London: Faber, 1999); Ronald James and Peter Williams, *A Guide to Improvisation: A Handbook for Teachers* (Banbury, UK: Kemble, 1980); Viola Spolin, *Improvisation for the Theatre: A Handbook of Teaching and Directing Techniques* (London: Pitman, 1973); Anthony Frost and Ralph Yarrow, *Improvisation in Drama* (Basingstoke, UK: Macmillan, 1990).

Chapter 5: Forming Habits

1. *The Oxford Dictionary of Quotations* (3rd ed., Oxford and New York: Oxford University Press, 1979), 567.

2. Donald Nicholl, *Holiness* (London: Darton, Longman & Todd, 1981), 54–55.

3. Matt. 25:1–13.

4. James Mackey, ed., *Religious Imagination* (Edinburgh: Edinburgh University Press, 1986), 23; Mary Warnock, *Imagination* (London: Faber, 1976), 10.

5. Nicholl, *Holiness*, 55–57.

6. John Irving, *A Prayer for Owen Meany* (London: Corgi, 1990).

7. Anthony Frost and Ralph Yarrow, *Improvisation in Drama* (Basingstoke, UK: Macmillan, 1990), 151–55.

8. Keith Johnstone, *Impro: Improvisation and the Theatre* (London: Methuen, 1981), 87–88. See the discussion of "being obvious" in chap. 4, above.

9. For a more extended treatment of the issues discussed in the following paragraphs, see my "How Common Worship Forms Local Character," *Studies in Christian Ethics* 15/1 (2002): 66–74.

Chapter 6: Assessing Status

1. I owe my understanding of status and the majority of what follows to Keith Johnstone, *Impro: Improvisation in the Theatre* (London: Methuen, 1981), 33–74, and *Impro for Storytellers: Theatresports and the Art of Making Things Happen* (London: Faber, 1999), 219–31 and 352–53.

2. Johnstone, *Impro*, 46.

3. This is adapted from ibid., 51.

4. See the discussion in Johnstone, *Impro*, 50–52.

5. In highlighting the way low-status behavior can be used to manipulate conflict, I am not making a moral judgment that one degree of status is superior to or more desirable than another. I am simply pointing out that power does not simply belong to the mighty. Hence this is part of a larger argument that the church should not assume it must become mighty (high-status) if it is to retain its integrity and have power. There is of course a longer discussion of the church's understanding of power to be had, but this is not the place for it. For a wonderful treatment of the way high and low status can alter in the same relationship in different contexts, see the portrayal of Mr. and Mrs. Merdle in Charles Dickens's *Little Dorrit*.

6. I have previously related this story in "Harry's Story: A Story of God's Power and Ours," *Christian* 99/3 (Autumn 1999): 10.

7. Johnstone, *Impro*, 61.

8. Often attributed to Cyprian but recorded by Augustine. See Geoffrey Parinder, ed., *The Routledge Dictionary of Religious and Spiritual Quotations* (London: Routledge, 2001), 20.

9. Michel de Certeau, *The Practice of Everyday Life*, trans. Stephen Rendall (Berkeley: University of California Press, 1984), 35–39, italics original.

10. De Certeau, *Practice*, 25–26, italics original.

11. James C. Scott, *Domination and the Art of Resistance: Hidden Transcripts* (New Haven, CT: Yale University Press, 1990), 198–99. Scott does not refer to either Johnstone or de Certeau. I owe my introduction to Scott's work to David Toole, *Waiting for Godot in Sarajevo: Theological Reflections on Nihilism, Tragedy, and Apocalypse* (Boulder, CO: Westview, 1997; London: SCM, 2001), esp. 232–48.

12. Scott, *Domination*, 18.

13. Scott, *Domination*, 2, 4.

14. Scott, *Domination*, 4–5, 191–92.

15. Scott, *Domination*, 5.

16. Mark 8:27–31.

17. John 11:35.

18. Mark 14:8.

19. John 13:14.

20. Mark 15:39 RSV.

21. Phil. 2:5–11.

22. Mark 10:43–44.

23. 1 Peter 4:13–14, 16.

Chapter 7: Accepting and Blocking

1. Keith Johnstone, *Impro: Improvisation in the Theatre* (London: Methuen, 1981), 92.

2. Johnstone, *Impro*, 131. Johnstone makes no attempt to identify what that outside force might be. In some Christian circles such a statement might evoke an immediate fear that he is talking about a demonic force. But his treatment is concerned with how actors can develop confidence in themselves and one another: the whole emphasis of his study is about the nurturing of this trust, and the irony is that fear of the demonic *inhibits* this trust, rather than facilitates it. In contrast I find Johnstone's last chapter, on the use of masks, less appropriate to the building of trust and I have chosen not to discuss it in this study.

3. Johnstone, *Impro*, 99–100.

4. This comes from a novel by Nicholas Mosley and is quoted in *Private Eye's Oxford Book of Pseuds* (London: Private Eye, 1983), 64–65.

5. Keith Johnstone, *Impro for Storytellers* (London: Faber & Faber, 1999), 34–36.

6. For this contrast, see John Howard Yoder, *The Royal Priesthood: Essays Ecclesiological and Ecumenical,* ed. Michael Cartwright (Grand Rapids: Eerdmans, 1994), 213. There is no doubt that Yoder's contrast is exaggerated: not all Native North Americans fought, for example.

7. James C. Scott, *Domination and the Art of Resistance: Hidden Transcripts* (New Haven, CT: Yale University Press, 1990), 18–19.

8. Scott, *Domination*, 19.

9. Scott, *Domination*, 132.

10. Scott, *Domination*, 203.

11. Scott, *Domination*, 205.

Chapter 8: Questioning Givens

1. John Milbank, "The Midwinter Sacrifice: A Sequel to 'Can Morality Be Christian?'" *Studies in Christian Ethics* 10/2 (1997): 13–38 at 25–26; italics original.

2. Milbank, "Midwinter Sacrifice," 26.

3. The analysis in these three paragraphs is largely shaped by David Kelsey, "Human Being," in *Christian Theology: An Introduction to Its Traditions and Tasks*, ed. Peter Hodgson and Robert King (London: SPCK, 1983), 141–67.

4. Perhaps those who have most vocally identified him in this way are Stanley Hauerwas, *With the Grain of the Universe: The Church's Witness and Natural Theology* (Grand Rapids: Brazos, 2001) and John Milbank, "The Poverty of Niebuhrianism," in *The Word Made Strange: Theology, Language, Culture* (Oxford, UK: Blackwell, 1997), 233–54.

5. Milbank, "Poverty of Niebuhrianism," 236–37; italics original.

6. Stanley Hauerwas, *With the Grain of the Universe: The Church's Witness and Natural Theology: Being the Gifford Lectures Delivered at the University of St. Andrews in 2001* (Grand Rapids: Brazos, 2001), 131, 136, 138.

7. Milbank, "Poverty of Niebuhrianism," 242, 250; italics original.

8. Matt. 18:23–35.

9. Matt. 20:1–16.

10. 2 Kings 7.

11. Gen. 45:7–8 and 50:20.

12. John Milbank, "Can Morality Be Christian?" in Milbank, *Word Made Strange*, 219–32.

13. Milbank, "Can Morality Be Christian?" 224–45; italics original. The references to world, time, and coyness allude to the opening words of Andrew Marvel's poem "To His Coy Mistress."

14. Martin Luther, *Treatise of Good Works*, quoted in Milbank, "Can Morality Be Christian?" 225.

15. Milbank, "Can Morality Be Christian?" 224.

16. Milbank, "Can Morality Be Christian?" 228–29; italics original. The reference to Gordonstoun may appear to challenge the way I presented the practice of formation at the start of chap. 6, when referring to the playing fields of Eton. But in fact Milbank's argument affirms the practice of formation, merely refining it as far as the content of that formation is concerned—and in a manner that clarifies the underlying purpose of my earlier argument.

17. Milbank, "Can Morality Be Christian?" 230–31; italics original.

18. I have found Robyn Horner a very helpful guide through these debates, and much of what follows derives from her treatment of the issues. See Robyn Horner, *Rethinking God as Gift: Marion, Derrida, and the Limits of Phenomenology* (New York: Fordham University Press, 2001).

19. Marcel Mauss, *The Gift: The Form and Reason for Exchange in Archaic Societies*, trans. W. D. Halls (London: Routledge, 1990). Subsequent anthropologists involved in the debate include Raymond Firth, Claude Levi-Strauss, and Marshall Sahlins.

20. Russell Belk, "The Perfect Gift," in *Gift-Giving: A Research Anthology*, ed. Cele Otnes and Richard F. Beltramini (Bowling Green, OH: Bowling Green State University Popular Press, 1996), 59–84, quoted in Robyn Horner, *Rethinking God as Gift*, 2.

21. Horner, *Rethinking God*, 4.

22. Horner, *Rethinking God*, 4–18 and 241–47. John Milbank sees return as a good thing, and seeks not "pure gift" but "purified gift-exchange," which he perceives as involving "delay and non-identical repetition." In other words he invokes the passage of time as a way out of Derrida's problems with return. In one passage he touches on the language of improvisation that I am employing in my argument in this book: "To be a Christian is not, as piety supposes, spontaneously and freely to love, of one's own originality and without necessarily seeking any communion. On the contrary, it is to *repeat differently*, in order to repeat *exactly*, the content of Christ's life, and to wait, by a necessary *delay*, the answering repetition of the other that will fold temporal linearity back into the eternal circle of the triune life." See John Milbank, "Can a Gift Be Given? Prolegomena to a Future Trinitarian Metaphysic," *Modern Theology* 11 (1995): 119–61 at 150. See also Jacques Derrida, *Given Time*, vol. 1, *Counterfeit Money*, trans. Peggy Kamuf (Chicago: University of Chicago Press, 1992) and Jean-Luc Marion, *Etant Donné* (Paris: Presses Universaires de France, 1997).

23. Garrett Green, *Imagining God: Theology and the Religious Imagination* (San Francisco: Harper & Row, 1989), esp. 137–45.

24. Walter Brueggemann, *The Bible and the Postmodern Imagination* (London: SCM, 1993), 15–16. See also André Brink, *A Change of Voices* (New York: Penguin, 1983) and David Bryant, *Faith and the Play of the Imagination: On the Role of Imagination in Religion* (Macon, GA: Mercer University Press, 1989).

Chapter 9: Incorporating Gifts

1. Anthony Frost and Ralph Yarrow, *Improvisation in Drama* (Basingstoke, UK: Macmillan, 1990), 59.

2. Ronald James and Peter Williams, *A Guide to Improvisation: A Handbook for Teachers* (Banbury, UK: Kemble, 1980), 49–52.

3. Keith Johnstone, *Impro: Improvisation in the Theatre* (London: Methuen, 1981), 100–101.

4. Johnstone, *Impro*, 101.

5. Johnstone, *Impro*, 102.

6. A similar practice is common among instrumental performers when they make mistakes in their play, incorporating what they call passing notes into their performance rather than calling a halt. A story is told of the violinist Itzhak Perlman. Once, while playing a violin concerto, he found that one of the strings snapped in the first movement. He continued as if nothing had happened, playing on with just the three strings. Speaking to the audience afterwards, he said, "Our job is to make music with what remains." (I owe this story to Rabbi Jonathan Sacks.) Likewise in the tradition of Eastern rug-making, mistakes must not be made, but, when they are made, they must not be unpicked: instead a new design emerges that incorporates the mistake into a new pattern.

7. Thomas Traherne, "Centuries of Meditations" 2/66 and 2/68, in *Selected Poems and Prose* (London: Penguin, 1991), 213–14.

8. Johnstone, *Impro*, 102.

9. John Milbank, *Theology and Social Theory: Beyond Secular Reason* (Oxford, UK: Blackwell, 1990), 5, 6, 402.

10. Pope John Paul II illustrates this point in his account of the demise of socialism in Eastern Europe, which has, he says, "been overcome by the non-violent commitment of people who, while always refusing to yield to the force of power, succeeded time after time in finding effective ways of bearing witness to the truth. This disarmed the adversary, since violence always needs to justify itself through deceit, and to appear, however falsely, to be defending a right or responding to a threat posed by others." *Centesimus Annus* in *Origins* 21/1 (May 16, 1991): 23.

11. Rowan Williams, "Interiority and Epiphany: A Reading in New Testament Ethics," in *On Christian Theology* (Oxford, UK: Blackwell 2000), 258–59. The citizens of Lockerbie responded to the savagery that brought a plane and its passengers down upon the town by choosing to make the careful restoration of the possessions of the passengers to their families their humble response. A prayer found written on a piece of wrapping paper in Ravensbruck, the largest of the concentration camps for women in Nazi Germany, goes as follows: "O Lord, remember not only the men and women of good will but also those of ill will. But do not remember all the suffering they have inflicted upon us; remember the fruits we bought, thanks to this suffering, our comradeship, our loyalty, our humility, the courage, the generosity, the greatness of heart which has grown out of this; and when they come to judgement, let all the fruits that we have borne be their forgiveness." Amen. (This prayer is in the Chapel of the Holy Innocents in Norwich Cathedral.)

12. Jer. 18:1–6.

13. The best studies of the political dimensions of this claim in New Testament perspective are David Toole, *Waiting for Godot in Sarajevo: Theological Reflections on Nihilism, Tragedy, and Apocalypse* (Boulder, CO: Westview, 1997; London: SCM, 2001), 232–48; and James C. Scott, *Domination and the Art of Resistance: Hidden Transcripts* (New Haven, CT: Yale University Press, 1990).

14. Stanley Hauerwas discusses the temptations in *The Peaceable Kingdom: A Primer in Christian Ethics* (London: SCM, 1983), 78–79, where he sees them as the recapitulation of God's way with Israel. My discussion is an improvisation on Hauerwas's approach.

15. Matt. 5:39–41.

16. A similar approach emerges in Paul's remarks about living as a slave in Eph. 6:5–6 ("Slaves, obey your earthly masters with fear and trembling, in singleness of heart, as you obey Christ; not only while being watched, and in order to please them, but as slaves of Christ, doing the will of God from the heart"). Augustine comments on this passage as follows: "What he means is if they cannot be set free by their masters, they themselves may thus make their slavery, in a sense, free, by serving not with the slyness of fear, but with the fidelity of affection, until all injustice disappears and all human lordship and power is

annihilated and God is all in all." Augustine, *Concerning the City of God against the Pagans*, trans. Henry Bettenson (London: Penguin, 1984), 19.15.

17. Mark 4:3–9 and 30–32; Toole, *Waiting for Godot*, 235–41; Ched Myers, *Binding the Strong Man: A Political Reading of Mark's Story of Jesus* (Maryknoll, NY: Orbis, 1988), 174–77; John Dominic Crossan, *The Historical Jesus: The Life of a Mediterranean Jewish Peasant* (New York: HarperSanFrancisco, 1991), 278–79.

18. Matt. 22:15–22.

19. John 8:2–11.

20. Mark 14:7.

21. Mark 10:35–45.

22. Mark 7:26–28.

23. For the former view, see the sources listed by Toole, *Waiting for Godot*, 250 and 312 nn 101, 102; for a blend of former and the latter view, see Myers, *Binding*, 299–304.

24. Mark 3:27.

25. Myers, *Binding*, 303–4.

26. Gen. 22:8.

27. Ian MacMillan, *Orbit of Darkness* (San Diego: Harcourt Brace Jovanovich, 1991). Again I am very much indebted to David Toole for my awareness and use of this story. See Toole, *Waiting for Godot*, 257–66.

28. Toole, *Waiting for Godot*, 262.

Chapter 10: Reincorporating the Lost

1. Quoted in *The Dorothy Day Book*, ed. Margaret Quigley and Michael Garvey (Springfield, IL: Templegate, 1982), 92.

2. F. L. Cross, ed., *The Oxford Dictionary of the Christian Church* (Oxford, UK: Oxford University Press, 1957), 790.

3. Keith Johnstone, *Impro: Improvisation in the Theatre* (London: Methuen, 1981), 112.

4. Johnstone, *Impro*, 116–17.

5. Johnstone, *Impro*, 116; my italics.

6. This is the all-too-common method of the child abuser. See Alistair McFadyen, *Bound to Sin: Abuse, Holocaust, and the Christian Doctrine of Sin* (Cambridge: Cambridge University Press, 2000), 57–79.

7. John Howard Yoder, *What Would You Do?* 2nd ed. (Scottdale, PA: Herald, 1992), 40. He goes on: "[Christians] guide their lives not so much by 'How can I avoid doing wrong?' or even 'How can I do the right?' as by 'How can I be a reconciling presence in the life of my neighbor?' From this perspective, I might justify firm nonviolent restraint, but certainly never killing."

8. "Only a clearly eschatological viewpoint permits a valid critique of the present historical situation and the choice of action which can be effective. . . . Significant action, for good or for evil, is accomplished by those whose present action is illuminated by an eschatological hope." John Howard Yoder, *The Original Revolution* (Scottdale, PA: Herald, 1977), 71. See also Charles R.

Pinches, *Theology and Action: After Theory in Christian Ethics* (Grand Rapids: Eerdmans, 2002), esp. 199–232.

Chapter 11: A Threatening Offer: Human Evil

1. William T. Cavanaugh, *Torture and Eucharist: Theology, Politics, and the Body of Christ* (Oxford, UK: Blackwell, 1998).
2. Cavanaugh, *Torture and Eucharist,* 80–81.
3. Cavanaugh, *Torture and Eucharist,* 82.
4. Cavanaugh, *Torture and Eucharist,* 85.
5. Cavanaugh, *Torture and Eucharist,* 93, 32–33.
6. Cavanaugh, *Torture and Eucharist,* 94.
7. Chilean Episcopal Conference "Declaration of the Permanent Committee of Bishops," in *Documentos del Episcopado: Chile 1975–80* (Santiago: Ediscones Mundo, 1982), 161, quoted in Cavanaugh, *Torture and Eucharist,* 105.
8. Ibid., "The Church: Its Mission Yesterday and Today," 183, quoted in Cavanaugh, *Torture and Eucharist,* 110.
9. Cavanaugh, *Torture and Eucharist,* 120.
10. Cavanaugh, *Torture and Eucharist,* 138.
11. Cavanaugh, *Torture and Eucharist,* 193.
12. Cavanaugh, *Torture and Eucharist,* 197.
13. Cavanaugh, *Torture and Eucharist,* 27.
14. Cavanaugh, *Torture and Eucharist,* 27–30.
15. Cavanaugh, *Torture and Eucharist,* 2.
16. Cavanaugh, *Torture and Eucharist,* 3.
17. Cavanaugh, *Torture and Eucharist,* 266.
18. Cavanaugh, *Torture and Eucharist,* 272.
19. Cavanaugh, *Torture and Eucharist,* 272.
20. See Cavanaugh, *Torture and Eucharist,* 226.
21. Cavanaugh, *Torture and Eucharist,* 229.
22. Cavanaugh, *Torture and Eucharist,* 251. The internal quotation is a reference to 1 Cor. 11:29. Cavanaugh argues that the "body" in this sense means the church, in the sense of the ingathered people of God, more than it means the transubstantiated elements of bread and wine.
23. Cavanaugh, *Torture and Eucharist,* 229–30, citing Augustine, *City of God,* book 10, chap. 6.
24. Cavanaugh, *Torture and Eucharist,* 230. Here he is following Dom Gregory Dix, *The Shape of the Liturgy* (New York: Seabury, 1982).
25. Cavanaugh, *Torture and Eucharist,* 237.
26. Cavanaugh, *Torture and Eucharist,* 242.
27. Cavanaugh, *Torture and Eucharist,* 117.
28. Cavanaugh, *Torture and Eucharist,* 263.
29. Cavanaugh, *Torture and Eucharist,* 12.
30. Cavanaugh, *Torture and Eucharist,* 30.
31. Cavanaugh, *Torture and Eucharist,* 14.
32. Cavanaugh, *Torture and Eucharist,* 14.
33. Cavanaugh, *Torture and Eucharist,* 275.

34. Cavanaugh, *Torture and Eucharist*, 276.
35. Cavanaugh, *Torture and Eucharist*, 277.
36. Cavanaugh, *Torture and Eucharist*, 277.
37. Cavanaugh, *Torture and Eucharist*, 277.
38. Cavanaugh, *Torture and Eucharist*, 279.

Chapter 12: A Threatening Offer: Flawed Creation

1. John 9:3.
2. Frances Young, *Face to Face* (London: Epworth, 1985). Reissued as *Face to Face: A Narrative Essay in the Theology of Suffering* (Edinburgh: T & T Clark, 1990). Page references are to the second edition.
3. Young, *Face to Face*, 9.
4. Margaret Spufford, *Celebration* (Glasgow, UK: Fount, 1989), 25–26.
5. Spufford, *Celebration*, 60.
6. Spufford, *Celebration*, 86.
7. Young, *Face to Face*, 99.
8. Young, *Face to Face*, 103–4.
9. Spufford, *Celebration*, 118.
10. Spufford, *Celebration*, 71–72.
11. Young, *Face to Face*, 109.
12. Young, *Face to Face*, 42.
13. Young, *Face to Face*, 36.
14. Young, *Face to Face*, 61–62, 64–65; italics original.
15. Spufford, *Celebration*, 26.
16. Young, *Face to Face*, 61.
17. Spufford, *Celebration*, 40.
18. Spufford, *Celebration*, 96–97.
19. Stanley Hauerwas, *Suffering Presence: Theological Reflections on Medicine, the Mentally Handicapped and the Church* (Notre Dame, IN: University of Notre Dame Press, 1986), 186.
20. Hauerwas, *Suffering Presence*, 207–8.
21. I chose to treat Margaret Spufford's account alongside Frances Young's not just because illness and disability offered different dimensions to the question of flawed creation, but also because in the perspective offered by considerations of status it seemed inappropriate to treat the account of a caregiver alone.
22. Spufford, *Celebration*, 110.
23. Young, *Face to Face*, 110–11.
24. Young, *Face to Face*, 191. These words are prefixed by the acknowledgement "I recognise that what I am about to suggest runs the risk of appearing sentimental."
25. Young, *Face to Face*, 143–44.
26. Young, *Face to Face*, 146.
27. Young, *Face to Face*, 204.
28. Young, *Face to Face*, 183; capitals original.
29. Young, *Face to Face*, 195.
30. Spufford, *Celebration*, 69–70.

31. Young, *Face to Face*, 203.

32. Spufford, *Celebration*, 115.

33. Young, *Face to Face*, 110.

34. Young, *Face to Face*, 172.

35. Young, *Face to Face*, 68. The reference is to Gen. 32:24–31.

36. Young, *Face to Face*, 71. The quotations come from a "rather soppy little poem" quoted in the text.

37. Spufford, *Celebration*, 74, quoting a passage of Pierre Teilhard de Chardin quoted and translated in Donald Nicholl, *Holiness* (London: Darton, Longman & Todd, 1987), 136.

38. Spufford, *Celebration*, 78–80, quoting W. H. Vanstone, *Love's Endeavour, Love's Expense: The Response of Being to the Love of God* (London: Darton, Longman & Todd, 1977), 47–48, 63–64.

39. Spufford, *Celebration*, 80.

40. Young, *Face to Face*, 74.

41. Spufford, *Celebration*, 92.

42. Young, *Face to Face*, 100.

43. Young, *Face to Face*, 179.

44. Hauerwas, *Suffering Presence*, 178, quoting Arthur McGill, *Suffering: A Test Case of Theological Method* (Philadelphia: Westminster, 1983), 75. See also Hans Reinders, *The Future of the Disabled in Liberal Society: An Ethical Analysis* (Notre Dame, IN: University of Notre Dame Press, 2000).

45. Young, *Face to Face*, 53–54.

46. Young, *Face to Face*, 3–4.

47. Young, *Face to Face*, 85–86.

48. Young, *Face to Face*, 103.

49. Young, *Face to Face*, 147.

50. Young, *Face to Face*, 176. The internal quotation is from Mary Douglas, *Purity and Danger* (London: Routledge, 1966).

51. Young, *Face to Face*, 184–85. She attributes these insights to Ian Cohen.

Chapter 13: A Promising Offer: Perfectible Bodies

1. The Sam and Kerry examples owe a great deal to Karen Lebacqz, "Genes, Justice, and Clones," in Ronald Cole-Turner, ed., *Human Cloning: Religious Responses* (Louisville: Westminster John Knox, 1997), 49–57.

2. I am especially grateful to Phil Jones for sharing his expertise in stem-cell research and thus greatly improving the scientific accuracy of this section.

3. I am grateful to Jo Hartley and Phil Jones for helping me think through the culture of health care in contemporary Britain in a more informed way.

4. This is the line taken by Joseph Fletcher. See his *Humanhood: Essays in Biomedical Ethics* (Buffalo, NY: Prometheus, 1979).

5. For the link with baptism, I am grateful to Stanley Hauerwas and Joel Shuman, "Cloning the Human Body," in Ronald Cole-Turner, ed., *Human Cloning*, 58–65. See also Dale Martin, *The Corinthian Body* (New Haven, CT: Yale University Press, 1995).

6. For further exploration of these issues, see Oliver O'Donovan, *Begotten or Made?* (Oxford, UK: Clarendon, 1984); Congregation for the Doctrine of the Faith, *Instruction on Respect for Human Life in Its Origin and on the Dignity of Procreation: Replies to Certain Questions of the Day* (Washington, DC: United States Catholic Conference, 1987); Richard A. McCormick, "Should We Clone Humans?" *Christian Century* (24 November 1993): 1148–9; Gilbert Meilaender, *Bioethics: A Primer for Christians* (Grand Rapids: Eerdmans, 1996); Ted Peters, *Playing God? Genetic Discrimination and Human Benefit* (New York: Routledge, 1997). I am grateful to Ian Thompson in helping me think through the issues raised in this chapter.

Chapter 14: A Promising Offer: Unlimited Food

1. The following treatments offer a general overview of this topic: Celia Deane-Drummond, *Theology and Biotechnology: Implications for a New Science* (London: Chapman, 1997); M. Reiss and R. Straughan, *Improving Nature? The Science and Ethics of Genetic Engineering* (Cambridge: Cambridge University Press, 1996); Darryl R. J. Maher, *Shaping Genes: Ethics, Law, and Science of Using Genetic Technology in Medicine and Agriculture* (Christchurch, New Zealand: Eubios Ethics Institute, 1990); and Earl J. Shelp, ed., *Theology and Bioethics: Exploring Foundations and Frontiers* (Dordrecht, Netherlands: Reidel, 1985).